The Unfinished Life of Benjamin Franklin

The UNFINISHED LIFE of *Benjamin Franklin*

DOUGLAS ANDERSON

The Johns Hopkins University Press
Baltimore

© 2012 The Johns Hopkins University Press
All rights reserved. Published 2012
Printed in the United States of America on acid-free paper
9 8 7 6 5 4 3 2 1

The Johns Hopkins University Press
2715 North Charles Street
Baltimore, Maryland 21218-4363
www.press.jhu.edu

Library of Congress Cataloging-in-Publication Data

Anderson, Douglas, 1950–
    The unfinished life of Benjamin Franklin / Douglas Anderson.
    p.   cm.
    Includes bibliographical references and index.
ISBN-13 978-1-4214-0523-0 (hdbk: acid-free paper)
ISBN-10 1-4214-0523-7 (hdbk: acid-free paper)
ISBN-13: 978-1-4214-0613-8 (electronic)
ISBN-10: 1-4214-0613-6 (electronic)
    1. Franklin, Benjamin, 1706–1790. Autobiography. 2. Franklin, Benjamin, 1706–1790.
3. Statesmen—United States—Biography. I. Title.
    E302.6.F8A58 2012
    973.3'092—dc23
    [B]   2011040332

A catalog record for this book is available from the British Library.

Special discounts are available for bulk purchases of this book. For more information, please contact Special Sales at 410-516-6936 or specialsales@press.jhu.edu.

The Johns Hopkins University Press uses environmentally friendly book materials, including recycled text paper that is composed of at least 30 percent post-consumer waste, whenever possible.

Contents

List of Illustrations   *vii*
Preface   *ix*
A Note to the Reader   *xi*

INTRODUCTION   Accident and Design   1

CHAPTER 1   Great Works and Little Anecdotes   13

CHAPTER 2   Imposing Forms   47

CHAPTER 3   The Scramble of Life   82

CHAPTER 4   *Litera Scripta Manet*   119

CHAPTER 5   Some Uses of Cunning   150

CONCLUSION   Segmented Serpent   182

Notes   *193*
Index   *209*

Illustrations

Frontispiece, *The Pilgrim's Progress*, third edition (1679)   20

Pieter Breughel the Elder, "Big Fish Eat Little Fish" (1556)   31

Description of the rowboat incident with John Collins, Franklin's manuscript   49

Franklin's daily schedule, Franklin's manuscript   69

Franklin's letter to his son, March 22, 1775, from "On board the Pennsylvania Packet"   107

"Hints for *Conversation*," insert in Franklin's letter to his son, March 22, 1775   110

Excerpt from Franklin's letter to his son, March 22, 1775   116

"Join, or Die," cartoon   183

Preface

This book proposes to illuminate the legacy of Benjamin Franklin by substituting his memoir for his life. The reverse is the customary scholarly practice: to sift the memoir for incidents and evidence that can illuminate our current understanding of the Atlantic world in Franklin's lifetime. No face in American history is more famous than his. Perhaps only Washington and Lincoln are equally recognizable, and equally mythic, figures. Since the bicentennial of the American Revolution, and the tercentennial of Franklin's birth, no other individual has prompted a similar outpouring of work by biographers, historians, political scientists, economists, and cultural critics—much of it of very high quality and eagerly consumed by a large community of readers who continue to be drawn to the story of Franklin's interests and achievements, his strengths and weaknesses.

But our collective story of Franklin's life is not his story. To the extent that I have been able to do so, I have set the historical presence of Benjamin Franklin to one side in order to concentrate on reading the pages of his incomplete memoir, an immersion in words that, I hope, is as rewarding as Franklin's own experience often proved to be, when as a sixteen-year-old apprentice he ate a simple and hurried lunch in his brother's Boston printing house and devoted the rest of his midday break to the complex pleasures of reading. From time to time, I have called attention to Franklin's personal or public circumstances during the course of discussing his book, but I have done so only when those circumstances seemed instrumental to understanding and enjoying Franklin's prose. These remarks will partly explain the selective nature of the notes that follow these chapters and provide a measure of necessary background for the introduction's opening sentence.

A NUMBER OF GENEROUS INDIVIDUALS offered their time, advice, and assistance as this book took final form. Olga Tsapina, Norris Foundation Curator of American Historical Manuscripts at The Huntington Library, made the process of securing illustrations from Franklin's manuscript a pleasure. Paul Hogroian and Bonnie Coles at the Library of Congress directed me to the 1973 printed guide of the library's Franklin holdings, much of which, including Franklin's 1775 voyage letter, is widely available on microfilm. The Imaging Services staff of the University of Georgia Library converted selections from the film into digital files. Carla Mulford kept me engaged with Franklin's work, despite the distractions of other writing interests, and gave a thoughtful assessment of the manuscript that prompted its complete reconsideration.

Robert J. Brugger at the Johns Hopkins University Press steered the book into the hands of Matt McAdam, an exemplary blend of advocate and critic throughout the acquisitions process. Brian MacDonald was both a patient and an exacting copy editor. Juliana McCarthy and Anne Whitmore, along with the rest of the editing and production staffs at the Johns Hopkins University Press, managed my authorial anxieties with tact and intelligence, as they ushered the book into being.

I continue to be grateful to the University of Georgia for its support of my writing through the resources of the Sterling-Goodman Professorship.

A Note to the Reader

Parenthetical citations identifying the source of Franklin's words refer either to *The Papers of Benjamin Franklin*, published by the Yale University Press and abbreviated as P, followed by volume and page number, or to the Yale edition of the *Autobiography* (A), edited by Leonard W. Labaree, Ralph L. Ketcham, Helen C. Boatfield, and Helene H. Fineman, published originally in 1964. Wherever my discussion of the *Autobiography* hinges on minute particulars of phrasing or word choice, I have checked these against the *Genetic Text* of Franklin's manuscript, prepared by Leo Lemay and P. M. Zall and published by the University of Tennessee Press (1981). Though the Yale edition may still retain a handful of transcription errors ("more than fifty" according to Lemay and Zall, though they do not undertake to list them), it remains an editorial monument of great importance, as well as a beautiful, compact, and readily available book. I prefer it for some of the same reasons that Franklin's imaginary neighbor once decided that he liked a speckled ax best. Parenthetical citations from *The Pilgrim's Progress* (PP) refer to the Oxford World's Classics paperback edition, edited by W. R. Owens.

The Unfinished Life of Benjamin Franklin

INTRODUCTION

Accident and Design

The following pages are about a book, not a man. Its author never gave his work a title, and though he wrote in English, part of his manuscript was first published in French translation in 1791, a year after his death. This initial appearance was quickly followed by German, Swedish, and English translations of the French fragment, one of which was serialized in eight installments of *The Lady's Magazine; or Entertaining Companion of the Fair Sex* in London beginning in January 1793. Twenty-five years and over one hundred English-language editions later, an 1818 version of the book based on what was thought to be a copy of the entire English original finally appeared, but even then the text was incomplete, with changes in wording that may have drawn, in part, on a transcription that has since disappeared. This irregular journey into print might well have delighted the author, editor, and publisher whose life story was in the process of making a haphazard return to its native tongue.[1]

Seventy-seven years after the book's initial, fragmentary publication, an American diplomat named John Bigelow produced a version drawn directly from the complete manuscript that Benjamin Franklin had left behind at his death. Bigelow's 1868 edition included all the major parts of the story that contemporary readers associate with the title that Bigelow adopted, the *Autobiography of Benjamin Franklin*, but his efforts drew criticism from subsequent editors, and though the title that he used has prevailed, his text has not. After more than a century of scholarly labor, it is still an unfinished life, with important pieces lost or scattered, partly by accident and partly not, much as its author must have expected would occur, given the turbulent world from which the book emerged and where it first appeared, in a city and a language where Franklin himself was, at best, only partly at home. *Mémoires de la vie privée de Benjamin Franklin, écrits par lui-même, et adressés a son fils* is what the 1791 translator had called Franklin's story, supplementing the narrative fragment with a "historical handbook" (*précis historique*) of Franklin's political views, as well as several additional items relating to this "father of liberty." Liberty had recently begun its violent reconstruction of French life as this early translation went to press. The publisher may have hoped that Franklin's measured performance would help shape the growth of his unruly ideological child.

Its opening pages, however, were at least nominally directed to Franklin's own unruly child, William, the royal governor of New Jersey at the time that Franklin sat down, during a brief holiday in 1771, to write him a letter explaining some aspects of his father's early life, perhaps as a means of bridging the widening political gap between them. The epistolary form was a well-established publication convention in Franklin's day, designed to evoke the thin illusion of private disclosure in a public medium. Franklin's contemporaries clearly recognized his "letter" as a benign disguise. A young English friend, Benjamin Vaughan, wrote to Franklin ten years later urging him to continue work on the book, calling it simply "your Biography." The first caretaker of the memoir whom scholars have been able to identify, a Philadelphia merchant named Abel James, termed it simply a "Work" and sent Franklin a brief description of the excitement he felt on examining a manuscript fragment that had come into his possession, late in 1782, in order to reawaken Franklin's interest in it:

> Some Time since there fell into my Hands to my great Joy about 23 Sheets in thy own hand-writing containing an Account of the Parentage and Life of thyself, directed to thy Son ending in the Year 1730 with which there were Notes likewise in thy writing, a Copy of which I inclose in Hopes it may be a means if thou continuedst it up to a later period, that the first and latter part may be put together, and if it is not yet continued, I hope thou wilt not delay it, Life is uncertain as the Preacher tells us, and what will the World say if kind, humane and

benevolent Ben Franklin should leave his Friends and the World deprived of so pleasing and profitable a Work, a Work which would be useful and entertaining not only to a few, but to millions. (A, 134)

Abel James had certainly read through Franklin's twenty-three handwritten sheets. A wry undertone in this passage suggests that he knew his correspondent's sense of humor quite well, and was even willing to mock his colloquial style, but wouldn't risk sending this precious record from Philadelphia to Paris while England and the United States were still officially enemies, over an ocean patrolled by hostile warships, a prey to storms and shipwreck. The author would have to make do with some scribbled notes and a crowded memory to carry on with the protracted letter to his son and to posterity that he had begun over a decade earlier.

Eventually Franklin took the advice of his two friends, and over the last six years of his life added sections to the book as his circumstances and his declining health permitted, more than doubling its length but falling far short of covering the whole of his extraordinary career. The narrative ends in 1760, leaving the last three decades of Franklin's life to the reconstructive energies of traditional biographers. But in setting out to continue his story, Franklin did something quite unexpected and surprising as well. Rather than simply put together the book's "first and latter part," as Abel James had hoped, Franklin provided for a highly conspicuous, even ragged, compositional seam. He indicated his wish to incorporate the letters from Abel James and Benjamin Vaughan directly into the body of his book, along with the pages of "Notes" that James had sent him to jog his recollection. These documents (Franklin indicated) would all appear sandwiched in between the portion of the story that Abel James had recovered near the end of the American Revolution and any new manuscript that Franklin might eventually live to add, carrying the narrative forward from 1730.[2]

Since 1818, when William Temple Franklin published the first version of his grandfather's book that included some of this later material, every subsequent edition of the memoir has followed the author's wishes and inserted the James and Vaughan letters where Franklin had wanted them to be. But no editor has printed the "Notes" alongside the letters. These loose manuscript sheets, rather oddly labeled Franklin's "Outline" by modern publishers, wind up in an appendix. Notes and outlines, after all, are extraneous to any writer's finished product, at least in the eyes of editors or executors. Surely so careful a stylist, and meticulous a printer, as Benjamin Franklin would have recognized this obvious fact and made a different decision about the placement of the notes before his book ever went to press. If he had been able to finish a complete draft that satisfied his intentions, the notes would have been superfluous and, perhaps, would have disappeared completely.

But the *Autobiography* never went to press in Franklin's lifetime, and though a large portion of the notes that Abel James sent to him in 1782 was eventually covered by the narrative that Franklin ultimately left behind, he never changed his mind about the role he wanted the notes themselves to play in his finished book. Many implications flow from this interesting gesture: Benjamin Franklin's apparent determination to confront his reader with the disruptions that plague the orderly writing of stories, or living of lives, and which the meticulously composed and carefully corrected nature of print inevitably conceals. "Join, or Die" is the motto Franklin famously gave to his drawing of a segmented snake in the 1754 editorial cartoon that he hoped might encourage some form of political union among the fractured British colonies of North America. The life story that he left behind at his death in April 1790 is yet another segmented snake, but one that he went to some trouble to avoid assembling from head to tail in an unbroken narrative stream. Moreover, the notes that Abel James copied and sent to him in 1782 display none of the architectural control of their subject that we customarily associate with the idea of an "outline." They are arranged in a sequential but fragmented line of brief phrases, names, and topics that Franklin must have prepared to use as a reference shortly after he began the sheets that eventually came into Abel James's possession.[3]

Some of the items that Franklin lists in his notes are quite specific, almost to the point of approximating sentences in a draft. Some are quite broad and vague, touching on extensive categories of experience rather than particular incidents. The document as a whole is an episodic ramble, a portrait of the memory in action rather than a selective and carefully structured aid to composition:

> My writing. Mrs Dogoods Letters Differences arise between my Brother and me (his temper and mine) their Cause in general. His News Paper. The Prosecution he suffered. My Examination. Vote of Assembly. His Manner of evading it. Whereby I became free. My Attempt to get employ with other Printers. He prevents me. Our frequent pleadings before our Father. The final Breach. My Inducements to quit Boston. Manner of coming to a Resolution. My leaving him

and going to New York. (return to eating Flesh.) thence to Pennsylvania. The Journey, and its Events on the Bay, at Amboy, the Road, meet with Dr. Brown. his Character. his great work. (A, 268)

The hints take up Franklin's life story some pages after the manuscript itself does, with his method of teaching himself how to write clear and graceful prose by segmenting and reassembling in various ways Joseph Addison's *Spectator* essays. They leap to the Silence Dogood letters (which the memoir itself does not identify by name) before making any mention of James Franklin's newspaper, the *New England Courant*, where those letters appeared, and ignore the early friendship with John Collins, as well as Franklin's boyish infatuation with Socratic argument. A bit later they refer to certain "Schemes" that Franklin entertained during the nineteen months he spent in London in 1725 and 1726: to the plays he attended, the books he read, and the preachers he heard. These intriguing details never appear in the pages he actually writes.

Franklin's notes allude somewhat cryptically to "Cornwallis's Letters" in connection with his 1724 London voyage. The reference is likely to puzzle readers who are unaware that "William Cornwallis" was a fraudulent identity assumed by William Riddlesden, the "complete rascal" whose correspondence Franklin inadvertently conveyed to a London recipient in 1724, hoping it might be some instructions from William Keith connected with the purchase of printing equipment. Riddlesden's actual name appears in the memoir, but his phony one remains in the notes.[4] If Franklin meant to address the general problem of counterfeit identities in his narrative, he gives no indication of his plans, but he clearly recalls the special nature of Riddlesden's deceit. He was "a very knave," the memoir rather stuffily observes, but its pages are oddly silent on the particular form of knavery that Riddlesden practiced.

At some point, Franklin meant to address the subject of "Children" in the early part of his story, a topic in which his surviving son William and daughter Sarah would have taken particular interest. But other than a poignant paragraph belatedly inserted into the margin of his manuscript discussing the 1736 death of Francis Folger Franklin, he decided not to do so. And even this brief reference omits the little boy's name or any account of the delightful personal qualities "Frankie" displayed that made his loss especially painful.[5] After Abel James sent a copy of the notes to France, Franklin added to it some subjects that he had initially overlooked and then proceeded to overlook them again as he expanded his manuscript. Near the entry where he had reminded himself to discuss a meeting with "Indians at Carlisle" he added "and at Easton." The Carlisle episode plays an important, and controversial, role in the long third portion of the memoir, but Franklin never elaborates on the equally complex circumstances surrounding his role at the Easton negotiations with the Delaware a few years later. Apparently he planned to transcribe a copy of the 1754 Albany Plan of Union into his book and then make "Remarks upon it." Would these have been more detailed than the brief discussion of this document that does survive in the book? We will never know.

Clearly the narrative took unexpected directions as Franklin both followed and departed from the track he laid out for himself. By including the notes that depict this sinuous track in the midst of his actual manuscript, along with the letters that accompany them, Franklin could expose the shifts, the interpolations, and the elaborations and omissions that characterize the unpredictable interplay between design and execution in any extensive piece of writing. The integration and disintegration of parts involved in the evolution of a complex story emerge as key features of the story itself: its theme as well as its textual background, the central psychological and moral lesson of an extraordinary life disguised as the patchwork preliminaries to a choppy draft. The verbal jigsaw puzzles that a teenage Franklin made out of Joseph Addison's paragraphs and ideas, in order to teach himself "Method in the Arrangement of Thoughts," almost inevitably invite comparison with the notes that Abel James sent to his seventy-six-year-old friend, urging him to take up yet another challenge in methodical arrangement. Just as inevitably, the extension of the notes well past the events of 1760 suggests Franklin's implicit recognition that he would never live to finish an account of his crucial role in what his manuscript termed the affairs of the Revolution.

Max Farrand observes, in his parallel text edition of *Benjamin Franklin's Memoirs*, that the handwriting as well as the ink of Franklin's instructions concerning the James and Vaughan letters indicate that he added the following brief explanation to his book not in 1784, when he first began to expand his story, but four years later, in rapidly declining health and with less than two years to live:

Memo.
    Thus far was written with the Intention express'd in the Beginning and therefore contains several little family Anecdotes of no Importance to others. What follows was written many Years after in compliance with the Advice contain'd in

these Letters, and accordingly intended for the Publick. The Affairs of the Revolution occasion'd the Interruption.

Letter from Mr. Abel James with Notes of my Life, to be here inserted. Also Letter from Mr. Vaughan to the same purpose. (A, 133)

It was August 1788, and Franklin was once again home in Philadelphia. The new Constitution that he had helped to draft a year earlier had been officially ratified by eleven states, two more than the nine-state minimum required to make it binding. Virginia and New York, two particularly vital members of the new union, had voted to adopt the Constitution in July. Franklin himself had completed his will in the same month and could now turn his attention to the unfinished account of his life that he had brought back from France. The eighty-two-year-old author of this memorandum, in nearly constant pain from kidney stones and gout, almost certainly recognized that another momentous interruption would very soon prevent him from completing the story that he had set out to tell. Because the notes that Abel James had sent him were likely to be all that the reader could ever expect to see of significant portions of his life, Franklin decided to include them here.

A second, brief book was to have served as an ethical and educational companion to Franklin's life story. In his own mind he had entitled it *The Art of Virtue* and intended it as a commentary on his system of daily self-examination and self-discipline, a routine that Franklin believed would be of more practical use than "the mere Exhortation to be good" that he found all too common in didactic literature. Benjamin Vaughan in particular hoped that this little manual, along with the finished autobiography, would help secure his hero's legacy and impact. But only its title survives. "I did indeed, from time to time put down short Hints of the Sentiments, Reasonings, &c. to be made use of in it," Franklin wrote, "some of which I have still by me" (A, 158). But he never linked these hints together, and he was never able to carry out the *"great and extensive Project"* to which *The Art of Virtue* was to have made an important contribution. A succession of private and public business intervened, Franklin explained, and these goals too remained unfinished.

In the weeks just before his death, Franklin was thinking about his unfinished life, his unwritten book, and the ambitious plans that he had once projected for the Society of the Free and Easy, a loose international organization of young men, schooled in virtue and public service, which he had postponed forming until he was too old and infirm to do so. He alluded to some of these truncated aspirations when Thomas Jefferson paid him a brief visit in March 1790, as Jefferson was traveling from Monticello to New York City to become George Washington's secretary of state. Franklin eagerly questioned Jefferson about his old acquaintances in Paris, which Jefferson had left six months earlier. How had they been coping with the instability and the danger of their own, great Revolution, Franklin wondered. The "rapidity and animation" with which he questioned his visitor, Jefferson remembered, were "almost too much for his strength."[6]

Like Abel James and Benjamin Vaughan before him, Jefferson then turned the conversation to the "history of his life" that he had heard Franklin was writing, possibly from some of their mutual friends in France:

> I cannot say much of that, said he; but I will give you a sample of what I shall leave: and he directed his little grandson (William Bache) who was standing by the bedside, to hand him a paper from the table to which he pointed. He did so; and the Doctr. putting it into my hands, desired me to take it and read it at my leisure. It was about a quire of folio paper, written in a large and running hand very like his own. I looked into it slightly, then shut it and said I would accept his permission to read it and would carefully return it. He said, "no, keep it." Not certain of his meaning, I again looked into it, folded it for my pocket, and said again, I would certainly return it. "No," said he, "keep it." I put it into my pocket, and shortly after took leave of him.

The pages that the dying man was so determined to give away, Jefferson discovered, contained an account of Franklin's last-minute efforts to negotiate a compromise between the American colonies and the British Ministry, "when he was endeavoring to prevent the contest of arms which followed." Perhaps he thought the nation's first secretary of state could profit from this extended story of abortive overtures and frustrated hopes.

When Franklin died a few weeks later, Jefferson scrupulously returned the sheets to his grandson, William Temple Franklin, who never bothered to include them in the life of his grandfather that he belatedly published twenty-eight years later. Nor has any subsequent editor done so, despite an addition that Franklin made to the end of the notes that Abel James had sent him in 1782 indicating his intention to discuss his "Negociation to prevent the War" should his manuscript ever reach that point in his life. It never did, but the pages that Franklin attempted to give to Thomas Jefferson survive in Franklin's papers in the form of a long letter, dated March 22, 1775, and addressed once again to his son, written as Franklin was sailing home from England after a decade's absence to take up a seat in the Continental Congress.[7]

The story the letter tells, interspersed with documents that Franklin intended to insert into the finished narrative, covers the events of a few months, between August 1774 and March 1775, when a variety of intermediaries tried to reengage Franklin in government discussions over British policy toward the colonies. Since his public humiliation before the Privy Council in January 1774, Franklin had broken with his political contacts in England. By late November, however, he was holding weekly meetings with private citizens and members of Parliament from both parties who were trying to grope their way toward an agreement that might mollify the Americans and preserve the dignity of the British Ministry. Franklin (they thought) had the best chance of bringing about this impossible result. The letter describing all this activity to William closely resembles the very brief fourth part of the memoir that touches on Franklin's first mission to England in 1757 as Pennsylvania's representative in its quarrel with the Penn family. Had he lived, it seems likely that the finished book would have contained equally detailed accounts of Franklin's public and private activity during the years of the Revolution in Paris and in Philadelphia, as well as in London—very different political worlds that he was in a unique position to portray and to contrast with the successive experiments in self-government that the first parts of the *Autobiography* bring vividly to life.

Jefferson himself was uncertain of Franklin's meaning when he handed this extraordinary manuscript to him and twice insisted, despite Jefferson's scruples, "No, keep it." Perhaps it is understandable, then, that the 1775 letter has never gained favor in the eyes of editors and publishers preparing modern versions of Franklin's autobiography. By contrast, the labeling of the story's main divisions in four "parts," followed by "Franklin's Outline" as an appendix, has become established publication practice, though Franklin never used these labels or endorsed this ordering of his book. Why would he have bothered to write a detailed letter to his son on this crucial episode of his life when he had every reason to anticipate seeing William Franklin in person when the 1775 voyage home had concluded? Why would he add the subject of these negotiations to his running "notes" if he had not intended to include the 1775 narrative in his life story? Why echo the opening format of the manuscript that he had begun only four years earlier if he did not see the 1771 and 1775 documents as closely related parts of a single literary enterprise?

These questions can never have definitive answers. But it is at least clear that within a few weeks of his death, Benjamin Franklin was dispersing rather than consolidating his written legacy, giving parts away rather than joining the pieces together, and imposing on his heirs (in the broadest sense of that word) the task of deciding how, or perhaps even if, the sections should be reunited. The caption to his drawing of the segmented snake, in other words, applies only in part to Franklin's book. Unlike the colonies whose union Franklin was among the first to urge, his life story must remain a series of provocative fragments in order to be complete, disassembled in order to be whole.

"In democratic countries," Alexis de Tocqueville wrote half a century after Franklin's death, "the science of association is the mother of all science," the "mother of action." Mutual assistance societies such as Franklin's famous Junto had taught Americans how to magnify the influence of private feelings into "a power seen from afar." "Among the laws that rule human societies," Tocqueville concluded, "there is one which seems to be more precise and clear than all the others. If men are to remain civilized or to become so, the art of associating together must grow and improve in the same ratio in which the equality of conditions is increased." Though he does not cite Franklin directly, Tocqueville's notes suggest that he drew on William Temple Franklin's 1818 edition of the memoir in preparing the second volume of *Democracy in America* (1840). Benjamin Franklin's book, in the form that he left it, is both a portrait of the associational arts that structured his life and a challenge to the associational instincts of his reader: an assortment of episodic fragments that dramatize and awaken the energies of combination.[8]

Both Abel James and Benjamin Vaughan envision Franklin's story as a verbal monument, a source of pleasure and profit to millions, as well as a barrier against the uncertainties of a post-Revolutionary future. But Franklin himself is profoundly skeptical of monuments. More than any other member of the Revolutionary generation to which he belonged, he recognized the inherent vanity of such building. No Greek revival temple or grand obelisk on America's national mall reminds tourists of Benjamin Franklin's formative influence on the imagination of his contemporaries. That influence resides, instead, in the subtle textures of an unfinished story that this book sets out to disclose.

THE FOLLOWING CHAPTERS CORRESPOND, very loosely, to the five major sections of Franklin's memoir that have survived: three fairly substantial narratives and two very brief ones, joining the 1775 voyage letter to the sections of the *Autobiography* with which most modern readers are familiar. But in every portion of the book I have not hesitated to draw together episodes or passages that Franklin may have written at intervals in his life many years and many thousands of miles apart from one another, if they seemed to invite a joint consideration. The chapter titles, however, are largely sequential, drawn from the sections of his memoir in chronological order of composition. "Great Works and Little Anecdotes," the title of the first chapter, points to a repeated motif of the pages in which Franklin described his early life in Boston, London, and Philadelphia, a pattern that the chapter sets out to explore. "Imposing Forms" and "The Scramble of Life," the titles of chapter 2 and chapter 3, both derive from the brief middle section of the book, in which Franklin literally imposes an ethical discipline on himself that Benjamin Vaughan hoped would deter the brutal scramble of appetites that the closing sentences of his letter envisioned.

"*Litera Scripta Manet*," a Latin proverb on the durability of the written word, points toward a consideration of speech and writing that Franklin repeatedly explores in the third part of his memoir but which also engages him in the first and second parts as well. "Some Uses of Cunning," the title of chapter 5, is drawn from Franklin's own characterization of his civic tactics as the inventory of these accumulates through the densely detailed texture of his book's longest section. But even this most public portion of Franklin's memoir is a tissue of great works and little anecdotes, of formal design amid the desperate scramble of history. The figure of the segmented serpent recurs as the title of my conclusion, but as a mnemonic emblem it shapes every page of the book, as this process of assembly and of disassembly moves forward. The entire performance should be sufficiently brief to satisfy Franklin's exacting standards of concision, and sufficiently long to do justice to one of the richest sources of instruction and happiness in American letters.

In writing each chapter, I have assumed a reasonable degree of familiarity with Franklin's memoir on the part of the reader, though I recognize that many may not have read the story for years, and many others may recall only anthology selections. But such handicaps are less crucial than they might seem. The memoir is by design episodic, as Franklin repeatedly but gently warns his reader, stressing his own tendency to digress or to violate "the order of time" in his presentation of events. My own discussion often violates the order of time as well—reserving a detailed look at the epitaph Franklin wrote for his parents, for instance, until the very end of the first chapter, rather than treating it very early in the book, as Franklin does; or concluding the second chapter with a lengthy discussion of a joke involving the eighteenth psalm that takes place during Franklin's first months in Philadelphia. If this approach proves occasionally confusing, my only excuse is that it exploits a structural feature to the memoir, highlighting the patchwork nature of writing and of memory on which the associational arts of reading ultimately depend.

CHAPTER ONE

Great Works and Little Anecdotes

Benjamin Franklin's memoir begins, inauspiciously, as the recollections of an amateur genealogist, tracing his origins in the English Midlands, sharing the experience with his son, and adding his own contributions to the family lore. The initial result, he suggests in retrospect, is a compilation of "little family Anecdotes of no Importance to others," a note of false modesty on the part of a writer who was already famous on both sides of the Atlantic Ocean when he began to tell his life story during a late summer holiday in 1771. Despite this apparent apology for the limited interest of his pages, Franklin clearly recognizes that his narrative amounts to momentous personal testimony: a public examination conducted before a tribunal far more extensive in its scope than the private judgments of his immediate descendants.

The book's first words strike a deliberately casual note. "I have ever had a Pleasure in obtaining any little Anecdotes of my Ancestors," Franklin writes his son: "You may remember the Enquiries I made among the Remains of my Relations when you were with me in England; and the Journey I took for that purpose. Now imagining it may be equally agreeable to you to know the Circumstances of my Life, many of which you are yet unacquainted with; and expecting a Week's uninterrupted Leisure in my present Country Retirement, I sit down to write them for you" (A, 43). The tone of these few sentences, however, is oddly guarded. Before any reference to the nature of the circumstances he hopes to describe or to the motives that lie behind such a belated disclosure to a child who is entering middle age, Franklin alludes to a time when he and his son were companions rather than distant correspondents whose increasing alienation from one another marks this opening reference to "my" ancestors, and "my relations," rather than yours or ours. Mutually agreeable feelings must first be imagined before they can be revived. What "remains" and what one remembers—categories that Franklin's initial words evoke—suggest a bitter contrast between desiccated bonds and living ones.

Even in the troubled year of 1771, William Franklin would have had little difficulty recalling the journey that he and his father took together thirteen years earlier in search of the family's English roots, but the memoir briefly revisits the excursion as if it were Franklin's alone, a lost opportunity rather than a fond memory.[1] Now that the stakes of mutual ignorance between father and son have increased, Franklin cannot be certain whether even this intimate a reader—or indeed any reader—is really equipped to understand the story of his early life, another variety of "journey" that may prove to be meaningful only to the one who takes it. The most important details will take only a week to record, Franklin disingenuously suggests, minimizing the complexity of a narrative that he must have suspected from the beginning would demand much more time to complete. He professes to anticipate no interruption or impediment to the telling of the tale, but uninterrupted leisure is clearly a rare commodity in his busy existence, an opportunity to seize while one can, knowing full well that experience almost always thwarts such sanguine expectations, as Franklin's book itself will ultimately demonstrate. Interruption is the nature of life and the essence of death, an existential truth that every child of New England's religious culture would immediately detect in the latent anxieties of Franklin's opening paragraphs. It is because he expects to be interrupted that he starts to write.[2]

A younger and more secular generation, however, would require a patient introduction to the special demands that Franklin's language will make as his story unfolds: to the subtle emotional inflections that a simple shift in modifiers can convey, or to the blend of documentary particulars and emblematic scope that often lends a surprising measure of suggestive power to inconsequential narrative details. Little anecdotes can unexpectedly acquire an expansive potential in Franklin's pages. Such evocative reserves call for a carefully schooled audience to register their impact. John Bunyan, one of Franklin's favorite writers, acknowledged a similar need very early in *The Pilgrim's Progress* by introducing his hero to the figurative tableaux of the Interpreter's House. Christian prepares for the ordeal ahead by reading a book and learning to "perceive" prophetic images by its meaning. Many of the memories that Franklin records in the first part of his own story are just such reading lessons, including the chance encounter with Bunyan's book that signals the beginning of his own pilgrimage. Franklin's little anecdotes draw his reader gradually, almost imperceptibly, back into the atmosphere of a tumultuous past, from the threshold of a tumultuous future.[3]

THE MEMOIR'S OPENING SALUTATION—"Dear Son"—is the first of several reminders, early in the narrative, that letters implicitly address an expanding circle of readers rather than a single recipient. Franklin anticipates that an unpredictably diverse and curious audience will be examining his son's mail, resulting in a "Sphere of Action" for his words that quickly comes to embrace all of his literal and figurative posterity, the indulgent (or indoctrinated) young of future generations, and a benevolent God. The epitaph Franklin writes for his parents' gravestone directs an equally sweeping appeal to the attention of every passing reader with the story and the moral that it offers. The "separate little Volumes" he buys as a boy pass through his hands into those of other readers so that he can afford to buy other books, the expression of an insatiable thirst that singles Franklin out for special attention but also links him to a social world that shapes every detail of his story. Through the first part of the memoir, the mobile culture of letters plays the role of Providence in Franklin's life, determining what he calls "the Complexion of my future Fortune" through agents who recognize the signs of a shared passion.

Among the episodes in his father's life that William Franklin had yet to hear about may have been one involving an early brush with authority. Dr. John Browne, a cosmopolitan innkeeper on the Burlington road, probably suspected that seventeen-year-old Benjamin Franklin was a runaway servant when he first began to chat with his guest on an October evening in 1723. Franklin was making his way from New York to Philadelphia, traveling light and much the worse for wear, with spare shirts and stockings stuffed in his pockets, when

Browne approached him to strike up a conversation and, perhaps, entrap him into disclosing his plight. But if that was Browne's original intention, he quickly changed his mind.[4]

"Finding I had read a little," Franklin remembers, his host "became very sociable and friendly." The young man's intelligence and conviviality quickly persuaded Browne to overlook his dubious appearance and embark on a lifelong friendship that eventually included sharing with Franklin a scurrilous poem he had written. "He had some Letters, & was ingenious," Franklin recalled, "but much of an Unbeliever, & wickedly undertook some years after to travesty the Bible in doggerel Verse as Cotton had done Virgil. By this means he set many of the Facts in a very ridiculous Light, & might have hurt weak minds if his Work had been published, but it never was" (A, 74). This wicked doggerel is the "great work" that Franklin alludes to when he mentions Browne in the notes that he made for himself as he wrote the first part of his memoir nearly fifty years later. The encounter must have been a pleasant surprise to them both, an unexpected reminder that inquisitive readers and ambitious writers could surface in unlikely places. A common appreciation for books forms a bond that even a subsequent difference of opinion on the merits of Browne's biblical travesty could not entirely undo.

The narrative quickly moves on toward a far more celebrated scene in Franklin's story describing his first arrival in Philadelphia—a family legend that William must have heard his father or his stepmother rehearse many times before—but the sociable innkeeper near Burlington left a lasting impression that Franklin goes out of his way to share, despite his disapproval of Browne's gregarious unbelief. "He had been, I imagine, an itinerant Doctor," Franklin concludes, "for there was no Town in England, or Country in Europe, of which he could not give a very particular Account." Nor is this the only encounter between intellectual and physical itinerants that the memoir's initial episodes record. Franklin's own Uncle Benjamin was a kind of pilgrim as well, though of a different ideological makeup from Dr. Browne's. Before emigrating to New England in 1715, at the age of sixty-five, to join his younger brother in Boston, he had assembled two formidable archives that reflected his zest for the explosive verbal output of the English Revolution and its cultural aftermath: a manuscript stock of shorthand sermons and more than thirty volumes of polemical pamphlets covering "Publick Affairs from 1641 to 1717." This encyclopedic textual repository must have impressed even its compiler as finally unreadable, for he left it behind in London when he sailed to America.[5]

Peter Folger, Franklin's maternal grandfather, had come to New England in 1635, six years before the appearance of the earliest of Uncle Benjamin's pamphlets, settling eventually in Nantucket, where he wrote a verse defense of "Liberty of Conscience" in 1675, supporting the various religious sects "that had been under Persecution" in Massachusetts. The "Decent Plainness and manly Freedom" of Folger's performance, in contrast to Browne's irresponsible mockery, prompted Franklin to memorize some of his lines. These brief portraits from the memoir's early pages suggest that Franklin's personal story of social and political mobility takes place side by side with many alternate versions of himself experiencing similar transformations. Peter Folger's commitment to liberty of conscience is the ancestor of Franklin's own lifelong suspicion of sectarian power. Uncle Benjamin's pamphlet archive suggests a fascination with the energy of the press with which his nephew's career would become virtually synonymous. Dr. Browne's scandalous poem anticipates the youthful Franklin's own scandalous pamphlet on Liberty and Necessity that succeeds in damaging at least a few weak minds before its chastened author manages (almost completely) to suppress it. All three men, like Franklin himself, were drawn to the power of print as a means of amplifying the individual voice in an age of democratic revolution.

Franklin and his genial host on the Burlington road belonged to the fraternity of strong-minded readers, able to withstand exposure to subversive ideas or caustic wit without moral or spiritual damage. But not every bookish mind was equally well equipped to profit from or to resist the extraordinary variety of paper currency that engulfed Franklin's world, much of which he surveys in the opening pages of his memoir: polemical divinity and crimp's bills, scurrilous satire and sober exhortations on the moral life in prose and verse, controversial pamphlets and sectarian histories, sermons and allegories, ballads and news digests, ancient works in translation and dietary advice, discourses, dialogues, grammars, self-help manuals. Novels would enter the mix in Franklin's youth—the memoir mentions *Robinson Crusoe* and *Moll Flanders* as especially engaging books—and Franklin himself would publish Samuel Richardson's *Pamela* in Philadelphia, four years before he retired from printing to conduct his electrical experiments and report on their progress in letters to learned correspondents in London, another literary genre of the day.

His childhood friend John Collins had entrusted his "pretty Collection of natural Philosophy and Mathematicks" books to Franklin when he set off from Boston to join his friend in Philadelphia. It may have been Collins's collection, in fact, that caught the eye of the governor of New York when he asked to meet the young custodian of such an impressive library who was making his way back to Philadelphia via New York City in 1724, after reconciling with his parents. Like Dr. Browne on Franklin's original excursion a year earlier, Governor Burnet took an interest in the fluid community of readers that came his way. The 1771 fragment of Franklin's narrative will conclude with a brief description of his plan for establishing a "Subscription Library" in Philadelphia, shortly after his marriage, but many of the episodes that fill this portion of the story already present Franklin's experience in the context of a mutually inquisitive and mutually supportive club of "subscribers" to the emerging circulating library of the eighteenth century.[6]

The bewildering variety of reading matter that Franklin consumes and produces in these early pages suggests that reading itself was a heterogeneous skill, unevenly distributed and unevenly practiced by a varied and busy population of readers who could not always be trusted to embrace an author's intentions. Even a modern sage was subject to the whims of a youthful audience, as Franklin half-wistfully recognized when he noted that his own memoir "may be read or not as anyone pleases" (A, 44). A pious clergyman setting out to combat heresy might create a heretic in the process, as the anti-Deist sermons that Franklin read in his father's "little Library" had made him, briefly, a Deist. Though style and substance were a single entity that Franklin learned to admire when he tutored himself in the delightful "manner" of the *Spectator* papers, amending his "faults" and inflaming his ambition in the process, even these resources could not prevent one's work from being misread by an unsympathetic audience. The transmission of experience or the teaching of life's lessons was not so straightforward an exercise as it might seem.

Many journeys preoccupy Franklin in the opening pages of his memoir, only one of which is the tale of personal and material success enshrined in popular myth. A more urgent story lies behind this familiar legend, one that requires Franklin to invoke a literary model early enough in the narrative to help shape its reception. Like the hero of John Bunyan's famous account of the soul's journey, Franklin too finds himself repeatedly confronted by interpretive challenges in his lifelong progress across the physical and metaphysical landscapes of the eighteenth century. He signals his interest in the parallel through an accidental discovery that his dissenting ancestors would not have hesitated to term providential. Thereafter, much of the structure that he imposes on the

1771 fragment of his manuscript springs directly or indirectly from the figurative instincts that this happenstance encounter awakens.

Shortly before sharing some cordial conversation with Dr. John Browne at his Bordentown inn, Franklin had endured a much less serene stage of his 1723 trip from Boston to Philadelphia. Unable to find work (as he had originally hoped) in a New York printing house, Franklin set out by boat for Amboy, New Jersey, only to be trapped all night on New York Bay by dangerously heavy surf and "a Squall that tore our rotten Sails to pieces." In the midst of the storm, a fellow passenger tumbled overboard, and when Franklin fished him out, he found a copy of *The Pilgrim's Progress* in the drunkard's pocket—a Dutch translation "on good paper with copper cuts," much more beautifully produced than the cheap editions of Bunyan's story that Franklin had read and enjoyed during his Boston boyhood. "I have since found that it has been translated into most of the Languages of Europe," Franklin wrote his son, half a century after rescuing the book's owner by his "shock Pate" and dragging him to safety. Largely as a result of its unique dramatic immediacy, Franklin suspects, *The Pilgrim's Progress* "has been more generally read than any other Book except perhaps the Bible" (A, 72).

This little anecdote is characteristic of many that lend the opening portion of Franklin's story its own dramatic appeal. It is characteristic too in the subtle ways that Franklin adapts Bunyan's work to a new narrative setting. The title page of *The Pilgrim's Progress* cites Hosea 12:10 to forewarn the reader of the book's allegorical method: "I have used Similitudes," the prophet explains, just as Bunyan will use them to portray the spiritual journey that he proposes to describe "from This World to That which is to come." Facing the biblical epigraph in every edition published after 1679 is the famous "sleeping" portrait of John Bunyan, reclining on top of the entrance to a dungeon where a crouching lion lurks, a "similitude" or figurative depiction of the concealed sins that every pilgrim must expect to confront. The City of Destruction lies in the distance, etched and labeled just behind Bunyan's shoulder, while a pilgrim has set out on his wanderings in the background, with a burden on his back and a book in his hand, all similitudes into which the dreamer's identity has briefly passed. The handsome copper cuts of the edition that Franklin undertook to dry for its hapless owner almost certainly included this image. In the memoir, Franklin fondly recalls how "Honest John," along with Defoe and Richardson, first gave him an appreciation for the mixture of narrative and dialogue in print.

Frontispiece, *The Pilgrim's Progress*, third edition (1679).

But more potent mixtures than this one are clearly at issue in the memoir itself. As Bunyan's sleeping portrait implies, readers, travelers, and dreamers have a great deal in common, particularly when the legacy of the past is heavy and pits or predators mark the way. Christian enters John Bunyan's dream as "a man clothed with rags" and stricken with anxiety, "standing in a certain place, with his face from his own home, and a great burden on his back." Like Christian, Franklin too is a disheveled traveler who has turned his face from home at this early point in his life, and though Boston in 1723 was hardly the City of Destruction that Bunyan's pilgrim flees, it was still (in Franklin's experience) all too "certain" a place: full of religious certitudes that he had come to doubt, sustained by an array of familial and civic authorities that seemed bent on thwarting his growth. The only figurative burden he carried, for the time being, was his own ambition, though in leaving Boston secretly he aroused a shipmaster's conspiratorial sympathy by pretending that he had "got a naughty Girl with Child," an echo of Christian's abandonment of wife and children as he flees the wrath to come.

A few months later when Franklin repeated this trip, after reconciling with his family, his guileless nature would invite a dubious sexual overture from two female passengers on a coastal packet sloop. "Young Man, I am concern'd for thee," remarks the Quaker matron who alerts Franklin to his danger, "as thou has no Friend with thee, and seems not to know much of the World" (A, 84). Franklin will soon confirm her judgment as he attempts to get a start in his trade: first as an unwitting party to James Ralph's desertion of his wife and child when he joins Franklin on a London voyage to purchase printing equipment, and later as the initiator of his own unwelcome sexual overtures to the "sensible and lively" young milliner who had become Ralph's lover. Franklin in turn had been enticed into this trip by the glib promises of William Keith, the governor of Pennsylvania and a good candidate for the roles of Mr. *Facing-bothways* or Mr. *Two-tongues* from the town of Fair-speech in Bunyan's fable. It was Keith who made the improbable offer of financing Franklin's start in business with an elaborate networking expedition to the heart of the British Empire.

Keith embodies the mix of benevolence and selfishness that will recur in many of the memoir's initial characters and anecdotes, as well as in their author. "Having little to give," Franklin notes, Keith "gave Expectations. He was otherwise an ingenious sensible Man, a pretty good Writer, and a good Governor for the People, tho' not for his Constituents the Proprietaries, whose Instructions he sometimes disregarded" (A, 95). Franklin too would make a career of thwarting the wishes and interests of the Penn family during his years in the Pennsylvania Assembly. The perplexing blend of good principles and ungovernable inclinations that make up Keith's Bunyanesque nature forms a mirror image, an ethical similitude, of the gullible young man whom he deceives.[7]

Once one begins to tug on the thread provided by the opportune appearance of *The Pilgrim's Progress* in Franklin's little anecdote, it quickly offers a number of unexpected hints on how to read the details and episodes that surround it: "Still as I pulled it came," John Bunyan recalled, describing the improbable growth of his famous book in words that Franklin will echo in the sly account he provides of retrieving Bunyan's popular allegory from a drunken Dutchman's pocket. Additional echoes follow that signal important formal parallels. In the verse "Apology" with which Bunyan prefaces his extraordinary dream, he offers a series of reflections on the untoward interaction of chance and design that frames Christian's story, and which Franklin in turn incorporates into the structure of his memoir:

> When at the first I took my Pen in hand,
> Thus for to write, I did not understand
> That I at all should make a little Book
> In such a mode; Nay, I had undertook
> To make another, which when almost done,
> Before I was aware, I this begun.   (PP, 3)

The creative process from which *The Pilgrim's Progress* emerges is thematically central to Christian's unpredictable journey: neither Bunyan nor his hero entirely appreciates the scope of what he has begun. Indeed, even before Christian reaches the narrow Wicket Gate where his pilgrimage is to start, he slips into the first of the moral quagmires that bedevil him, a Slough of Despond that cannot be filled despite the "Twenty thousand Cart Loads" of good advice that have been dumped into the mire "for above this sixteen hundred years." The "Art of Virtue" that Franklin once proposed to draft aimed to avoid the fate of these cartloads by substituting practical behavioral tactics for exhortations, but this book too is swallowed even before it could be written. The "Slow" of Despond is a consumer of libraries, as well as souls, a destiny that both Franklin and Bunyan hope to thwart by more carefully attuning their words to the reader's strengths and weaknesses (PP, 17).

The memoir depicts its own share of quagmires, great and small, throughout the course of a story that, much like Christian's, proves to be a series of inadvertent interruptions and narrow escapes: from drowning, from sickness or imprisonment, as well as from an array of alternative futures as a swimming instructor, a wandering compositor, or a Barbados merchant. Moreover, Franklin and Bunyan present the process of writing as a similar collaboration between accident and intention. While working on one task, Bunyan unwittingly stumbles across "twenty things" that take on a compositional life of their own, the first signs of a long, unforeseen digression that will eventually grow into the tale of Christian's pilgrimage. Rather than simply ignore these prolific "sparks," Bunyan sets them off by themselves and adds to them during "vacant seasons" only, strictly for diversion or pleasure:

> . . . but yet I did not think
> To shew to all the World my Pen and Ink
> In such a mode; I only thought to make
> I knew not what: nor did I undertake
> Thereby to please my Neighbour; no not I,
> I did it mine own self to gratifie.   (PP, 3)

For Franklin too, digression is design. Like Bunyan, he collects the incidents and details that begin to multiply as he writes, storing them in the notes that Abel James would later find with the first twenty-three sheets of his narrative, pages that Franklin wrote during his own vacant season of "Country Retirement" at Twyford. Like Bunyan once again, he writes at least in part to gratify his own vanity as much as the curiosity of his reader.

Bit by bit *The Pilgrim's Progress* grew, as Bunyan put what he termed its various "ends" together, until it attained an impressive degree of "bigness" that led him to ask some friends whether the result should be printed, a question that Abel James and Benjamin Vaughan answer at some length for Franklin. The story is "dark," some of Bunyan's preliminary readers complain, and its incidents are "feigned." Similitudes can deter weak minds, one friend insists: "Metaphors make us blind." Bunyan's verse "Apology" argues strenuously for the advantages of his method. A literary vehicle and its spiritual content may be quite different from one another, he suggests. In fact the difference is critical if an author hopes to catch the attention and win the assent of a wide variety of readers: some birds can be snared only with pipe and whistle, Bunyan explains;

some fish must be tickled before they can be caught. Listless men learn more from homely figures of speech than from sober sermons: "Be not too forward therefore to conclude, / That I want solidness, that I am rude," Bunyan cautions, "All things solid in shew, not solid be; / All things in parables despise not we" (PP, 6).

Franklin's famous contrast between the stubborn imperfections of character and the progressively more correct editions of a printed book is a deft emblem of resignation and hope, mixing simplicity and subtlety much as Bunyan's similitudes often do in *The Pilgrim's Progress*. It would be a great advantage, Franklin confesses in his heavily edited memoir, to be able to edit the "sinister Accidents and Events" of the past—to repeat the human pilgrimage in modified form, as Bunyan does when he has Christiana retrace Christian's steps in the second part of his allegory. But even without the possibility of issuing a corrected "edition," Franklin confesses, he would have no objection to reliving his life, sinister accidents and all. "Faults" and "errata" are the most frequent terms that he applies to these unhappy memories, but Franklin also stresses the deeper layers of regret that shape this language. He has played a role in sinister things, he admits, in a letter to the illegitimate son whose obscure origins clearly remain a significant mental burden. "Sir," Christian replies to Evangelist, when this all-important guide first detects his inner distress, "I perceive, by the Book in my hand, that I am Condemned to die, and after that to come to Judgment; and I find that I am not willing to do the first, nor able to do the second" (PP, 11). Franklin's opening paragraphs delicately restage this encounter, as he finds himself poised between impossible emotional and political alternatives, facing condemnation on either hand, once the bonds between Britain and America, as well as those within his own family, begin to fray. Like Christian, he is reviewing his existential accounts, though he quickly recognizes that no one is obliged "to give me a Hearing."[8]

This last term too is a miniature similitude. The bitterest hearing of Franklin's life had yet to take place when he began the memoir. In 1771 Alexander Wedderburn's withering examination of his conduct before a gloating Privy Council was still several years in the future. On that subsequent occasion Franklin would maintain a stoic silence, as Wedderburn repeatedly attacked his character for the role he had played in conveying Thomas Hutchinson's private correspondence into the Boston press. But during the Stamp Act crisis, five years earlier, Parliament had indeed given Franklin a careful hearing as he explained the passionate resistance with which the colonies had greeted

England's revenue policies, reminding the members of the House of Commons that deep affections once treated with scorn could quickly change into equally deep resentments. "What was the temper of America towards Great-Britain before the year 1763?" the members of the House wished to know, when they met with Franklin as a committee of the whole in February 1766:

> A. The best in the world. They submitted willingly to the government of the Crown, and paid, in all their courts, obedience to acts of parliament. Numerous as the people are in the several old provinces, they cost you nothing in forts, citadels, garrisons or armies, to keep them in subjection. They were governed by this country at the expence only of a little pen, ink and paper. They were led by a thread. They had not only a respect, but an affection, for Great-Britain, for its laws, its customs and manners, and even a fondness for its fashions, that greatly increased the commerce. Natives of Britain were always treated with particular regard; to be an Old England-man was, of itself, a character of some respect, and gave a kind of rank among us.
> Q. And what is their temper now?
> A. O, very much altered. (P, 13.135)

An English government that had once struck Americans as "the great bulwark and security of their liberties and privileges," Franklin continued, was on the verge of squandering this goodwill. The thread was about to break.[9]

"See that ye refuse not him that speaketh," Evangelist warns Christian, dismissing the shallow views of Worldly-Wise Man and directing Christian's attention once more to his indispensable book: do not "draw back thy foot from the way of peace" (PP, 23). By 1771 the English Ministry and its American supporters (William Franklin among them) had embarked on just such a fatal misreading of their true interests, in Franklin's eyes. The Boston Massacre in the spring of 1770, a little over a year before he began writing the first portion of the memoir, offered a glimpse of the future if the contentious parties proved unable to change course. The opening sentences of Franklin's book address this complex texture of associations with considerable figurative economy, borrowed in part from the example of John Bunyan's suggestive tale. The similitudes Franklin employs here have an exacting literary cast that draws on the extraordinary popularity of one pilgrimage to illuminate the circumstances of another.

Like Bunyan too, along with many contemporary moralists, Franklin recognized both the social uses and the ethical threat of vanity, but the memoir expresses this commonplace conviction in suggestively militant terms, echoing and modifying the traditional trope of the armor of virtue in its lifelong battle with vice. "Most People dislike Vanity in others," Franklin writes as he begins his famous book, "whatever Share they have of it themselves, but I give it fair Quarter wherever I meet with it, being persuaded that it is often productive of Good to the Possessor and to others that are within his Sphere of Action" (A, 44). This reference to "fair Quarter," like the pun on "hearings," is both casual and telling—a similitude, or a miniature fable, that offers a wide-ranging context for the gentle didactic strategy of Franklin's Uncle Benjamin in the two poems addressed to his four-year-old namesake aimed, in part, at discouraging the boy's interest in being a soldier. Franklin slipped both poems into the manuscript of the memoir late in his life, long after the Revolution had born out his uncle's warnings. The first set of cautionary verses has a simple grandeur that would not be out of place in John Bunyan's dream:

Beleeve me Ben. It is a Dangerous Trade—
The Sword has Many Marr'd as well as Made.
By it doe many fall, Not Many Rise;
Makes Many poor, few Rich and fewer Wise;
Fills Towns with Ruine, fields with blood beside;
'Tis Sloth's Maintainer, And the Shield of pride;
Fair Citties Rich to Day, in plenty flow,
War fills with want, Tomorrow, and with woe.
Ruin'd Estates, The Nurse of Vice, broke limbs and scarts
Are the Effects of Desolating Warrs.   (A, 48)

A birthday acrostic from the same year (1710) administers a litany of his uncle's orthodox advice that may have puzzled the boy at the time, counseling him to keep his "Dealings" free of fraud and falsehood, and to resist sloth, lust, and pride—a battery of precocious sins more suited to John Bunyan's savage vision of Vanity Fair than to the repertoire of a four-year-old. "Above all Ills be sure Avoide the shelfe," Franklin's uncle enigmatically concludes: "Man's Danger lyes in Satan, sin and selfe." Clumsy though they may be, these lines distill the lessons of a complex political and religious inheritance. They are both a legacy and a reading lesson.

Uncle Benjamin was "much of a Politician," Franklin recalls in the opening pages of his book: "too much perhaps for his Station." This apparently casual observation strikes very close to home. By 1771 Franklin's own transgressions against the privileges of "station" were becoming increasingly pronounced to members of the English Ministry. By contrast, Uncle Benjamin wrote amateurish poetry and kept scrapbooks. His involvement in politics took the form of the fervor with which he assembled a vast pamphlet collection documenting the fierce ideological battles of the seventeenth century, a polemical library that reflected his insatiable appetite for controversy. "A Dealer in old Books met with them," Franklin reports of these thirty-two bound volumes, "and knowing me by my sometimes buying of him, he brought them to me. It seems my Uncle must have left them here when he went to America, which was above 50 years since. There are many of his Notes in the Margins" (A, 50).

This exhaustive archive ultimately seems expendable to everyone who handles it: its original compiler, an opportunistic bookseller, and Franklin himself, to whom the collection seems little more than a curiosity. The pamphlets and their marginalia are the residue of old quarrels, the fruitless animosities against which Uncle Benjamin's simple poems had sought to warn his four-year-old American nephew. Like his uncle, Franklin too chooses to jettison these verbal remains in favor of some snippets of birthday verse on the desolation that results from the "trade" of war. Truth "in Swadling clouts," John Bunyan insisted, was better suited to appease our troubles than "lies in Silver Shrines."

As two "Bookish" and highly competitive boys in Boston, Franklin and his friend John Collins reconstructed their own version of the pamphlet wars that Franklin's uncle had observed in England, with Collins usually proving to be the victor in their debates. He "bore me down more by his Fluency than by the Strength of his Reasons," Franklin recalls, an experience that eventually leads him to adopt the role of "humble Inquirer and Doubter" as a substitute for the unproductive results of contradiction and conflict. Disputatious habits, Franklin observes, are a vice of the educated—"Lawyers, University Men, and Men of all Sorts that have been bred at Edinborough"—and to underscore the point he sets a simple trap for the educated reader as he concludes this set of anecdotes in the memoir. To consolidate the hard-won lesson that a combative manner is self-defeating, Franklin mangles two couplets, from two different poets, into a single adage that mimics the boyish struggles where he had learned the dangers of passionate fluency: "Immodest words admit *but this* Defence," Franklin declares, "That Want of Modesty is Want of Sense" (A, 66). Keen-witted students of poetry (he realizes) will probably sort out the misattribution in his rhyme, as he too had once been fond of pouncing upon an opponent's errors in argument. But the resulting surge of editorial triumph will simultaneously expose the habitual intellectual immodesty that the couplet strives to correct. In the ethical universe that Bunyan and Franklin share, foolish things often prove to be wise ones in disguise. This anecdote is both a memory and a similitude for the lesson in gentle tactics that it strives to teach.[10]

The most provocative emblem that Franklin offers for the recurrent mixture of great works with little anecdotes in his book is his family legend about the Bible and the joint stool:

> This obscure Family of ours was early in the Reformation, and continu'd Protestants thro' the Reign of Queen Mary, when they were sometimes in Danger of Trouble on Account of their Zeal against Popery. They had got an English Bible, and to conceal and secure it, it was fastned open with Tapes under and within the Frame of a Joint Stool. When my Great Great Grandfather read in it to his Family, he turn'd up the Joint Stool upon his Knees, turning over the Leaves then under the Tapes. One of the Children stood at the Door to give Notice if he saw the Apparitor coming, who was an Officer of the Spiritual Court. In that Case the Stool was turn'd down again upon its feet, when the Bible remain'd conceal'd under it as before. This Anecdote I had from my Uncle Benjamin. The Family continu'd all of the Church of England till about the End of Charles the 2ds Reign, when some of the Ministers that had been outed for Nonconformity, holding Conventicles in Northhamptonshire, Benjamin and Josiah adher'd to them, and so continu'd all their Lives. The rest of the Family remain'd with the Episcopal Church. (A, 50)

This passage combines both a reading device and a reading lesson. The Bible in its simple sling of tapes beneath a stool—"under and within the Frame"—calls to mind the process of carefully wedging pages of type into wooden forms before sliding them under and within the frame of a press. It is easy to picture the scene, and just as easy to elaborate on the figurative implications that John Bunyan would have appreciated: an elaborate similitude depicting the great work cleverly disguised and protected by a piece of ordinary household furniture, always near at hand though readily concealed, always open even when it is completely hidden.

When the Bible rests on the reader's lap, it is still carefully secured within its wooden enclosure. Franklin's ancestor is sitting, not deferentially kneeling, as he reads, and the safety of the entire family depends on the vigilance of one of the children, who must watch and listen with equal care if they are all to avoid imprisonment. The mutual reliance of experience upon innocence and vice versa plays a key role in the anecdote's suggestive scope. Turning the pages beneath the tapes would clearly not be casually or quickly managed, encouraging just the kind of deliberative reading that the Apparitor was charged to prevent. At any point the consideration of a chapter or a book might be interrupted and the Bible left literally suspended in its hiding place while the household went about its ordinary chores, superficially indifferent to the stool in the corner, but inwardly attentive to its presence, as well as to the inward-working experience that it conceals.

Twice in the passage Franklin stresses that his family maintained the practices that his uncle's anecdote depicts across formidable generational divisions and in the face of considerable danger. His ancestors "continued all" in the Protestant faith until larger fractures in the Stuart succession radiate outward toward their Northhampstonshire home. The clever contrivance of the Bible and the joint stool presides over the first part of the story, bridging a considerable span of time between the middle of the sixteenth century and the closing decades of the seventeenth before the protective framework breaks down, "outing" some dissenting ministers to whom the brothers Benjamin and Josiah Franklin "adhere" when they join the more radical conventicles that refuse to conform to the strictures of episcopal government. These stubborn adherents in turn "continued all their lives" in a new course, and ultimately in a new home, while their relatives remained where Franklin and his son would discover them or their descendants on the genealogical tour to which the memoir's opening sentence alludes.

Nonconformity and continuity collaborate in the compact picture of transmission and decline that this episode depicts. The resolute behavior of Benjamin and Josiah captures their determination to distinguish between the essential and the superficial features of their religious inheritance. Despite more than a century of experience as zealous Protestant readers, the balance of their family gradually settles by stages into the liturgical conventions of the Episcopal Church. But this pair of younger siblings, though they are "outed," remained securely fastened within the homely framework of conscientious dissent for which the joint stool becomes a convenient emblem. This memory too invites William Franklin to "read" himself in the lessons of his great uncle's anecdote, but as an emblem of strenuous reading its range is wider than the obscure family whose fate it describes. What imaginative purpose do riddles or parables really serve, John Bunyan once complained at the beginning of *The Pilgrim's Progress*: "happy is he / That finds the light, and grace that in them be" (PP, 6). The light and grace that Franklin captures in Uncle Benjamin's story links intergenerational bonds and personal growth to a pattern of reflective reading captured in a simple dramatic prop, a template for the subtle formal relationship between homely means and extraordinary ends that the language of Franklin's memoir and of Bunyan's fable exemplify.[11]

A MORE FAMOUS EXAMPLE of Franklin's figurative tactics at work, in the opening pages of his book, is his deliberate misapplication of an ancient proverb to solve a dietary dilemma that he faces during his first voyage to New York. Like his calculated mismanagement of Pope's didactic couplet earlier in the memoir, this lapse too is a similitude of much more profound human failings. The expression "big fish eat little fish" is as old as Hesiod, a blunt summary of the relations that prevail between kings and subjects, nobles and commoners, Spiritual Courts and humble Christians bent on exercising their own religious judgment. Wycliffe, Lydgate, and Shakespeare all employ the saying. Roger Williams alludes to it in *The Bloudy Tenant of Persecution*. Pieter Breughel the Elder illustrated the proverb in a 1556 drawing that, in its engraved version, circulated widely throughout Europe long before Franklin decided it would be a useful excuse for breaking his vegetarian habits and eating some savory fried cod that his fellow passengers had caught. His description of this decision introduces a pair of psychological antagonists that lie behind many of the disruptions that shape the first portion of the memoir.[12]

As Franklin presents the story, he disguises the proverb just enough to allow it to fit unobtrusively into the narrative, but it is hard to imagine any of Poor Richard's contemporaries failing to detect its presence:

> I believe I have omitted mentioning that in my first Voyage from Boston, being becalm'd off Block Island, our People set about catching Cod and hawl'd up a great many. Hitherto I had stuck to my Resolution of not eating animal Food; and on this Occasion, I consider'd with my Master Tryon, the taking every Fish as a kind of unprovok'd Murder, since none of them had or ever could do us any Injury that might justify the Slaughter. All this seem'd very reasonable. But I had formerly been a great Lover of Fish, and when this came hot out of the Frying Pan, it smelt admirably well. I balanc'd some time between Principle and Inclination: till I recollected, that when the Fish were opened, I saw smaller Fish

"Big Fish Eat Little Fish" (1556) by Pieter Breughel the Elder after a lost original by Hieronymous Bosch. Engraving by Pieter van der Hayden published by Hieronymous Cock, Antwerp, 1557.

taken out of their Stomachs: Then thought I, if you eat one another, I don't see why we mayn't eat you. So I din'd upon Cod very heartily and continu'd to eat with other People, returning only now and then occasionally to a vegetable Diet. So convenient a thing it is to be a *reasonable Creature*, since it enables one to find or make a Reason for every thing one has a mind to do. (A, 88)

The generous margin of Franklin's manuscript would have allowed him to introduce this incident at the point in his narrative where it actually occurred, during the original three-day voyage to New York that followed his surreptitious departure from Boston. But the memoir only reports that "a fair Wind" hurried Franklin along on his momentous escape, depositing him abruptly "near 300 Miles from home, a Boy of but 17, without the least Recommendation to or Knowledge of any Person in the Place, and with very little Money in my Pocket" (A, 71). These words stress the bewilderment of the little fish at a particularly telling juncture in Franklin's life. When he elaborates on this experience many pages later, he imposes a reflective "calm" on the events that stresses a different lesson, one depicting the subtle counterpoise of principle and inclination into which memory and reason may be drawn.[13]

There is nothing inherently reasonable in Franklin's self-serving change of diet. If anything his blithe suggestion, in this passage, that wholesale slaughter might, under certain circumstances, seem justifiable casts a monstrous shadow over the anecdote's superficially innocent goals, one that springs directly from the gruesome nightmare of Breughel's famous image. Situated where the episode is in the memoir, however, it provides an interpretive key—a reader's guide—to the incidents immediately surrounding it, as well as to the fragile balance that marks this section of Franklin's story. He has just described the first phase of his acquaintance with William Keith, the worldly patron who first enticed Franklin to draw up "an Inventory of a little Printing House" that Keith would import from England at his own expense to set Franklin up in business. No sooner had Franklin done so than Keith followed his grand gesture with the still more remarkable offer to send Franklin to London himself to select his equipment "on the Spot" and establish business connections. Little fish that he was, Franklin rejoiced in his spurious good fortune: "I believed him one of the best Men in the World." The result would turn out to be not the dramatic commercial boost that Franklin expected but a costly interruption in his Philadelphia career.

Another little fish, Franklin's boyhood friend John Collins, had just departed for Barbados under similar fortuitous circumstances to become "a Tutor for the Sons of a Gentleman." A ship captain commissioned to find a suitable teacher, "happening to meet with him, agreed to carry him thither." Collins accepted the offer, partly as a desperate effort to recover his bearings after failing to find work in Philadelphia and partly as a result of a bitter break in his friendship with Franklin. Despite "a wonderful Genius for Mathematical Learning" and the encouragement of some prominent figures in Boston, Collins had begun to drink and to behave "very oddly," Franklin recalled, "for when a little intoxicated he was very fractious." A quarrel in a rowboat on the Delaware resulted in Franklin pitching Collins overboard and then helping to lift him back in the boat, when it became clear that Collins would rather drown than take a turn at the oars (A, 86). Talents alone can't keep Collins afloat—another common similitude in these early sections of the memoir—and he disappears from the story without a trace.

These details involving Collins and Keith immediately precede Franklin's apparently casual insertion of the cod anecdote into his narrative, as if to prepare the reader to consider a number of variations on the roles of the eater and the eaten in Franklin's life: on the tendency of inclination to overwhelm principle whenever passion or desire momentarily displaces judgment, as they do when Collins and Franklin fight or when Keith's empty promises lure Franklin to London with no letters of credit to redeem for printing equipment. All of these relationships are circumstantial enactments of the cannibalistic fish that Franklin had observed off Block Island. His comic account of duping Samuel Keimer into adopting a vegetarian diet immediately follows his description of how he convinced himself to abandon his meatless principles when the odor of fried cod sharpened his hunger. This episode too is a parable of consumption, a mockery of Keimer's gluttony that recoils on Franklin himself as it probes more deeply into the ethical paradoxes entailed in being a "reasonable Creature."

The collaboration between the two men had been unstable from their first meeting, when Franklin stood quietly by while crafty old William Bradford, the New York printer, enticed Keimer into revealing his plans for driving Bradford's son out of the Philadelphia printing business, another instance of the human propensity to devour one another. Keimer was clearly "a mere Novice" at this game, Franklin immediately concluded, "who was greatly surprised when I told him who the old Man was." The novice was savvy enough, however, to test Franklin's skills before agreeing to employ him by putting "a Composing Stick in my Hand to see how I worked." And he was deft enough to compose an elegy "out of his Head" on the death of Aquila Rose, the promising young printer whom Franklin hoped to replace. Keimer set his elegy directly into type without even bothering to write it out beforehand. "He had been one of the French Prophets," Franklin recalled, "and could act their enthusiastic Agitations. At this time he did not profess any particular Religion, but something of all on occasion; was very ignorant of the World, and had, as I afterwards found, a good deal of the Knave in his Composition" (A, 79).

Keimer's ability to "act" religious enthusiasms that he may not really experience closely resembles the willingness that Franklin himself will soon show to participate, however facetiously, in framing and defending doctrines that he does not believe. In their joint lack of a particular religious affiliation, but their interest in "all on occasion," Franklin and Keimer mirror one another almost perfectly, as they do in their comparative ignorance of the world and in the mixed "Composition" of their characters. Little wonder, then, that Franklin is able to report that he and Keimer "liv'd on a pretty good familiar Footing and agreed tolerably well" at the outset of their working relationship. But this cordial teamwork, too, is based upon a measure of knavery on Franklin's part. At this point in his story, he has already agreed with William Keith to equip a new printing house that will threaten Keimer's livelihood, but for the time being he is keeping his plans to himself. Keimer "suspected nothing of my Setting up" (A, 88).

On this uneasy foundation, the memoir reports, these two nonsectarian spirits agree to establish a new religious sect. Both men loved "Argumentation" (as Franklin puts it), but Keimer had acquired a hard-earned appreciation for Franklin's ability to "trapan" his intellectual adversaries, and Keimer's equivocal background with the French prophets had equipped him with a number of "old Enthusiasms" to which he still remained firmly attached. This blend of talents and convictions made for a perfect counterpoise:

> He was to preach the Doctrines, and I was to confound all Opponents. When he came to explain with me upon the Doctrines, I found several Conundrums which I objected to unless I might have my Way a little too, and introduce some of mine. Keimer wore his Beard at full Length, because somewhere in the Mosaic Law it is said, *thou shalt not mar the Corners of thy Beard.* He likewise kept the seventh day Sabbath; and these two Points were Essentials with him. I dislik'd both, but agreed to admit them upon Condition of his adopting the Doctrine of using no animal Food. I doubt, says he, my Constitution will not bear that. I

assur'd him it would, and that he would be the better for it. He was usually a great Glutton, and I promis'd my self some Diversion in half-starving him. (A, 88)

Distinguishing the diversion from the devotion in these words is a conundrum in itself. Franklin has set out to ensnare (or trepan) his sectarian partner at the same time that he proposes to collaborate with him, but neither is entirely cynical about their exchange. Despite the superficial nature of Keimer's religious loyalties, he is not merely frivolous in his beliefs, and Franklin is at least partly sincere in his conviction that a vegetarian diet has important moral, physical, and economic benefits to confer.

But principle is hopelessly (and deliberately) entangled with inclination in this passage—a trap far more cunning in nature than Franklin's silly negotiation with Keimer over their religious doctrines. The memoir makes it far from clear whether either party to the plan takes it seriously and, in doing so, briefly confers a playful quality on their relationship, mixed with the deep-seated antagonisms that will ultimately doom it, another human conundrum in which Franklin and his son might easily recognize themselves. Before very long, self-denial once more gives way to the allure of a savory odor. The partnership that Keimer and Franklin had established apparently had a social as well as a religious side, but when a roast pig that Keimer had ordered to entertain Franklin and "two Women Friends" arrives prematurely on the table, he devours it all himself with the same gusto that Franklin had dined on his fresh cod. In recording this episode, Franklin contrasts Keimer's gluttony with his own lifelong ability to keep even the strictest Lent without the "least Inconvenience," but this double-edged observation is itself a kind of diversion—even a kind of trap—because Lent is intended to impose, not to mitigate, the fleshly "inconveniences" that Franklin claims he is able to avoid.

The little fish outwits his employer in this anecdote, but the memoir's wording casts considerable doubt on the purity of Franklin's principles. "I us'd to work him so with my Socratic method," Franklin gloats of Keimer's gullibility, "that at last he grew ridiculously cautious, and would hardly answer me the most common Question, without asking first, *What do you intend to infer from that?*" The same uncertainty confronts the memoir's reader in evaluating the proverb of the cod, the puzzle of William Keith's character, or the odd blend of strengths and weaknesses in Collins, Keimer, and Franklin himself. What does this sequence of episodes and portraits encourage us to infer from the repeated triumph of appetite over reason that they depict?

A final contest between principle and inclination concludes this carefully interwoven portion of Franklin's narrative. Like its companion episodes, this one too is linked to the challenge of distinguishing between sincerity and insincerity on the tantalizing basis of inference alone. In the months immediately following Franklin's arrival in Philadelphia, his courtship of Deborah Read had progressed to the point where marriage was the logical next step: "I had a great Respect and Affection for her," Franklin wrote of this tentative romantic understanding, "and had some Reason to believe she had the same for me." The wording is both a gentlemanly euphemism and a tacit acknowledgment of the difficulty of assessing human motives. Love too would appear to pose inferential difficulties that "Reason" alone is not adequate to resolve. Deborah's mother intercedes between Franklin and her daughter "to prevent our going too far at present," perhaps as much for selfish as for practical reasons. Governor Keith's overtures of support had encouraged Franklin to plan a voyage to London that might require him to spend some time abroad purchasing printing equipment for his new business. Unlike Samuel Keimer, the Reads were clearly privy to at least some of Franklin's plan for setting up and may have harbored doubts about its success. Moreover, the prospective husband and wife were still only eighteen years old. A marriage would be more "prudent," Mrs. Read believed, after Franklin's return and his successful establishment as a printer. "Perhaps too," Franklin infers, "she thought my Expectations not so wellfounded as I imagined them to be" (A, 89).

It is, at the very least, unusual for the times that Mrs. Read alone, rather than her husband or both parents together, would exercise this decisive influence over her daughter's plans. John Read, Deborah's father, died in 1724, the year that Franklin sailed to London on the expedition that seems to have aroused Mrs. Read's skepticism. The chronology of the memoir is too imprecise to make clear whether Mrs. Read was a widow when she imposed this delay on the couple's marriage, and Franklin himself takes no notice of Mr. Read's death at any point in his story, though that event almost certainly played a key role in the hasty marriage that Deborah eventually made, perhaps in part for economic reasons, while Franklin was abroad. The memoir shows little interest in explaining the background to this latest of the many interruptions that mark Franklin's narrative. Perhaps Mrs. Read had a better grasp of Governor Keith's improvident nature than Franklin was willing to admit; or she may have had a richer experience of the vulnerability of the imagination to bitter disappointments: so convenient a thing it is to be a reasonable creature and found elaborate hopes on empty promises. Behind this little episode, too, lies a rich tapestry of inference—an index of the interpretive challenges with which Franklin strives to entice his reader at every point in his story.[14]

AS THE EVENTS OF FRANKLIN'S FIRST YEARS in Philadelphia unfold, Deborah Read's mother proves to be a composite figure in her own right, partly the principled governor of her children's impetuous desires and partly impetuous herself. When the Read family learns that Franklin is not likely to make a prompt and triumphant return from London, her mother persuades Deborah to accept the overtures of another suitor, a potter named Rogers, "a worthless Fellow, tho' an excellent Workman" (Franklin remembers) and quite possibly a bigamist whom Deborah ultimately leaves, refusing "to bear his name." The memoir does not stress the emotional trauma of this period in Franklin's life or call attention to the speed with which the Read family gave up on Benjamin Franklin as a future son-in-law, but the picture is clear enough. Franklin arrived in London in late December 1724, planning to purchase a press and types, establish some professional contacts, and return to open his own business in Philadelphia in a matter of a few months. All these plans were rudely disrupted by the deceit of William Keith. Franklin was forced to live by his wits for over a year and a half in England, earning his own passage home if possible, while Deborah Read was quickly pressured into an unhappy marriage.

In the long run, these blows to the future prospects of two young lives prove to be temporary rather than decisive, but this early experience of the fragility of human happiness partly explains the unusual prayer that Franklin inserts into the opening paragraphs of his book, as both an expression of grateful dependence and an acknowledgment that life is as much a record of reverses as a celebration of triumphs. Though the first sentences of the memoir had already offered a formulaic acknowledgment of the "Blessing of God" that lay behind Franklin's extraordinary success story, he quickly returns to the theme of the unpredictable collaboration between individual fortunes and divine favor in a digression that dramatizes the instability to which it points:

> And now I speak of thanking God, I desire with all Humility to acknowledge, that I owe the mention'd Happiness of my past Life to his kind Providence, which led me to the Means I us'd and gave them Success. My Belief of this, induces me to *hope*, tho' I must not *presume*, that the same Goodness will still be exercis'd towards me in continuing that Happiness, or in enabling me to bear a fatal Re-

verse, which I may experience as others have done, the Complexion of my future Fortune being known to him only: and in whose Power it is to bless to us even our Afflictions. (A, 45)

Though Franklin presents this passage as an afterthought, it neatly disrupts the stream of his narrative much as an unexpected reversal of fortune can disrupt any human design. The combination of circumstances that thwarts his initial romantic interest in Deborah Read is not the first such reverse that he records in his memoir, but it is clearly among the most meaningful ones, entangled as it is with William Franklin's illegitimate birth and with the complex relationship that eventually developed between Deborah Franklin and her stepson. The consequences do not prove to be fatal, but they entailed a mix of blessings and afflictions that the memoir takes pains to expose.

The collapse of her first marriage left Deborah "generally dejected, seldom chearful," and socially isolated, Franklin recalled: "I consider'd my Giddiness and Inconstancy when in London as in a great degree the Cause of her Unhappiness." Mrs. Read ultimately accepted a greater share of the blame for her daughter's depression, but the legal repercussions of the first marriage were potentially very serious and combined with its psychological consequences to make Deborah, at first, an object of pity in Franklin's eyes after his return (A, 129). He is able to reestablish his friendship with the family, in part by filling some of the advisory vacuum that John Read's death had clearly created, and to revive his relationship with Deborah, correcting "that great *Erratum* as well as I could." This observation falls within two paragraphs of the conclusion of the memoir's first part and is carefully phrased to acknowledge a legacy of pain that could never be completely eradicated. Deborah was still alive in 1771, as Franklin began his book. Her implicit presence, as a reader, shapes these closing pages, just as William's explicit presence shapes the opening ones. Together their influence establishes the emotional framework for the first portion of Franklin's story.

The chastened expression of thanks that Franklin offers at the beginning of his autobiographical "letter" gives voice to the complex lessons of his domestic experience, a study in the interrelationship between accident and design that all the members of the Franklin household were in a unique position to appreciate. These are not feelings that lend themselves to a conventional enumeration of blessings and transgressions, or to the personal calculus of happiness and affliction, failure or success, with which Benjamin Franklin is so often associated. Character is to be judged not by what one has or achieves but by what one is able to bear with humility and patience. We can hope, Franklin stresses, but we can never presume, that "Goodness" will continue to be good to us. We can plan, but we can never rely on the efficacy of our "Means."

Separation and dispersal are the governing energies of these opening portions of the memoir: dictating the fragmented state of Franklin's manuscript, marking the legacy of his Northamptonshire relatives, and shaping the wayward journey from "religious Impressions" to "written Resolutions" that characterized the first years of his life. Despite the best efforts of his parents, Franklin was "scarce 15" (the memoir reports) when he began to stray from the "Dissenting Way" in which he had been raised. Some of the Boyle tracts attacking Deism that he found in his father's library had the paradoxical effect of drawing Franklin to the Deists, whose arguments eventually prompted him to produce his own "great work" in the freethinking tradition, *A Dissertation on Liberty and Necessity, Pleasure and Pain*, which Franklin wrote and printed in London in 1725. The smug certitudes that this pamphlet sought to endorse—"that nothing could possibly be wrong in the World, and that Vice and Virtue were empty Distinctions"—prove as unsatisfactory to Franklin himself as the orthodox convictions of his parents or the polished arguments of the Boyle lectures.

Ultimately he falls back on a set of convictions suggestively similar to the doggerel advice that his uncle had offered when he was four years old—"that *Truth, Sincerity and Integrity* in Dealings between Man and Man, were of the utmost Importance to the Felicity of Life." Franklin returns, in brief, to the lessons depicted in the similitude of the Bible beneath the joint stool: a practical, domestic respect for the wisdom of an old book, shorn of the superstitious attributes imposed on it by all sorts of spiritual courts or priestly authority:

> Revelation had indeed no weight with me as such; but I entertain'd an Opinion, that tho' certain Actions might not be bad *because* they were forbidden by it, or good *because* it commanded them; yet probably those Actions might be forbidden *because* they were bad for us, or commanded *because* they were beneficial to us, in their own Natures, all the Circumstances of things considered. And this Persuasion, with the kind hand of Providence, or some guardian Angel, or accidental favourable Circumstances and Situations, or all together, preserved me (thro' this dangerous Time of Youth and the hazardous Situations I was sometimes in among Strangers, remote from the Eye and Advice of my Father) with-

out any *wilful* gross Immorality or Injustice that might have been expected from my Want of Religion. (A, 115)

The opinionated young man this passage describes has cut himself loose from the "weight" of traditional piety but not from an interest in what revelation might permit us to infer. Providence is a kind persuader, Franklin concludes, not a dictator. The equivocal agents of good luck and a guardian Angel combine with the parental benevolence of a distant but not indifferent Creator in order to preserve some individuals, at least, from inflicting or suffering lasting harm.[15]

John Dryden's lines celebrating "the equal Beam" of the scales of Providence had attracted Franklin in his Deist phase, when he was arguing for the moral equivalence of virtue and vice, until it became clear that the cosmic poise was neither as equal nor as consoling as it had first seemed, when measured against the circumstantial fluctuations of existence. The dispassionate Chain and Beam of omniscient Design depict a judgmental apparatus that is largely unconcerned with the limitations of "purblind Man" and unresponsive to the needs of individuals caught in the crossfire between principle and inclination that permeated life. By contrast, Franklin's spiritual journey ultimately teaches him to value a very different kind of moral interchange, one receptive to precisely the sort of guidance and kindness that Franklin captures in the elaborate portrait of his father that he presents in the memoir's opening pages.[16]

Josiah Franklin gives circumstantial form to the complete human pilgrimage that Franklin's book sets out to describe. In a handful of pages, the memoir charts the course of Josiah's entire life, from his 1682 emigration to New England to his death in 1745, beginning with Franklin's childhood memory of a family reunion in which thirteen of Josiah's seventeen children were "sitting at one time at his Table," an assembly in which Franklin himself was the "youngest Son and the youngest Child but two" (A, 51). In the anecdotes that follow, Josiah becomes a great work in his own right, a dramatic similitude for the conjunction of virtues to which his son will later aspire. As Franklin first introduces him, however, Josiah seems to be both an authoritarian and an indecisive parent—a compound of opposite attributes much like the compound characters of Dr. Browne, Samuel Keimer, or Mrs. Read. "My early Readiness in learning to read," Franklin recalls, originally prompted his father to prepare the boy to be a minister. But in less than a year, Josiah changed his mind, interrupting Franklin's extraordinary run of success at the Boston Grammar School to place him in less prestigious, though perhaps kinder, hands at George Brownell's School for Writing and Arithmetic.

The explanation that Josiah gave his friends (in Franklin's "hearing") for altering his "first Intention" is clearly intended for both public consumption and the private instruction of his son: college is expensive, Josiah complains, and in the end the ministry is a "mean Living." But neither of these discouraging observations had any influence with him a few months earlier, when he first decided to designate his youngest son "for the Service of the Church." Despite Franklin's clear aptitude for the Grammar School curriculum, Brownell's "mild encouraging Methods" prompt a sudden and decisive change in his father's plans. The memoir highlights this quick and tactful decision to choose mildness over family vanity or future status.

The episode of stealing building stones to make a wharf on the Boston Mill Pond immediately follows this first illustration of Josiah's parental tactics and principles. Franklin is the ringleader who organizes his "Playfellows" to relocate the stones from the site of a new house one evening after the workmen had gone home, filling in the "mere Quagmire" the boys had made as they fished from the Mill Pond's bank. When the workmen return to find their construction supplies missing, Franklin and his friends are called to account by their fathers. "I pleaded the Usefulness of the Work," Franklin recalls, but his own father "convinc'd me that nothing was useful which was not honest" (A, 54). Josiah Franklin was fifty-one years old when his youngest son was born, certainly around sixty when he corrected him for stealing building stones, and sixty-three when he set out to prevent Franklin from running away to sea by enticing the restless twelve-year-old to become an apprentice in his brother's printshop. The blend of grandfatherly restraint with paternal authority in the portrait of Josiah that these early passages offer may reflect the generational complexity posed by their respective ages, but it is partly too an outgrowth of the generational complexity surrounding the memoir itself. In 1771 Franklin is writing to a child of his own who is long past the age of discipline but not beyond the reach of a persuasive parental voice.

"I think you may like to know Something of his Person and Character," Franklin suggests, as he prepares to describe the only living grandfather whom his son William had ever known. Josiah did not die until January 1745 (1744 by the Old Style calendar), when his grandson was around fifteen years old. The two had never met, but surely stories featuring Josiah had played a role in William's boyhood. On the genealogical expedition to which the memoir's opening sentences allude, Franklin and "Billy" (along with Franklin's black servant Peter) canvassed every one of the family's English relatives they could find in several counties and towns, taking an occasional gravestone rubbing and collecting anecdotes from many a "good natured chatty old lady," as Franklin put it in a 1758 letter to Deborah describing the trip. "Mrs. Salt is a jolly, lively dame," he wrote of one of these informants, "both Billy and myself agree that she was extremely like you . . . exactly the same little blue Birmingham eyes" (P, 8.144). "Billy" clearly shared his father's pleasure in ancestral lore, as well as being an observant student of family traits.

When the memoir sets out to describe Josiah to his grandson, however, Franklin writes as if he were introducing his son to a total stranger:

> He had an excellent Constitution of Body, was of middle Stature, but well set and very strong. He was ingenious, could draw prettily, was skill'd a little in Music and had a clear pleasing Voice, so that when he play'd Psalm Tunes on his Violin and sung withal as he sometimes did in an Evening after the Business of the Day was over, it was extreamly agreable to hear. He had a mechanical Genius too, and on occasion was very handy in the Use of other Tradesmen's Tools. But his great Excellence lay in a sound Understanding, and solid Judgment in prudential Matters, both in private and publick Affairs. In the latter indeed he was never employed, the numerous Family he had to educate and the straitness of his Circumstances, keeping him close to his Trade, but I remember well his being frequently visited by leading People, who consulted him for his Opinion in Affairs of the Town or of the Church he belong'd to and show'd a good deal of Respect for his Judgment and Advice. (A, 54–55)

This passage stresses the mix of unusual interests and strengths in Josiah's nature: the excellent, the sound, and the solid elements of his character providing a stable matrix for the personal warmth with which Franklin recalls the deftness of his father's drawing and the soothing nature of his voice. As Franklin himself would later prove to be, Josiah too is handy in the use of other tradesmen's tools. His well-set constitution and memorable strength echo the physical determination of Franklin and his playfellows, pitted "like so many Emmets, sometimes two or three to a Stone" as they build their wharf, filling in the "Quagmire" they had made on the edge of the salt marsh.

The memoir's account of Josiah's musical talents invites the reader to link the overmatched boys and their construction stones to the psalmist's mythic life, to the figurative "rock" of his faith, and to the judgmental firmness that makes both Josiah Franklin and his son into reservoirs of advice for their peers. Franklin had clearly listened with great care and intense pleasure to his father's singing and noted with interest and with pride the way in which Boston's "leading people" had treated this gifted tradesman. Though he presents these details without fanfare, they too join the list of partial self-portraits with which the 1771 fragment of the memoir is filled, aimed at forming a mirror in which Franklin and his son might gauge the present state of their own feelings for one another.

When Franklin describes his father's dinner table customs, he recasts his uncle's story about the Bible and the joint stool in a secular setting that welcomes the presence of outsiders to the domestic circle. Instead of focusing on a biblical lesson, however, Josiah raises "some ingenious or useful Topic for Discourse" when the family sits down to eat, as often as possible inviting "some sensible Friend or Neighbour" to join them:

> By this means he turn'd our Attention to what was good, just, and prudent in the Conduct of Life; and little or no Notice was ever taken of what related to the Victuals on the Table, whether it was well or ill drest, in or out of season, of good or bad flavour, preferable or inferior to this or that other thing of the kind; so that I was bro't up in such a perfect Inattention to those Matters as to be quite Indifferent what kind of Food was set before me; and so unobservant of it, that to this Day, if I am ask'd I can scarce tell, a few Hours after Dinner, what I din'd upon. (A, 55)

Religious orthodoxy is not entirely absent from this passage, but its influence, like Josiah's own, is subtle and indirect. The conduct of life and the food on the table appear to echo the opposition between flesh and spirit that preoccupied Franklin's pious ancestors in their long struggle to take control of sacramental life. In similar fashion, Josiah's simple ritual converts the meal into the eating of symbols rather than of "victuals"—a point that Franklin scarcely needs to stress to contemporary readers. Moreover, the scene inverts the story that Franklin tells later in the memoir about enjoying fried cod off Block Island. It is, he observes then, a "convenient Thing" to be a reasonable creature, as he contrives a flimsy excuse for a trivial transgression. The lesson that his father teaches produces a different order of convenience through a higher use of reason. The episode is part of a series of similitudes that undergird the memoir's opening pages: a great work hidden in a homely memory.

Significant disappointments (if not quite fatal reverses) have lasting effects on Josiah Franklin's life that test his spiritual and personal resources. He had to give up his trade as a cloth dyer when he emigrated to New England and support his family as a "Tallow Chandler and Sope-Boiler," steady but dirty work that all but alienated his youngest son. The Franklins were by no means poor, but if Josiah ever had any ambitions to play a more prominent role in civic or church affairs in Boston, his son makes it clear that he had to give up those as well. "To his great Vexation," Franklin remembers, a son and namesake from his first marriage ran away to sea and ultimately disappeared. Josiah and his nephew Samuel had a falling out over a fee that Samuel hoped to receive for training Franklin in "the Cutler's Trade," a rupture that may have played some role in Uncle Benjamin's eventual decision to leave Josiah's house, despite the "particular Affection" that Franklin remembers the brothers once had for one another.

The epitaph that Franklin wrote for his parents and carefully transcribes into the memoir hints at other painful experiences in their lives:

> Josiah Franklin
> And Abiah his Wife
> Lie here interred.
> They lived lovingly together in Wedlock
> Fifty-five Years.
> Without an Estate or any gainful Employment,
> By constant labour and Industry,
> With God's Blessing,
> They maintained a large Family
> Comfortably;
> And brought up thirteen Children,
> And seven Grand Children
> Reputably.
> From this instance, Reader,
> Be encouraged to Diligence in thy Calling,
> And distrust not Providence.
> He was a pious & prudent Man,
> She a discreet and virtuous Woman.
> Their youngest Son,
> In filial Regard to their Memory,
> Places this Stone.

More than one of the Franklin children must have disappeared, or become incapable of managing a family, for these seven grandchildren to have come under Josiah and Abiah's care. Only their youngest son remains to memorialize his parents, instructing an anonymous "Reader" to pay careful attention to the memory that this stone records, while underscoring the hidden attrition among Franklin's siblings. The epitaph points to a surprisingly modest moral: "Be encouraged," Franklin writes, and "distrust not Providence." But Josiah's prudence and Abiah's discretion also remind us that distrust is an inevitable feature of life and may have played an important complementary role in sustaining this loving partnership for fifty-five years. In its own way the epitaph too is both a discreet and a pious work.

Like Franklin himself, Josiah had an innate appreciation for the challenges of managing the young, for curtailing their natural impatience not so much by blunt opposition but by careful handling. The approach that he takes when he removes Franklin from the Boston Grammar School is an instance of this trait. When he finds Franklin and John Collins engaged in their private pamphlet wars, he attends to his son's method and manner of writing, as well as to his lapses in "elegance of Expression," to encourage the same sort of literary ambitions that he had appeared, rather curtly, to discourage when he ridiculed Franklin's early poetic performances. Fearing he might lose another son to the sea, and having some experience with the untoward effects of coercion, Josiah took Franklin on walks around Boston to watch other tradesmen at work, hoping to find a skill that attracted the boy more than soap boiling and candle making. Pleasure in skill itself is one lasting result of these walks, Franklin reports, as well as a knack for using tools that would eventually enable him to manage "little Jobs" around the house or "to construct little Machines for my Experiments while the Intention of making the Experiment was fresh and warm in my Mind" (A, 57). Josiah too is managing a kind of experiment in this episode, trying as best he can to "fix" his youngest son's interests and intentions on a trade that will tie him to the land.

When James Franklin's return to Boston in 1717 made printing a possible channel for Benjamin's energy, Josiah grew impatient to complete the apprenticeship arrangements, Franklin remembers, but not so impatient as to neglect the importance of Inclination in the long-term success of his plan. Franklin was only eleven when James brought his press and equipment home from England, but even so the boy's consent mattered to his father: "I stood out some time," Franklin remembers of this critical period, "but at last was persuaded and signed the Indentures, when I was yet but 12 Years old." At this important juncture in his son's life, Josiah seems to have appreciated the necessity that the boy agree to commit himself almost completely to his brother's control until he was twenty-one, an eternity in the eyes of a twelve-year-old. For good reason, the term "Indenture" in the early eighteenth century applied equally to the documents that controlled the life and labor of a "bought Servant" as well as to apprentices who expected to be trained in a skill in return for the fee paid to the master craftsman. But the power to enter into this legal agreement belonged to Josiah and to James, not to the boy whose future they were deciding. That Franklin "stood out" from endorsing this plan until he was "persuaded" to do so is some measure of the determination and the patience that both the father and the child brought to their extraordinary relationship.

The "flat Denial" that Josiah gives to William Keith's proposal that he set his eighteen-year-old son up in business stands in stark contrast to this background of mutual consideration and concern. But his father's response was not as peremptory as Franklin seems to imply. Josiah took Keith's suggestion under consideration and inquired discreetly into his character before making a decision that he promptly followed with a "civil" letter of thanks to Franklin's Pennsylvania patron, as well as a private expression of pleasure that his son had been able to make such a favorable impression in his new home. Avoid "lampooning and libelling," he advised Franklin, "telling me, that by steady Industry and a prudent Parsimony, I might save enough by the time I was One and Twenty to set me up, and that if I came near the Matter he would help me out with the rest" (A, 83). Along with the love, approbation, and blessing of his parents, Franklin writes, "this was all I could obtain" before leaving Boston for a second time to pursue his prospects in Philadelphia. But this "all" is both less and more than Franklin had a right to expect, an exercise of goodness that both retards and advances his future fortunes. The words are a harbinger of the epitaph that Franklin would compose for his parents more than thirty years later, celebrating the blend of love, prudence, faith, and discretion that constituted their invaluable legacy.

CHAPTER TWO

Imposing Forms

Franklin's memoir dramatizes a remarkable range of experiments in association, large and small, nearly all of which incorporate the shifting proportions of stability and instability reflected in the epitaph that he wrote for his parents. Social compacts of all sizes are repeatedly established, broken, modified, and remade in his pages, often for reasons that have little to do with matters of principle. The secret apprenticeship that Franklin exploits when he leaves his brother's printing house is an instance of this volatility on a diminutive scale. The intellectual bonds he had formed with his childhood friend Collins ultimately disintegrate not over ideological differences but in a trivial temperamental outburst, exacerbated by drink, after the two of them reunite in Philadelphia in 1724:

> Collins wish'd to be employ'd in some Counting House; but whether they discover'd his Dramming by his Breath, or by his Behaviour, tho' he had some Recommendations, he met with no Success in any Application, and continu'd Lodging and Boarding at the same House with me and at my Expense.... His drinking continu'd about which we sometimes quarrel'd, for when a little intoxi-

cated he was very fractious. Once in a Boat on the Delaware with some other young Men, he refused to row in his Turn: I will be row'd home, says he. We will not row you, says I. You must or stay all Night on the Water, says he, just as you please. The others said, Let us row; what signifies it? But my Mind being soured with his other Conduct, I continu'd to refuse. So he swore he would make me row, or throw me overboard; and coming along stepping on the Thwarts towards me, when he came up and struck at me I clapt my Hand under his Crutch, and rising pitch'd him head-foremost into the River. (A, 85–86)

"We hardly exchanged a civil word afterwards," Franklin remembered, once his struggling friend returned to the boat. The unstable mix of drunken arrogance, a sour mind, and mild exasperation that brings on this crisis underscores the system of physical imbalances that Franklin depicts as Collins advances along the unsteady pathway of the thwarts. "What signifies it?" the others ask as they prepare to indulge Collins's demand: what difference does it make if we row while he refuses? But Franklin's sense of an interesting story almost always involves its capacity to signify issues larger than itself.

Five decades later, as Franklin is returning to America after the failure of his efforts to mitigate Parliament's harsh colonial policies, he describes for his son a very similar breakdown in social balances. The long letter that he addresses to William on March 22, 1775, from his cabin on the *Pennsylvania Packet*, skips ahead more than forty years from the point where the first part of the memoir had ended in order to capture in detail his recent diplomatic frustrations. The 1771 fragment of Franklin's book concludes by describing his role in establishing the Library Company of Philadelphia, among the earliest and most successful of the many cooperative societies in which he would play a formative role, "the Mother of all the N American Subscription Libraries now so numerous" (A, 130). These institutions, Franklin believed, had prepared Americans for self-government and had fortified them in their recent "Stand" against the British Ministry. It makes perfect sense, then, that Franklin would take up the broken thread of his story fours year later by depicting this political stand in action: another act of exasperated resistance to an irrational demand.[1]

Unlike the episode on the Delaware with John Collins, this account depicts a rupture of momentous significance. A series of "severe Acts" of Parliament directed against Massachusetts had finally alarmed the moderate opposition in England, Franklin wrote, "For they saw in the Violence of these American Measures, if persisted in, a Hazard of Dismembring, Weakning, and perhaps

Description of the rowboat incident with John Collins, Franklin's manuscript, p. 40. Reproduced from HM 9999 by permission of the Huntington Library, San Marino, California.

Ruining, the British Empire." Franklin shared this anxiety and did what he could, through private conversation, to encourage the moderate minority in the Houses of Parliament not to permit "so glorious a Fabric to be demolished by these Blunderers" (P, 21.545). Just as he had with the recalcitrant Collins fifty years earlier, Franklin once more finds himself nursing a sour mind as he begins the voyage letter narrative. He had temporarily withdrawn from diplomatic life in response to the grievances incurred when the king's solicitor general had humiliated him in a public hearing before the Privy Council. The March 22 letter candidly depicts his brooding:

> From the Time of the Affront given me at the Council Board in January 1774, I had never attended the Levee of any Minister. I made no Justification of my self from the Charges brought against me: I made no Return of the Injury by abusing my Adversaries; but held a cool sullen Silence, reserving my self to some future Opportunity.... Now and then I heard it said, that the reasonable Part of the Administration were asham'd of the Treatment they had given me. I suspected that some who told me this, did it to draw from me my Sentiments concerning it, and perhaps my Purposes: But I said little or nothing upon the Subject. In the mean time their Measures with regard to New England failing of the Success that had been confidently expected, and finding themselves more and more embarrass'd, they began, (as it seems) to think of making use of me, if they could, to assist in disengaging them. But it was too humiliating to think of applying to me openly and directly; and therefore it was contriv'd to obtain what they could of my Sentiments thro' others. (P, 21.545–46)

Wounded pride and diplomatic guile combine to sustain this cool, sullen performance. As Franklin's long letter unfolds, his last-ditch efforts are repeatedly thwarted less by political differences than by the temperamental ones that had played so prominent a role in the personal collisions of his earliest years in Boston and Philadelphia.

"Providence is an excellent artist," Jonathan Shipley ultimately writes a deeply discouraged Franklin shortly before his departure from England, "and can perform very admirable Works with very wretched Tools" (P, 21.540). The words are intended to console an old friend, in the face of what Shipley hoped would be a temporary, if devastating, reverse. But they are also a beautiful similitude: a figurative emblem in the tradition of *The Pilgrim's Progress* that points directly toward Benjamin Franklin's lifelong struggle to harness the essential "tool" of his own nature in the service of constructive ends. That struggle is on display, both for better and for worse, as Franklin describes his state of mind on the threshold of the Revolution. In his efforts to alleviate the differences dividing Americans from Englishmen, Franklin is not always successful in curbing his own resentments or abiding by the elaborate system of precepts and personal rituals that he had built for himself at the beginning of his business career in Philadelphia, long before he had any intention of entering public life. This system too represents a delicate act of accommodation to the unstable interplay between passion and principle in human behavior. The opening of the 1775 voyage letter, like the memoir as a whole, portrays that interplay as vividly as Franklin does the instabilities of a rowboat full of quarrelsome young men on the Delaware River.

When a printer imposes his forms, he wedges his lines of carefully set type firmly in place so that the press can pull a clean and near-perfect image from the inked surfaces of the letters: an admirable work, Jonathan Shipley might have observed, produced with wretched tools. But character is not so simple a medium to manage. Franklin's craft had taught him to appreciate the intricate and often frustrating relations between the process and the product, a double nature that the printer's finished page conceals.[2]

The sheets of unruled paper that make up the memoir's manuscript are a conventional adaptation to the double nature of authors and of the books they make. Like many writers before and after him, in the centuries preceding electronic composition, Franklin divided his pages into equal halves with a single vertical fold, in effect creating an expanded margin to one side of the main column of his draft. The unimpeded flow of Franklin's memories, directed in part by his stream of suggestive notes, filled half of each manuscript sheet. The other half remained available to accommodate large-scale corrections or changes that might occur as the narrative progressed, like the proliferating "sparks" of thought or dialogue that kept presenting themselves to John Bunyan as *The Pilgrim's Progress* grew to presentable dimensions. The detailed discussion of Peter Folger's "homespun Verse" in defense of religious liberty is one such interpolated detail, inserted beside the main body of the story. So is the brief entry, early in the third fragment of the book, in which Franklin describes the death of his four-year-old son during a smallpox outbreak in 1736. The scene in which Franklin throws John Collins into the Delaware River is another, a story that spills out into the broad margin of the sheet much like Collins spills out of the boat when Franklin unexpectedly seizes him by the "crutch" and throws him off balance.[3]

This simple provision for handling one's manuscript was an effective means of providing for the mix of addition, elaboration, and revision that go into the writing process, particularly in an era of expensive paper. But it is also an effective emblem for the restless counterpoises of character and experience that never lost their fascination for Franklin. Mrs. Read, for instance, as Franklin portrays her in the first part of his story, is both astute and imprudent when she evaluates Franklin's promise as a potential son-in-law and ultimately risks her daughter's happiness on a bad match. Samuel Keimer is an equally complicated human composition, both inept and perceptive in his appreciation for Franklin's argumentative and technical gifts. The account of Franklin's marriage with which the 1771 fragment of the memoir closes is a love story like few others, blending as it does long-standing reserves of mutual affection and respect with the burdens of guilt and dejection stemming from the Read family's precipitous interest in a worthless suitor, while a mercurial Benjamin Franklin steeped himself in the cultural resources of London. The complex legal obstacles to Deborah's remarriage (not to mention the existence of Franklin's illegitimate son William) combine to suggest the depth of the erotic quagmire into which Franklin and Deborah had tumbled and from which both were struggling to free themselves as they revived their relationship.[4]

Ultimately they are able to form a bond that approximates the durability of Josiah and Abiah Franklin's lifelong partnership, but the comparison is only approximate, marked by the array of contingencies and qualifications that complicate all emotional or moral accountings. Every dimension of Franklin's story invites the reader to assess the individuals whom it introduces or the scenes that it describes on finely graduated scales of character or principle, not unlike those which Franklin applies to himself throughout the narrative, beginning with the bodily scale that presswork routinely imposed on a journeyman printer. Walking up and down a flight of stairs in Watts's London printing house in 1725, Franklin had startled his fellow pressmen by his surprising ability to carry "a large Form of Types in each hand" to and from the composing room. The Water-American, as they called him, deriding Franklin's abstemious drinking habits, was able to distribute across the fulcrum of his shoulders and back two sets of lead letter, locked into pages and ready for the press, weighing as much as seventy or eighty pounds apiece.

This memory too has a figurative double life in Franklin's book. In effect, the anecdote depicts Franklin as a bodily scale under considerable strain, sustaining formidable amounts of weight on either hand, as he moves through the divided world in which he finds himself: master and worker, pressman and compositor, writer and printer, English and American. The striking of precarious balances is an ongoing preoccupation of Franklin's story, a delight and a challenge to the intellectual and physical vigor that he brings to his experience. Like much of the memoir, these scales and balances too have their origins in the tradition of moral discrimination that John Bunyan presents in *The Pilgrim's Progress*. The engaging mixture of narration and dialogue had first attracted Franklin's interest in the dramatic immediacy of Bunyan's book, but incessant mixture itself proves to be the more influential feature of Bunyan's example: a conceptual and imaginative bent that eventually sustains Franklin's moral performance in an equivocal world.[5]

THE VILLAGE OF ECTON in Northamptonshire that Franklin visited in July 1758 to collect information about his English ancestors is less than twenty miles northwest of Bedford, the town where John Bunyan's nonconformist congregation met and where Bunyan spent over a decade in jail, in the years following the Restoration, for illegal preaching. Josiah Franklin was six years old and living with his family of staunch dissenters in Ecton when Bunyan was first imprisoned in 1661. Eleven years later, when Bunyan resumed his interrupted career, Josiah was seventeen—the same age as Benjamin Franklin when he first left Boston—and, like his own son, Josiah too was apprenticed to an older brother, John Franklin, a dyer in Banbury, a little over thirty miles west of Bedford. When *The Pilgrim's Progress* first appeared in 1678, Josiah was twenty-three, two years into what he had called "a man's estate" when he declined to support William Keith's premature investment proposal for his youngest son's future. By that time Josiah's apprenticeship was over, though he probably remained a journeyman in his brother's Banbury shop, close enough to experience the influence of Bunyan's Bedford meeting.

The religious circles in which the Franklins of Ecton moved, during Josiah's formative years, as well as their proximity to the town and the dissenting congregation made famous by such a celebrated figure make it quite likely that Josiah knew of John Bunyan as he grew up and may well have heard him preach during these troubled years. Bunyan's fame derived in part from his own itinerant life, first as a tinker and then as a preacher who traveled an informal circuit, meeting with groups of nonconformist worshipers in the immediate vicinity of his home, as well as preaching from the pulpits of sympathizers in London. Certainly some of Bunyan's sermons would have been included among the shorthand stock that Franklin's uncle hoped to bequeath his gifted nephew, when it seemed for a time that he too might become a preacher. Uncle Benjamin was a connoisseur "of the best preachers," Franklin noted in the memoir, and John Bunyan was clearly in that class, even before *The Pilgrim's Progress* gave evidence of quite different literary gifts.[6]

Bunyan's personal example, however, is less important to the emerging design of Franklin's memoir than are the methods and the fruits of self-examination that Hopeful touches on while he and Christian are warding off sleep as they walk through the Enchanted Ground, one of the figurative environments that tests their vigilance on the route to the Celestial City. Even saints are prone to drowsiness, and Hopeful proposes that the two pilgrims "lie down here and take one Nap" before proceeding on their journey (PP, 130). To resist this fateful urge and to pass the time, Christian asks his companion for a kind of spiritual memoir: "*How came you to think at first of doing as you do now?*" Hopeful had been a contented resident in the city of Vanity and a customer at its famous fair when Christian and Faithful originally arrived there. The spectacle of Faithful's martyrdom and Christian's fortitude gradually brought him to the same state of anxiety that marked Christian at the beginning of his pilgrimage, but at this point in the book Bunyan expands on the psychological process of awakening that takes hold in Hopeful's mind: a contest between Principle and Inclination, in which Hopeful only gradually comes to recognize the intractable nature of the spiritual troubles that sometimes recede from his mind, as he takes steps to change his life, only to come "tumbling on me again, and that over the neck of all my Reformations" (PP, 133).

Even the fear of damnation is insufficient to prompt us to "mend" our lives once and for all. Old sins cannot be erased, Hopeful ultimately concludes, and new ones cannot be evaded, no matter how exacting one's self-examination might be: "if I look narrowly into the best of what I do now, I still see sin, new sin, mixing itself with the best of what I do" (PP, 133). Franklin's own discoveries about himself and others spring from the same method of narrow ethical inquiry, leading to much the same conclusion that Bunyan's characters reach: a stubborn impurity is latent even in the best that human beings strive to do. This insight is particularly congenial to the exacting trade that Franklin finally adopts after he signs his indentures and goes to work for his brother in Boston. He stresses the link very early in his memoir when he calls many of his regrets and misdeeds "errata," a printing term that seems at first to diminish the weight of the guilt that Franklin feels for his transgressions, signaling his escape from the religious world that John Bunyan and his Ecton ancestors shared. Hopeful offers Christian a detailed account of how he came to accept the necessity for Christ's imputed grace if he were ever to overcome the persistent sin in his nature. No such conversion experience influences the systematic process of "amendment" that Benjamin Franklin designs for himself.

At the same time, however, Franklin embraces the central perception that Hopeful describes. Our motives and our actions are never entirely free of the influence of self-interest, part of the trio of spiritual dangers that his uncle's birthday acrostic had cautioned him to avoid: Satan, sin, and self. Vanity is a key motive for most human endeavor, Franklin admits in the opening sentences of the memoir, and is often "productive of good" despite its equivocal origins. Pride and humility may be ethical opposites, but in life (Franklin acknowledges) they are often inextricably entangled with one another. Mixtures of this kind are intrinsic to human nature. Even Josiah Franklin briefly thinks about his own financial necessities when he declines to support William Keith's plan to set his son up in Philadelphia. Franklin deleted from the memoir Josiah's admission to his son-in-law Robert Homes that "he had advanc'd too much already to my Brother James" to allow him to make a similar commitment to support his youngest son's ambitions. His father "was clear in the Impropriety" of turning an expensive new business over to the untested judgment and skill of an eighteen-year-old, but a sense of impropriety is not the sole reason for Josiah Franklin's decision. He is simply short of funds. In suppressing this detail, Franklin risks making his father appear unsympathetic in order to heighten the contrast between Josiah's parental principles and William Keith's shallow permissiveness—scales of character that are critical to the lessons that Franklin hopes his own son, William, will take to heart.[7]

Like Bunyan's Hopeful, Franklin too eventually embarks on an elaborate effort at personal reformation, instituting a systematic and narrow scrutiny of his daily actions only to find that his success is limited at best. But success, surprisingly enough, is of secondary importance to the ethical journey that parallels the more familiar tale of material progress that Franklin's story often appears to embody. The anecdote of the speckled ax—another of the memoir's many parables—illustrates this point with an economy and wit that John Bunyan might have admired. Hopeful's discouragement at the persistent presence of new sin mixed with his "late amendments" invites comparison to the frustration Franklin claims to have felt at the incorrigible nature of his own "faulty Character." With time and effort his various transgressions did indeed seem to diminish, but they never entirely disappeared. When his attention lapsed, new faults would crop up in place of the old ones. Franklin was ready to content himself with imperfection:

> Like the Man who in buying an Ax of a Smith my neighbour, desired to have the whole of its Surface as bright as the Edge; the Smith consented to grind it bright for him if he would turn the Wheel. He turn'd while the Smith press'd the broad Face of the Ax hard and heavily on the Stone, which made the Turning of it very fatiguing. The Man came every now and then from the Wheel to see how the Work went on; and at length would take his Ax as it was without farther Grinding. No, says the Smith, Turn on, turn on; we shall have it bright by and by; as yet 'tis only speckled. Yes, says the Man; but—*I think I like a speckled Axe best.* (A, 155–56)

A fatiguing stint at the grinding wheel makes short work of the love of dazzling appearances. Foppery in morals is ultimately ridiculous, Franklin concludes. And, at any rate, it is prudent to tolerate some flaws in one's character in order to avoid arousing the envy of one's neighbors.

But these are not the only lessons—or even the most interesting ones—that this little story tells. *The Pilgrim's Progress* is full of similar spiritual exempla presented in the form of tableaux or exhibits for the instruction of Bunyan's travelers. Some of these are little more than inspiring museum curiosities, like Moses's rod or the sling and stone with which David slew Goliath, inspirational objects that Christian views on his visit to the House Beautiful. Others are proverbs or verbal emblems, like those that Prudence, one of the mistresses of the House Beautiful, introduces to Christiana's children, in the second part of Bunyan's book, when she invites her young visitors to pose "profitable" questions that she can turn into instructive similitudes of the spiritual life. "Why doth the Fire fasten upon the Candle-wick?" Christiana's oldest son Matthew asks, taking up Prudence's invitation: "To shew that unless Grace doth kindle upon the Heart, there will be no true Light of Life in us," she replies (PP, 218).

More elaborate scenarios or instructive scenes call for a seasoned interpreter to unravel. Early in Christian's journey, for instance, as he rests at the Interpreter's House, he visits one of his host's "Significant Rooms" to watch a man with a broom energetically sweeping a parlor and stirring up choking clouds of dust in the process, until a "Damsel" appears to sprinkle the room with water, allowing it to be thoroughly cleaned. What does the little tableau mean? Christian asks. His guide informs him that the parlor is an image of the heart and the dust is sin, which can never be finally swept away until it has been sprinkled with the waters of Grace.

The original sweeper, the Interpreter continues, represents the futility of the moral Law without the assistance of the power of the Gospel to subdue the heart's native corruption. Franklin may have had this little skit in mind, later in his memoir, when he describes the odd origin of his proposal for sweeping London's perennially dusty streets. That "significant" scene too begins with an energetic street sweeper, a feeble old woman, whose efforts enjoy a miraculous success once Franklin arranges to pay her a fair wage for her work. In the second part of Bunyan's allegory, Christiana is often very good at interpreting riddles on her own, but even she needs help with deciphering the emblem of a great spider hanging unnoticed upon the wall of the best room in the Interpreter's array of meaningful exhibits. As he did for her husband, Christiana's host explains its surprising significance—"that how full of the Venome of Sin soever you be," he observes, "yet you may by the hand of Faith lay hold of and dwell in the best Room that belongs to the King's house" (PP, 189).

The man shopping for a new ax in Franklin's seemingly innocent story is not preoccupied by the venom of sin, but he does find himself in the presence of a surprisingly astute smith—a kind of successor to John Bunyan's canny Interpreter—who is as good at teaching lessons as he is at metalwork. In the simplest, most circumstantial sense, it would be perfectly appropriate for this tradesman to point out to his customer, with some exasperation, that an ax is a working tool, not an ornament, made for hard use and not for show. It does not need to be uniformly bright to serve its ends. Or the smith might simply comply with his customer's impractical desire in return for a higher price and ask an apprentice to turn the heavy wheel while the purchaser waits. But neither of these plausible outcomes occurs. By situating this story in a place that purports to be his own neighborhood, Franklin is inviting the reader to imagine more realistic exchanges between the two characters that, in turn, highlight its "significant" departures from the ordinary.

In reality, the story is an emblem of instruction as well as the vehicle of a lesson. How its participants behave, how the narrative is worded, and what it omits are as interesting as what the two men finally agree to accept about human imperfection. Even a speckled ax may have a keen edge. A brightly polished "face," however broad or flawless, is not always a sign of inward perfections. Regardless of what we claim to "think" we like, our actual thoughts and reflections are almost certainly more complex than our words reveal.

These lessons too extend the scope of Franklin's simple story. "Something that pretended to be Reason," he continues, was skeptical of the kind of "extreme Nicety" in morals that the speckled ax story purports to illustrate, but it actually illustrates a more provocative range of perceptions than this premature conclusion suggests. Neither the wily smith nor his chastened customer ever clearly explains his motives to the other or itemizes the different meanings to which their encounter lends itself, but the anecdote confers on each participant an ethical depth and narrative interest that the brevity and everyday nature of the story would appear to preclude.[8]

Franklin offers the scene as an encapsulation of the blend of success and failure that his experience taught him to expect from the struggle to shape his character to an ideal standard. The expression of modest diffidence with which the smith's customer accepts his speckled ax—his affirmation of what he "thinks" he likes—signals the close identification of this make-believe neighbor with the restraints that Franklin had first applied to his own youthful love of argument and later adapted to the broad exercise in self-discipline that he began during his first years in Philadelphia: the celebrated pursuit of moral perfection, which he takes up in the second section of his memoir. This "bold and arduous Project" emerges from the accumulated frustrations that he had encountered in his relations with institutionalized religion, beginning with his Boston childhood and extending into his adult encounters with the clerical establishment of Philadelphia. Some of the dogmas of his parent's church "appear'd to me unintelligible," Franklin recalled in the memoir, others seemed merely doubtful, while still others he never ceased to accept throughout the course of his religious pilgrimage. He never doubted the existence of God, Franklin insisted, or the immortality of the soul, or the Providential government of creation and its enforcement of justice "either here or hereafter," according to our behavior in life (A, 146).

In this carefully scaled response to inherited religious conviction, the unintelligible and the unquestionable counterbalance one another at either extreme, like the heavy forms of lead type on either hand that Franklin carried through Watts's printing house, with "doubtful" doctrines poised between. A similar scale of responses extends to Franklin's view of the other religious sects with which he found himself surrounded in the heterogeneous sectarian culture of Philadelphia. Nearly all of them endorsed the essentials of belief that Franklin too never ceased to affirm, but all of these confessional systems were likewise "more or less mix'd with other Articles which without any Tendency to inspire, promote, or confirm Morality, serv'd principally to divide us and make us unfriendly to one another" (A, 146). Franklin does not calibrate his support for public worship in conformity with these fine discriminations of mixture or division, but neither does he commit himself to any single sect's support beyond the "Mite" that he says he extends to any religious body that promises some degree of "good Effects" from the construction of a church. Each group that solicits his help gets an equal measure of endorsement—the accounts are balanced—but the aggregate effect of these many "mites" reflects Franklin's ongoing reluctance to align himself with any particular sectarian persuasion.

This wary posture is quite easy to confuse with the kind of religious equivocation that John Bunyan scorns, very early in *The Pilgrim's Progress*, when he has Evangelist administer a stern lecture to Christian about his apparent willingness to settle for a nice house in the village of Morality, rather than pursuing the hardships of pilgrimage. Worldly-Wiseman had given Christian this self-serving advice when he observed "his laborious going . . . his sighs and groans" as he struggled toward the Wicket Gate at the outset of his journey. A citizen of the great town of Carnal-Policy, "hard by" the City of Destruction, Worldly-Wiseman had heard of Christian's quest for eternal life and had set out across the fields deliberately to intercept him and suggest a less arduous alternative. "Pray Sir open this secret to me," Christian eagerly asks:

> Worldly-Wiseman: *Why in yonder Village, (the Village is named* Morality*) there dwells a Gentleman, whose name is* Legality, *a very judicious man (and a man of a very good name) that has skill to help men off with such burdens as thine are, from their shoulders: yea, to my knowledge he hath done a great deal of good this way. . . . His house is not quite a mile from this place; and if he should not be at home himself, he hath a pretty young man to his Son, whose name is* Civility, *that can do it (to speak on) as well as the old Gentleman himself. There, I say, thou mayest be eased of thy burden, and if thou art not minded to go back to thy former habitation, as indeed I would not wish thee, thou mayest send for thy wife and Children to thee in this Village, where there are houses now stand empty, one of which thou mayest have at reasonable rates: Provision is there also cheap and good, and that which will make thy life the more happy, is, to be sure there thou shalt live by honest neighbors, in credit and good fashion.* (PP, 19–20)

Bunyan's village of Morality bears a striking resemblance to the Philadelphia that Franklin describes in the early pages of the memoir: reasonable rents and cheap provisions (if the price of bread is a reliable index), honest neighbors like the young Quaker who steers Franklin to a reputable inn after he falls asleep in Sunday meeting, and an abundance of vacant real estate that alarms the gloomy Samuel Mickle when he informs Franklin in his newly opened print-shop that he has cast his economic lot in a "sinking Place." This half-whimsical, half-troubling parallel is probably not lost on Franklin himself, as he is drawing it in 1771.

Eventually Franklin too will a have "pretty young man to his Son," one accomplished in the civil graces, who is ready to make a career in this compliant and comfortable world. A complacent Legality seems, at first glance, to be the very destination that Franklin aims at in his own religious aspirations. But he quickly signals the reader of the memoir that his personal understanding of moral life has very little in common with the kind of shallow, outward conformity to Law that Worldly-Wiseman recommends. Franklin in fact attacks mere Legality with nearly as much zeal as Bunyan's Evangelist. In response to the frequent urging of Philadelphia's sole Presbyterian minister, he occasionally attended Presbyterian services during his first years in the city, partly perhaps out of deference to his New England roots. Once (Franklin brags) he appeared at these weekly "Administrations" for "five Sundays successively," a comment aimed at stressing the superficial nature of religious conformity. The sermons invariably disappointed him. The minister's "Discourses were chiefly either polemic Arguments, or Explications of the peculiar Doctrines of our Sect, and were all to me very dry, uninteresting and unedifying" (A, 147). Sectarian discipline rather than "moral Principle" seemed to be their goal: a kind of legalism intended to shore up congregational solidarity for its own sake, "their Aim seeming to be rather to make us Presbyterians than good Citizens."

This objection is not as secular as it first appears to be. Franklin did not attend church to brush up on the particulars of the catechism, but neither did he go for a Sunday civics lesson. Like many of his peers in the years immediately preceding the Great Awakening, he was interested in the state of the heart, in its capacity to lend an inward energy to the kind of "mere speculative conviction" that often left religious doctrine or moral principle a dead letter in most people's lives, a matter of tabulating church attendance for its own sake, rather than attending to the substance of their religious lives. "Why doth the Fire fasten upon the Candle-wick?" Christiana's son inquires when Prudence invites him to pose emblematic questions. Why do some spirits burn with fervor or inner purpose, consuming "the Wick and Tallow and all," the boy continues, while others flicker out? The questions intrigue Franklin as well, and when his minister announces that a forthcoming sermon will address Philippians 4:8, he is hopeful. The memoir quotes a close paraphrase of the verse, apparently from memory and not strictly by the book, so that Franklin's reader can appreciate the grounds of his anticipation: "*Finally, Brethren, Whatsoever Things are true, honest, just, pure, lovely, or of good report, if there be any virtue, or any praise, think on these Things*" (A, 147).

Very little in this verse would appear to invite a narrow sectarian reading, but neither is it directed strictly at the formation of good citizens. The pure, the lovely, and the true are central to its focus, along with the more public or civic attributes of justice, honesty, and "good report." Half of the Philippians passage looks outward toward social values, and half turns inward toward more mysterious resources linked to spiritual perception and, in doing so, asks the listener (or the reader) to think, not to do. Reflection as well as action seems to be the goal of these words—a counterpoise between the outer and the inner life—as if some transformational experience or insight shares equal importance with behavior in the mind of its author. A complex interchange between physical and metaphysical, between secular and spiritual ends, is at issue in the verse. It does not refer openly to grace, as Prudence so candidly does in the House Beautiful, but it points toward the same mental and emotional terrain over which Bunyan's pilgrims traveled. Like Bunyan's similitudes, it is an effort to shape consciousness or to foster a special kind of awareness, rather than to prescribe behavior.[9]

When Philippians 4:8 elicits only another doctrinaire sermon from Philadelphia's Presbyterian minister, Franklin reports that he abandoned the church meetings in disgust—a surprisingly strong term for this master of modest diffidence—and returned to the exercise of a private liturgy that he had devised for himself shortly after his return from London in the autumn of 1726. A few fragments of this private worship system remain in the memoir, but Franklin's chief interest in the brief section of his book that he wrote at Passy in 1784 was to explain the reasoning behind a list of virtues that he had made, and to describe a tablet of "accounts" that he kept, in an effort to restrict his habits within a specific array of moral boundaries. This attempt begins in the same tabulating spirit that Franklin derides when he recalls his successive Sundays of church attendance, but it quickly outgrows this shallow stage:

> I wish'd to live without committing any Fault at any time; I would conquer all that either Natural Inclination, Custom, or Company might lead me into. As I knew, or thought I knew, what was right and wrong, I did not see why I might not *always* do the one and avoid the other. But I soon found I had undertaken a Task of more Difficulty than I had imagined. While my Care was employ'd in guarding against one Fault, I was often surpris'd by another. Habit took the Advantage of Inattention. Inclination was sometimes too strong for Reason. I concluded at length, that the mere speculative Conviction that it was our Interest to be compleatly virtuous, was not sufficient to prevent our Slipping, and that the contrary Habits must be broken and good ones acquired and established, before we can have any Dependence on a steady uniform Rectitude of Conduct. (A, 148)

The language in this passage is both unobtrusive and highly charged, from the perspective of the religious world in which Franklin was raised. The familiar antagonism between Inclination and Reason carries over directly from the 1771 fragment of the memoir, where Franklin discusses his dietary qualms over eating freshly caught cod, but Prudence's examination of Christiana's children in the second part of *The Pilgrim's Progress* also includes the doctrinal reminder that Man was created, by design, a "Reasonable Creature" intended, above all, for "everlasting Happiness," both terms central to the ethical enterprise that Franklin describes in the memoir. A respect for reason alone does not signal Franklin's unmixed humanist or Enlightenment loyalties, particularly in view of his implicit recognition that reason often "sleeps" (as Hopeful had wanted to do in the Enchanted Ground) or loses its contest with the irrational forces of Natural Inclination. Other terms in the passage do appear deliberately intended to exclude a conventional religious analysis of the inner life. Faults, rather than sins, are the target of Franklin's efforts at reformation; good habits, rather than Grace, are the necessary auxiliaries that reason requires if it hopes to "conquer" appetite and desire. Rectitude of conduct is Franklin's nominal goal, a phrase that Worldly-Wiseman might applaud.

Once Franklin turns to his collection of virtues and precepts, however, he moves steadily if subtly closer to the psychological heart of John Bunyan's world. To begin with, a kind of balancing act dictates the formation of Franklin's list of ethical goals, one closely related to the interchange between narrow inquiry and outward performance that troubles Hopeful during his pilgrimage. Franklin's research into the "Catalogue" of virtues derived from his reading produces a problem at the outset: ideas and names (or labels) appear to be inconsistently arranged, with a "more or less numerous" roster of virtues linked to "more or fewer Ideas" of what any particular authority believed a particular ideal to include. The conceptual and the moral "books" that he examined were in disarray. Cataloging alone is clearly the wrong approach to managing the complex relationship between conscience and conduct. In framing his own list of ideal attributes, Franklin chooses to align fewer ideas with more names, for the sake of "Clearness" (he claims in the memoir), and prepares a list of twelve initial virtues, which grows eventually to thirteen when a Quaker friend points out a conspicuous deficiency.

The original twelve had formed an all-too-obvious Christological echo that the awkward addition of a thirteenth virtue at first disrupts, but Franklin is pointedly indifferent to symbolic numerology as well as to folk superstition. Twelve, after all, was also the number of original members in Franklin's Junto, his young men's club for moral improvement and mutual education, and dictated the familiar structure of his annual almanacs, as well as being an appealing even number that lent itself to a variety of symmetrical and asymmetrical groupings of the sort that might have delighted the fussy mathematician, Thomas Godfrey, a Junto member and for some years a tenant in Franklin's printshop. "Clearness" alone is much too simple a criterion to account for the original design of Franklin's ethical program, but neither is it immediately clear what instincts ultimately influence its shape.

To each virtue Franklin then "annex'd" a short "Precept" to illustrate its "Extent." These three terms from the memoir appear carefully selected to avoid the implication that Franklin was aiming at the kind of prescriptive definition to which the cataloging mind inclines. Each ethical ideal on Franklin's list has territorial scope. Moreover, the precepts themselves are worded so as to discourage the love of legalism, or the merely technical compliance with a public code, that makes the village of Morality such an appealing destination for human pilgrims. Each virtue requires that a thoughtful interaction take place between the subjective and the objective spheres of moral life. Temperance, for instance, stipulates that Franklin "Eat not to Dulness. Drink not to Elevation," a double exhortation calling for careful attention to one's interior condition long before a drinking or dining companion might be inclined to express some concern over one's obvious excesses. Dullness and elevation are subtle, affective states as complicated in their own ways as the meaning of temperance itself. The precept for Silence addresses a similar division between behavior that others might readily observe and feelings or intentions that only the moral agent is in a position to examine: "Speak not but what may benefit others or yourself. Avoid trifling Conversation." As Franklin presents it, this virtue can only manifest itself through the way in which one manages its audible opposite. Mere silence can be a form of selfishness, as it is in the early sentences of the 1775 voyage letter, a kind of "trifling" with the responsibilities that the gift of language imposes.

Sincerity, the seventh virtue on Franklin's list, is by definition rooted in intentions that are invisible to others and often hidden even from ourselves. It can be a notoriously difficult attribute to assess. For this reason, the precept that Franklin annexes to it establishes its claims in unusual terms, substituting accessible ideas for inherently elusive ones. "Use no hurtful Deceit," the motto for Sincerity begins, immediately conceding that deceit itself is often an inescapable feature of social existence, even for the sincere, and may in fact be put to generous uses. "Think innocently and justly," Franklin continues, "and, if you speak, speak accordingly" (A, 150). These words presuppose the presence of an inner monitor charged with overseeing the manner in which one thinks or speaks, not the essence of one's thought: an interior performance which recognizes that an exhaustive command over our motives is unattainable.[10]

Justice and Moderation, the eighth and ninth virtues on Franklin's list, have precepts that mix familiar public ideals with private criteria of judgment, redirecting their straightforward application from visible to invisible forums. The just must be wary of "omitting the Benefits that are your duty," as well as careful to "Wrong none," Franklin insists, envisioning a code of behavior that sets aside a conventional list of infractions or crimes in favor of discovering the benefits that we "owe" to one another. This standard has next to nothing in common with the appeal to mere legality that John Bunyan scorns. The moderate must "Avoid Extremes," Franklin's precept for his ninth virtue predictably (and moderately) declares, before making a surprising concession to the struggle with private resentments that lies behind all acts of moderation: "Forbear resenting injuries so much as you think they deserve." Moderation strives to smother these resentful fires, as Franklin himself attempted to do after the bitter public chastisement of January 1774, but his precept concedes that one cannot reasonably expect to extinguish them.[11]

At several points in this portion of the memoir, Franklin refers to the list of virtues and precepts, along with the booklet that he made to track his daily behavior, as his "Scheme." The term suggests to readers today an ingenious plan or devious plot, confirming a predisposition to view Franklin's ethical interests as purely manipulative. But he is using the word in an older sense to describe an elaborate and ambitious mnemonic device. John Bunyan uses it this way in the second part of *The Pilgrim's Progress* when he has Piety present Christiana with a "Scheme" of all the objects and emblems that she and her children have seen at the House Beautiful "for when thou findest thyself forgetful" (PP, 221). Franklin's bold and arduous project too is a compact tool for fending off forgetfulness. A virtue that hardens into a mere label risks losing its claim on our attention without a concise reminder of the interplay between thought and action, consciousness and conduct, that the practice of virtue entails. Franklin's interest in forming virtuous "habits" suggests that he aims at an automatic or unreflective version of morality, but nothing in the precepts that he writes for his personal catalog of ethical goals lends itself to the merely habitual anymore than mere speculative conviction alone was adequate to govern the conduct of life.

The number and the sequence of the original twelve virtues, as well as Franklin's daily, weekly, and yearly systems of ethical accounting, exert a variety of subtle claims on human attention. By beginning his list with Temperance and ending it with Chastity, for instance, Franklin shapes the sequence into a circle or a spiral of behavioral goals that imbeds a system of mutual reinforcement into the collective arrangement. Temperance, he explains, is a precondition for the "Coolness and Clearness of Head" that careful compliance with all the following virtues will demand, but it is also a close relative of the tempered sexual appetites that Chastity, the last of the original twelve, hopes to encourage. In a similar way, Silence and Tranquillity, the second and eleventh virtues on the list, are natural pairs, with the second of the two a direct, if higher, successor to the first. Order and Cleanliness, the third and the tenth virtues, are likewise cognate goals—ethical similitudes of one another applied to different aspects of existence. The first three virtues on Franklin's list, in conjunction with their later partners, function much like a trio of concentric ethical circles inscribed around the six interior and socially oriented attributes of Resolution, Frugality, Industry, Sincerity, Justice, and Moderation. Franklin's arrangement, in other words, has an inside and an outside, as well as a beginning and an end, just as each precept seeks to mix interior and exterior life.

Once Franklin was persuaded to add Humility as his thirteenth virtue, this apparent asymmetry produced a convenient outcome: he could now use the little booklet that he had prepared for keeping track of his ethical lapses to organize four, thirteen-week "Courses" of moral reform in a year, concentrating each of the fifty-two weeks of the calendar on one of his virtues and its accompanying precept. The booklet included a verse motto from Joseph Addison's *Cato* and a prayer of Franklin's own to help remind him of the ontological context for his project. The first was very much an outer, and the second an inner, exhortation. "Here will I hold," Addison's Roman hero proclaims: "If there is a Pow'r above us, / (And that there is, all Nature cries aloud / Thro' all her Works) he must delight in Virtue, / And that which he delights in must be happy." Franklin's prayer, by contrast, puts aside the defensive stoicism of Addison's lines in favor of Franklin's recognition that the motives and the self-understanding that shape our deeds call for metaphysical reinforcement:

> *O Powerful Goodness! bountiful Father! merciful Guide! Increase in me that Wisdom which discovers my truest Interests; Strengthen my Resolutions to perform what that Wisdom dictates. Accept my kind Offices to thy other Children, as the only Return in my Power for thy continual Favours to me.* (A, 153)

These words appear to suggest an exchange of services, rather than a sincere expression of gratitude for blessings, a tradesman's utilitarian piety aimed at enhancing worldly interests in return for kind offices. But just as with the memoir's suggestively imperfect quotation from Philippians, this prayer requires a deliberative reading.[12]

Franklin is projecting a kind of unconventional trinity with these words as well as introducing his booklet of virtues, offering three versions of the Deity that mingle identities and attributes in provocative ways. Goodness is the locus of power in this prayer, not the mythic Father: an inner and to some degree an abstract entity from which bounty and mercy flow. But bounty and mercy are not the prayer's objects. Wisdom is, and wisdom in turn is necessary to distinguish one's "truest" interests from the many lesser ones that preoccupy or distract the human pilgrim. When Alexis de Tocqueville commented on the principle of mutually advantageous self-interest, as "the American moralists" understood and applied it, he quite clearly had Benjamin Franklin in mind:

> In the United States hardly anybody talks of the beauty of virtue, but they maintain that virtue is useful and prove it every day. The American moralists do not profess that men ought to sacrifice themselves for their fellow creatures *because* it is noble to make such sacrifices, but they boldly aver that such sacrifices are as necessary to him who imposes them upon himself as to him for whose sake they are made. . . . They therefore do not deny that every man may follow his

own interest, but they endeavor to prove that it is the interest of every man to be virtuous. (2.2.8)

Tocqueville's words (and the suggestive emphasis of Henry Reeve, the young Englishman whom Tocqueville selected as his first translator) indicate that he paid close attention to Franklin's insistent sense of ethical causality in the first section of the memoir: that certain actions were "forbidden *because* they were bad for us," or commanded *because* they were good, by the Providential intelligence that designed the world with human well-being in mind (A, 115). But Tocqueville goes on to wonder whether the outcome of this philosophic principle will be to purge the world of extraordinary virtues as well as extraordinary vices:

> The principle of self-interest rightly understood produces no great acts of self-sacrifice, but it suggests daily small acts of self-denial. By itself it cannot suffice to make a man virtuous; but it disciplines a number of persons in habits of regularity, temperance, moderation, foresight, self-command; and if it does not lead men straight to virtue by the will, it gradually draws them in the direction by their habits. (2.2.8)

These words, once again, appear to be in close dialogue with parts of Franklin's memoir, but the appeal to "Powerful Goodness" with which Franklin's book of virtues begins makes extraordinary moral demands, as well as minor or pragmatic ones, operating on a vast rather than a diminished metaphysical stage. In some respects the prayer is framed as carefully as the ethical precepts accompanying each of the virtues that it introduces, aiming not simply at the accumulation of good or beneficial habits but at the wisdom to discern the truest from the merely expedient interests of existence.[13]

The prayer, in turn, links Franklin's booklet of ethical accounts to the structure that he imposed on his daily schedule, presented in the memoir as a column of numbers enclosed in squares for every hour of the day, beginning at five o'clock. An extract from Pythagoras's "Golden Verses" that he intended to transcribe in this section of the book suggests the necessity for some narrow daily examination to work in tandem with Franklin's weekly and yearly plans: "Let not the stealing God of Sleep surprize,/ Nor creep in Slumbers on thy weary Eyes,/ Ere ev'ry Action of the former Day,/ Strictly thou dost, and righteously survey." Accordingly to the left of Franklin's schematic column of hours, he inserts morning and evening questions—"What Good shall I do this

Day?" "What Good have I done to day?"—and begins his workday routine with a recitation of the Powerful Goodness prayer, along with a handful of largely practical chores: rise, wash, "contrive the Day's Business," study, "and breakfast" (A, 154). Temperance, Cleanliness, two forms of Resolution, and a prayer expressive of Humility—all important entries on Franklin's list of thirteen virtues—play a part in getting his day underway. Indeed, this group draws from the beginning, the middle, and the closing sections of the list of virtues, as if the morning hours have a more comprehensive scope than the evening ones do.

Franklin's time line makes no provision for an evening prayer to balance the morning one, an intriguing decision since it seems to echo the conventional emblematic significance of wakefulness and sleep that John Bunyan's allegory repeatedly stresses. Sleep is nearly always an outward sign of spiritual blindness in *The Pilgrim's Progress*. Staying awake is the mark of an attentive and watchful soul. Bunyan's characters often find themselves holding religious discussions or deciphering pious riddles all night during their journey. In part two of the story, no one in Christiana's large party of pilgrims sleeps at all after they arrive in the Land of Beulah, immediately adjacent to the border of the Celestial City. When a travel-worn Christian and Hopeful originally rested there, "they talked more in their sleep ... then ever they did in all their Journey," a phenomenon that puzzles Bunyan until Beulah's Gardener explains the reason: "It is the nature of the fruit of the Grapes of these Vineyards to go down so sweetly, as to cause the lips of them that are asleep to speak" (PP, 147).

The original twelve virtues, in fact, appear to parallel the hours of the waking day, as well as observing the order of progressive facility in which Franklin claims to have arranged them: a cumulative tactic whereby mastering the first virtue assists in addressing the second, which helps in turn with the third, and so on. This staircase model appears arbitrary at best the more closely one examines it, but the progression of the virtues across the private and public phases of the day is striking. The first four on Franklin's list—Temperance, Silence, Order, and Resolution—all play important roles in the morning ritual that Franklin allots to the hours between five and eight o'clock, with the Powerful Goodness prayer serving as the beneficial speech prescribed by Silence, and breakfast offering the first opportunity to eat and drink in moderation. "Take the resolution of the day," Franklin instructs himself, as he prepares for work, perhaps as a reminder to read over the precept for the virtue that is the object of the present week's "strict Attention" as he leaves for the printshop or

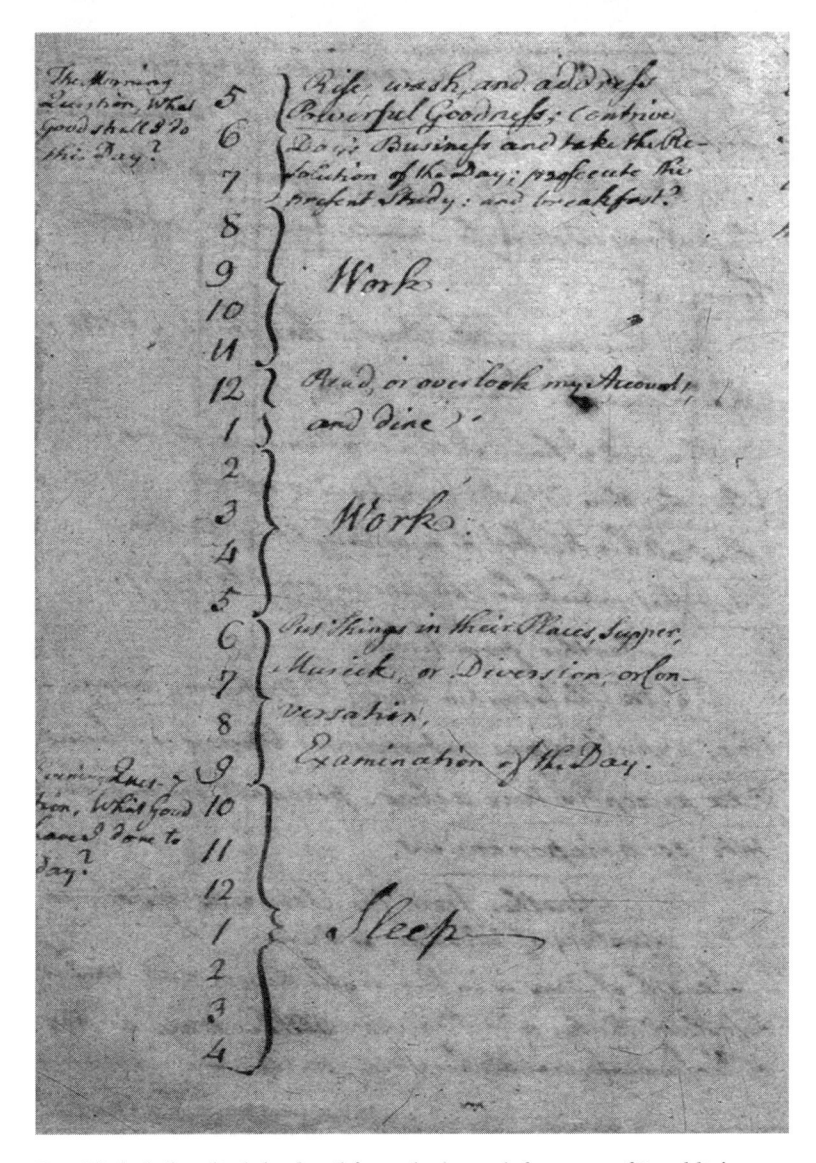

Franklin's daily schedule, detail from the lower left corner of Franklin's manuscript, p. 99. The left margin reads, "The Morning Question, What Good shall I do this Day" and "Evening Question, What Good have I done to day?" Reproduced from HM 9999 by permission of the Huntington Library, San Marino, California.

the Assembly, where the civic virtues of Frugality, Industry, Sincerity, Justice, and Moderation find a natural theater for their activity.

Cleanliness, Tranquillity, and Chastity, the last of the original twelve, are correspondingly tied to the evening hours: a reflective and traditionally intimate period of the day. "Rarely use Venery but for Health or Offspring," Franklin admonishes himself in the precept for Chastity, "Never to Dulness, Weakness, or the Injury of your own or another's Peace or Reputation," words that carefully echo the precept for Temperance to which Chastity corresponds in the concentric behavioral circles that Franklin has arranged. But this sexual advice is not exclusively marital in its focus (as the bawdy pun on "piece" may be meant to suggest) and embraces the view that one's sexuality is not strictly a provision for procreation. This hard-to-be-governed passion (as Franklin called it) has an important bearing on the complex form of emotional well-being associated with peace of mind and, as such, is more closely tied to Tranquillity than people customarily acknowledge. Cleanliness would appear to be out of place in this evening group, but "Uncleanness" referred to the full range of sexual transgressions in Franklin's day, rather than simply to hygiene. Avoiding the erotic disorder that this word implied would have struck Franklin's contemporaries as critical to the achievement of long-lasting happiness in such a vital sphere of existence.

Humility and its precept, "Imitate Jesus and Socrates," conclude the list of virtues after one of Franklin's acquaintances convinces him that he is frequently "overbearing and rather insolent" in discussions. The steps he took to try to modify his manners, if not his private opinion concerning the "Absurdity" of other people's ideas, required Franklin's attention across the entire range of his revolutionary working day and throughout his life. It is the only virtue of the thirteen that appeals to human models in its precept, and the two extraordinary beings whom Franklin names as its exemplars suggest the difficulty that he expected to encounter in trying to master it. But even in the face of such an impossible standard, Franklin concludes, his collective efforts at observing what he terms "the whole Mass of the Virtues" brought him happiness, wealth, reputation, and "Weight with my Fellow Citizens," in spite of the political handicaps that plagued him: "For I was but a bad Speaker, never eloquent, subject to much Hesitation in my choice of Words, hardly correct in Language, and yet I generally carried my Points" (A, 160). To possess this kind of exemplary weight is a prerequisite to carrying the consent of others. The broad-shouldered young pressman in Watts's printing house, over a long and varied career, found ways to adapt his strength to the balancing of intangible burdens.[14]

FRANKLIN ADHERED TO HIS SYSTEM of narrow self-scrutiny and moral reformation for a much longer period than he allotted to the public administrations of Philadelphia's Presbyterian church. Five successive Sundays of disappointment was all it took to drive him out of a sectarian congregation and back to his private prayer, his daily questions, and a weekly charting of the ethical lapses that he committed. The paper records he kept repeatedly wore out, and he replaced them with an ivory-leaved booklet containing weekly tables for each of the thirteen virtues inscribed in durable red ink on its pages. The lead pencil marks of his faults could then be conveniently wiped away with a sponge and a new course of watchful accounting begun. Gradually his devotion to maintaining this record through four complete cycles of thirteen virtues a year also understandably waned: "After a while I went thro' one Course only in a Year, and afterwards only one in several years; till at length I omitted them entirely, being employ'd in Voyages and Business abroad with a Multiplicity of Affairs, that interfered." This effort too, like the memoir itself, falls victim to the incessant interruption that cuts through life.

But the apparent displacement of Franklin's private ethical ambitions by his public responsibilities is partly a fulfillment rather than a rejection of the virtues and the precepts he had framed. The prayers, the goals, and the daily distribution of Franklin's time always assumed the kind of active engagement in life that his conception of Providence required: "kind Offices" to other human beings, not ecstatic withdrawal into contemplative isolation. Christian and Faithful in *The Pilgrim's Progress* agree: "The Soul of Religion is the practick part." Deeds, not verbal profession or the mastery of a catechism, are the spiritual essentials. At Judgment Day, Christian insists in a formulation that Franklin paraphrases many times in his life, fruits alone will matter: "It will not be said then, *Did you believe*? but Were you *Doers* or *Talkers* only? and accordingly shall they be judged" (PP, 78). When Franklin pockets his ivory memorandum book, then, and enters into the world of "Affairs," he is striking a sound balance rather than compromising his principles. "I always carried my little Book with me," he writes, even when it ceased to be the central focus of his day, as if its presence alone still represented a significant counterweight to the visible demands of business.

Indeed, though thirteen years separate the writing of the memoir's first two fragments, Franklin often seems to have his ivory memorandum book in mind, as well as in his pocket, as he reviews for his son the events of his months in London in 1725 and 1726 or tells the story of his gradual establishment in Philadelphia throughout the first section of his book. He carries his points among the compositors in Watts's London printing house, for instance, very much as he does among the citizens of Philadelphia later on, through a combination of virtues that enhances the weight of his example: temperance, moderation, justice, industry. Once he got on a "fair Footing" with his English co-workers by contributing to the Composing Room drinking fund, he was able to propose "some reasonable Alterations in their Chapel Laws" and win their adoption "against all Opposition," both because the changes were sensible and because many members of the "Chapel" relied on weekly loans from Franklin to pay their alehouse bills (A, 101).

Originally something of an outcast amid this tightly knit fraternity of English workmen, Franklin rather quickly begins to influence their daily habits, establishing a breakfast cooperative, among other improvements, in order to replace the compositors' traditional morning pint with a concoction of "hot Water-gruel, sprinkled with Pepper, crumb'd with Bread, and a Bit of Butter in it," made to Franklin's order. In addition to this savory gruel recipe, Franklin's fellow workers soon acquire a taste for his abilities as a "jocular verbal satirist," an interesting mix of comic and caustic gifts, part of which Franklin would ultimately try to restrain when he came to frame the precept for Silence in his moral program, in the hope of breaking the habit of "Prattling, Punning, and Joking" that he had fallen into.

But a "trifling" wit had its uses at Watts's printing house. Franklin was able to draw on the goodwill it produced in order to change some bad laws for better ones in the whimsical, pseudo-sacred order that governed their workplace. Temperance, Silence, Frugality, Industry, and Moderation all play important roles in the design of this brief episode in Franklin's early working life. Even the "little Pieces of private Mischief" that Franklin endured at the hands of the "Chapel Ghost" when he first moved from presswork to setting type—"mixing my Sorts, transposing my Pages, breaking my Matter"—did not so much provoke his anger as teach him "the Folly of being on ill Terms with those one is to live with continually." The price of foppery in morals could be unpleasant and unproductive, just as the speckled ax story suggests; the advantages of sacrificing a bit of principle in return for good social relations could amplify rather than diminish one's influence for good (A, 100).

A similar mix of ethical accountings extends to Franklin's other London household during this critical interval in his life. For most of his stay in the city, and for nearly all the time that he worked for John Watts, Franklin lodged with a Catholic landlady who lived "two pair of stairs backwards at an Italian Warehouse" with her daughter and a maid:

> She was a Widow, an elderly Woman, had been bred a Protestant, being a Clergyman's Daughter, but was converted to the Catholic Religion by her Husband, whose Memory she much revered, had lived much among People of Distinction, and knew a 1000 Anecdotes of them as far back as the Times of Charles the Second. She was lame in her Knees with the Gout, and therefore seldom stirr'd out of her Room, so sometimes wanted Company; and hers was so highly amusing to me; that I was sure to spend an Evening with her whenever she desired it. Our Supper was only half an Anchovy each, on a very little Strip of Bread and Butter, and half a Pint of Ale between us. But the Entertainment was in her Conversation. (A, 102)

Trapped by age, gout, and two flights of "backwards" stairs, Franklin's companionable host has an agile and amusing mind—far more attractive a partner (it would appear) than the daughter or the maid, neither of whom receives much attention from a nineteen-year-old lodger who has just been slapped down by the lively young milliner, Mrs. T, with whom Franklin had attempted some unwelcome "Familiarities."

By contrast, familiarity proves to be a source of great pleasure in these casual relations with his landlady. Like the "elderly" man who is now recalling her place in his life, she is an avid collector of anecdotes and something of a religious itinerant, having journeyed from one devotional extreme to another over the course of her experience, living up and down the scale of social distinction, since the early years of the Restoration, in a fashion that recalls the several flights of backwards stairs that lead to her present lodgings. She prizes good character, male protection, and intelligent conversation so highly that when Franklin finds cheaper rooms that might help him save more money, she cuts her rent to keep him. Together they feast on words, as much as bread, butter, ale, and anchovies, echoing the experience of Josiah Franklin's Boston dinner table or the hot-water-gruel society in Watts's composing room.

Among the anecdotes that Franklin's landlady shares with him is a joke she tells about a maiden lady recluse now living in her garret, venerating Saint Veronica, and devoting her inherited income to charity. Hoping to be a nun but unable to find a nunnery in a country that agreed with her, she had returned to England as a young woman to set up a personal cloister above the Italian warehouse:

> Accordingly she had given all her estate to charitable Uses, reserving only Twelve Pounds a Year to live on, and out of this Sum she still gave a great deal in Charity, living her self on Water-gruel only, and using no Fire but to boil it. She had lived many Years in that Garret, being permitted to remain there gratis by successive Catholic Tenants of the House below, as they deem'd it a Blessing to have her there. A Priest visited her, to confess her every Day. I have ask'd her, says my Landlady, how she, as she liv'd, could possibly find so much Employment for a Confessor? O, says she, it is impossible to avoid *vain Thoughts*. (A, 103)

The landlady's mild joke points to another, comic instance of foppery in morals in the memoir, one similar to the anecdote of the chastened neighbor who wanted his ax to be as bright as a mirror until experience taught him to check his own idealism. Franklin and this reclusive lady share an appreciation for the pervasive presence of vanity in life, as well as a taste for hot water-gruel. Like Franklin, too, she is living out a bold and arduous project in the pursuit of moral perfection, embodying a number of the virtues that Franklin will later enumerate in the second fragment of the memoir: temperance, frugality, cleanliness, and humility, as well as chastity and tranquillity, judging from the "cheerful and polite" demeanor with which she entertains an inquisitive young guest. They are, in some respects, mirrors of one another.

When Franklin pays her a visit, he surveys her austere surroundings as if he were taking the measure of one of the Interpreter's "significant" exhibits in *The Pilgrim's Progress*: "The Room was clean," he recalls, "but had no other Furniture than a Matras, a Table with a Crucifix and Book, a Stool, which she gave me to sit on, and a Picture over the Chimney of St. Veronica, displaying her Handkerchief with the miraculous Figure of Christ's bleeding face on it, which she explained to me with great Seriousness." The import of this scene both echoes and inverts Uncle Benjamin's ancestral anecdote of the Bible and the joint stool, grouping the book and the stool with other ordinary items of furniture, rather than presenting them as emblems of an intense inner life. Even in her retirement, Franklin's devout hostess takes external display with an alarming degree of seriousness—a fact that the memoir quietly stresses by reducing to mere externals the significance of her pious example. "She look'd pale," Franklin remarks as he concludes the account of his visit, "but was never sick, and I give it as another Instance on how small an Income Life and Health may be supported."

Franklin himself quickly proves to be much the greatest curiosity in this compact section of the memoir. The Water-American transmits his swimming skills, in only two miraculous lessons, to a fellow worker from Watts's printing house named Wygate, with whom he shared a love of languages and reading. With some of the fervor of Saint Veronica's devotee, the pupil soon urges his teacher to demonstrate his abilities to a company of "Gentleman" as they are all returning from a rowing excursion on the Thames:

> I stript and leapt into the River, and swam from near Chelsea to Blackfryars, performing on the way many Feats of Activity both upon and under Water, that surpriz'd and pleas'd those to whom they were Novelties. I had from a Child been ever delighted with this Exercise, had studied and practis'd all Thevenot's Motions and Positions, added some of my own, aiming at the graceful and easy, as well as the Useful. All these I took this Occasion of exhibiting to the Company, and was much flatter'd by their Admiration. And Wygate, who was desirous of becoming a Master, grew more and more attach'd to me, on that account, as well as from the Similarity of our Studies. He at length propos'd to me travelling all over Europe together, supporting ourselves everywhere by working at our Business. (A, 104)

"Our Business" was journeyman compositor, a skill with a long-standing tradition of itinerancy behind it, as talented pressmen wandered from city to city, across Europe, to meet the shifting demands of the printing industry. This triumph of external display in the Thames, however, briefly tempts Franklin to capitalize on his mastery of motions and positions by becoming a swimming instructor to the sons of English gentlemen, a shallow destiny that neatly captures the superficial nature of Franklin's London attachments. His confidante and adviser, Thomas Denham, has little difficulty replacing Wygate's prospective business proposal with another, enticing Franklin to abandon printing altogether and return to Philadelphia as his merchant clerk. Like Collins before him, Wygate represents another of the impermanent emotional bonds with which Franklin fills the first fragment of the memoir. But unlike Thomas Denham, Wygate's commitment to this friendship seems implicitly self-centered rather than disinterested, a speculation conducted on his own "account" rather than an outgrowth of strong personal feeling.

Not all the emotional bonds in this section of Franklin's story are equally impermanent. Among the anecdotes from his early years that he shares with his son, one episode in particular captures his remarkable ability to impose dramatic form on the interplay between inner and outer life that characterizes his ethical experience: to link an outward propensity for display, with its attendant hunger for admiration, to more substantial inner attributes. This memory too involves the subtle exchange of identities that Franklin had begun to explore in the 1771 fragment of the memoir with his portraits of William Keith or Samuel Keimer and that continues with his amusing London landlady, her saintly lodger, and Wygate. Like those portraits, too, this passage invokes a broader biographical perspective, addressing the full scope of Franklin's life, as well as focusing on the obscure people and unimportant events from his youth that he appears to dismiss in 1784, as he prepares to take up later, more public portions of his story.

Shortly before the abortive voyage to England that interrupts his marriage plans with Deborah Read, Franklin develops a close friendship with three young Philadelphia clerks that anticipates the much larger, more formal, and more celebrated Junto that he will organize among his friends a few years later. Charles Osborne, Joseph Watson, and James Ralph, along with Franklin, are drawn together by their common love of reading and by the enjoyment of one another's company. But these four readers differ from, as well as resemble, each other. Each of their characters, too, is a compound of precarious balances, and the incident with which Franklin brings them to life illustrates the precariousness of life itself.

Osborne and Watson both clerk for the Philadelphia scrivener, Charles Brockden, and apparently hope to make careers in law or politics. Ralph clerks for a merchant, but as Franklin quickly makes clear, in the concise portrait that he offers of this group, they form an inherently unstable quartet, in spite of these superficially clear career paths:

> Watson was a pious sensible young Man, of great Integrity. The others rather more lax in their Principles of Religion, particularly Ralph, who as well as Collins had been unsettled by me, for which they both made me suffer. Osborne was sensible, candid, frank, sincere, and affectionate to his Friends; but in litterary Matters too fond of Criticizing. Ralph, was ingenious, genteel in his Manners, and extreamly eloquent; I think I never knew a prettier Talker. Both of them great Admirers of Poetry, and began to try their Hands in little Pieces. Many

> pleasant Walks we four had together on Sundays into the Woods near Skuykill, where we read to one another and conferr'd on what we read. (A, 90)

James Ralph's conspicuous skill as a "Talker" is the first disquieting sign in Franklin's pages that he possesses a more superficial nature than either Osborne or Watson; "Were you Doers or Talkers only?" is the dismissive question that awaits John Bunyan's pilgrims at Judgment Day. The memoir's quick descent from the eloquent to the pretty, in its characterization of Ralph's gifts, anticipates the more crucial descents of Ralph's subsequent experience. The anecdote that follows pays tribute to Ralph's talents, at the same time that it separates these four companions along lines that roughly correspond to the inward and outward spheres of experience that Franklin will build into his system of virtues and precepts.

The two admirers and practitioners of poetry, Ralph and Osborne, are direct and envious competitors. Watson—by far the least verbal presence in this episode—brings the least contaminated character to the group. Franklin is an agent of ethical unsettlement, perhaps, but his expressive abilities, like Watson's, appear to fall short of the standards that Osborne and Ralph apply to one another. These two ultimately spark a quarrel over the practicality of poetry as a profession, leading to an ingenious contest and a memorable joke:

> Ralph was inclin'd to pursue the Study of Poetry, not doubting but he might become eminent in it and make his Fortune by it, alledging that the best Poets must when they first began to write, make as many faults as he did. Osborne dissuaded him, assur'd him he had no Genius for Poetry, and advis'd him to think of nothing beyond the Business he was bred to; that in the mercantile way tho' he had no Stock, he might by his Diligence and Punctuality recommend himself to Employment as a Factor, and in time acquire wherewith to trade on his own Account. I approv'd the amusing one's self with Poetry now and then, so far as to improve one's Language but no farther. On this it was propos'd that we should each of us at our next Meeting produce a Piece of our own Composing, in order to improve by our mutual Observations, Criticisms and Corrections. (A, 90)

The list of virtues from the second part of the memoir is once more in evidence here, as if Franklin had his ivory memorandum book of ideals and precepts handy as a narrative guide. The voice of Moderation in this little scene belongs to Franklin himself, who is clearly echoing the dismissive views of his father, but without Josiah's contemptuous conviction that "Verse-makers were generally Beggars." Watson is Silent, out of his reserves of good sense perhaps, while Osborne endorses Frugality and Industry, at the same time that he disparages Ralph's dream for its implicit vanity as well as for its imprudence. Order and Resolution play modest roles in the group's plan to come up with a way of testing various claims for and against the study of poetry and improving by one another's criticisms.

Faults and corrections, beauties and defects, are the objects of this composition contest, but they are equally attributes of character in each of its participants. In his piety and integrity, Watson possesses the most potent virtues of the four, but one might argue that his personal reserve prevents him from exerting an influence for good on the others that might counteract the effects of Franklin's corrosive skepticism. "Speak not but what may benefit others or yourself," is Franklin's motto for Silence; Watson seems deficient in beneficial speech. Osborne's candor and sincerity are obvious counterweights to Watson's reticence, but his critical spirit—like the insolent and overbearing behavior that leads Franklin to add Humility to his list of virtues—is the source of the mild atmosphere of antagonism that ignites the competition. While a middle ground of sorts, Franklin's own lukewarm approval of poetry as a device for improving vocabulary has no effect whatever on either of his voluble companions. It is a forecast of his complete failure to produce a poem for the others to judge, the first of a series of broken promises on which this complex memory turns.

But the poem itself hovers over this story like the presence of the now-famous writer who is composing it. Though the memoir does not say as much, it may have been the pious and sensible Watson who suggested that each contestant produce a version of the eighteenth psalm as a display of his verbal powers. The choice of text is ambitious and significant, invoking another of the great works with which the 1771 fragment of the memoir repeatedly invites the reader to collate the autobiographical narrative in which it appears. Franklin rather blandly observes that these lines describe the "Descent of a Deity," but any contemporary reader of his story would quickly recognize the inadequacy of that description. The eighteenth psalm is one of the few that appear twice in the Bible, once in the book of Psalms itself, detached from any specific narrative context, but once much earlier in the Old Testament as well, near the end of 2 Samuel, where its lines compose a verse memoir of David's entire life, a summation of his outward trials and triumphs, as well as a retrospective assertion of the ethical and spiritual attributes that had sustained him.

The story of David's reign is almost complete when the psalm begins. The rebellion of Absalom is over, and at long last the king has recovered and ceremonially reinterred the bones of Saul and Jonathan, imposing a degree of closure on his experience by honoring the remains of his oldest patron and enemy, as well as his most beloved friend. The memoir will serve some of the same purposes for Franklin, too, when he laments Watson's premature death. The psalm takes stock of David's achievements by describing the Lord's fiery descent to deliver his servant from danger:

> *In my distress I called upon the Lord, and cried to my God: and he did hear my voice out of his temple, and my cry did enter into his ears.*
> *Then the earth shook and trembled; the foundations of heaven moved and shook, because he was wroth.*
> *There went up a smoke out of his nostrils, and fire out of his mouth devoured: coals were kindled by it.*
> *He bowed the heavens also, and came down; and darkness was under his feet.*
> *And he rode upon a cherub, and did fly; and he was seen upon the wings of the wind.*
> *And he made darkness pavilions round about him, dark waters, and thick clouds of the skies.*
> *Through the brightness before him were coals of fire kindled.*
> *The Lord thundered from heaven, and the most High uttered his voice.*
> *And he sent out arrows, and scattered them; lightning, and discomfited them.*
> *And the channels of the sea appeared, the foundations of the world were discovered, at the rebuking of the Lord, at the blast of the breath of his nostrils.*
>
> 2 Samuel 22:7–16

Over fifty exultant verses allow the singer to dwell at some length on the abasement of David's enemies, the humbling of the Philistine and Canaanite kings with whom he had fought all his life. To Franklin and his three young friends, the psalmist's experience is equally foreign subject matter, making it all the more useful for the purposes of their poetic contest. But Franklin himself must have appreciated the uncanny pertinence of the lines to his complex circumstances in 1771, surrounded by real and potential enemies in the capital of a monarch who is hostile to the political aspirations that he represents.

This pertinence would clearly not be lost on a careful reader of the memoir who took the trouble to collate Franklin's public record with these snippets of private recollection. Lightning is Franklin's ally and protector, too, at this hazardous stage of his career, conferring on him a cultural authority derived from his scientific achievements that no colonial contemporary could equal in his negotiations with the British Ministry. As James Ralph's joke unfolds, this as-yet-to-be-realized affinity makes itself felt in the dramatic flair that Franklin brings to his role in Ralph's plan. In order to trick Osborne into revealing an unbiased opinion of Ralph's talents, Franklin agrees to present Ralph's version of the psalm as if it were his own. In the memoir Franklin retells the story with obvious pleasure, stressing the critical touch he contributed to Ralph's ruse by immediately transcribing the poem "that it might appear in my own hand." By 1771, Franklin is the last surviving participant of the scene that follows:

> Watson's Performance was read; there were some Beauties in it: but many Defects. Osborne's was read: It was much better. Ralph did it Justice, remark'd some Faults, but applauded the Beauties. He himself had nothing to produce. I was backward, seem'd desirous of being excus'd, had not had sufficient Time to correct; &c. but no Excuse could be admitted, produce I must. It was read and repeated; Watson and Osborne gave up the Contest; and join'd in applauding it immoderately. Ralph only made some Criticisms and propos'd some Amendments, but I defended my Text. Osborne was against Ralph, and told him he was no better a Critic than Poet; so he dropped the Argument. As they two went home together, Osborne express'd himself still more strongly in favour of what he thought my Production, having restrain'd himself before as he said, lest I should think it Flattery. But who would have imagin'd says he, that Franklin had been capable of such a Performance; such Painting, such Force! Such Fire! he has even improv'd the Original! In his common Conversation, he seems to have no Choice of Words; he hesitates and blunders; and yet, good God, how he writes! (A, 91)

Ralph's words are responsible for the quality of the writing that Osborne admires, but Franklin's "performance" brought the lines to life, beginning with his sham excuses and extending through a defense of "his" text against the changes suggested (sincerely or not) by the poem's actual author. Though a bumbling speaker on "common" occasions, Franklin implies that he is capable of remarkable expressive powers on uncommon ones, eclipsing the Bible itself in Osborne's overwrought opinion.

The episode concludes with a rapid disposition of the lives of its participants. Ralph is "cur'd" of his delusive poetic dreams by a disparaging couplet in Pope's *Dunciad*—a kind of death that precedes his much more prosaic success as a London pamphleteer. But even this equivocal form of immortality is denied Franklin's other two friends. Watson "died in my Arms a few Years after," he writes, the only hint that the memoir offers of the depth of this particular friendship but all the more telling a disclosure for the unexpected glimpse of intimacy that it provides. He was "much lamented," Franklin confesses, "being the best of our set" (A, 91). After establishing a successful legal career in the West Indies, Osborne too died young. He and Franklin, however, shared a final joke between them. They agreed before Osborne's departure that the first to die was pledged to visit the survivor "and acquaint him how he found things in that Separate State," but Osborne "never fulfilled his Promise." Franklin's inconspicuous pun captures the playful irreverence of this youthful friendship, along with a much older writer's wistful recognition of life's indifference both to individual promise and to our promises, an outgrowth of the half century of experience with his own limited powers of amendment that Franklin brings to the telling of this story.

CHAPTER THREE

The Scramble of Life

*O*sborne, Watson, and Ralph compose Franklin's second experiment in the formation of a mutual improvement society. The first, his friendship with Collins, had begun in much the same way as the bond among the four "Lovers of Reading" who debated the usefulness of poetry during their Sunday walks. But Collins had disappeared in the West Indies where Osborne's promising legal career would come to a premature end; Watson died young; and James Ralph took his unchastened literary ambitions to England, when Franklin went to London in 1724, and never returned to America. In the autumn of 1727, Franklin tried a third time to collaborate with a group of friends whose interests extended beyond the professions or the trades in which they hoped to make a living. Shortly before he left Samuel Keimer's printshop once and for all to open his own business, Franklin assembled the Junto, uniting "most of my ingenious Acquaintance" among the city's young tradesmen with the three apprentices whom he was training for Keimer: Hugh Meredith, Stephen Potts, and George Webb.

The Junto too becomes the focus of an intriguing group portrait in the memoir's pages, beginning with Keimer's apprentices. As Franklin presents them, these first three are, in various ways, unstable blends of principle and inclination, partly equipped to thrive in life and partly destined to fail by some of the same bad habits or personality flaws that Franklin was trying to purge from his own character. Hugh Meredith, nine years older than Franklin, was hoping to make a belated transition from "Country Work" to a skilled trade in the city. Franklin's thumbnail portrait of him is a telling memorandum of strengths and weaknesses. Meredith was "honest, sensible, had a great deal of solid Observation, was something of a Reader, but given to drink" (A, 108). Though not as volatile as Collins, he suffered from the same debilitating addiction. Potts had a similarly mixed nature, joining "uncommon natural Parts" and a good sense of humor to laziness. Webb was an Oxford scholar whose background Franklin summarizes in some detail, both because it echoes quite closely Franklin's own experience as a runaway and because it dramatizes how swiftly a promising future could deteriorate into a desperate scramble for survival:

> He was not more than 18 Years of Age, and gave me this Account of himself; that he was born in Gloucester, educated at a Grammar School there, had been distinguish'd among the Scholars for some apparent Superiority in performing his Part when they exhibited Plays; belong'd to the Witty Club there, and had written some Pieces in Prose and Verse which were printed in the Gloucester Newspapers. Thence he was sent to Oxford; there he continu'd about a Year, but not well-satisfy'd, wishing of all things to see London and become a Player. At length receiving his Quarterly Allowance of 15 Guineas, instead of discharging his Debts, he walk'd out of Town, hid his Gown in a Furz Bush, and footed it to London, where having no Friend to advise him, he fell into bad Company, soon spent his Guineas, found no means of being introduc'd among the Players, grew necessitous, pawn'd his Cloaths and wanted Bread. Walking the Street very hungry, and not knowing what to do with himself, a Crimp's Bill was put into his Hand, offering immediate Entertainment and Encouragement to such as would bind themselves to serve in America. He went directly, sign'd the Indentures, was put into the Ship and came over; never writing a Line to acquaint his Friends what was become of him. (A, 109)

Franklin's deft review stresses Webb's Hogarthean progress from the point at which he abandoned his promising future at Oxford to the point at which he wanted bread on the streets of London—an inverse reflection of Franklin's fortuitous discovery, in 1723, that Philadelphia was a city where bread was cheap.

Though a witty and "pleasant Companion," Franklin concludes, Webb was "thoughtless and imprudent to the last Degree," traits that anticipate Franklin's own imprudence when he blithely confides his plans for starting a newspaper to the unreliable Webb, perhaps in the hope that Webb's education would make him a useful partner in the venture. Webb, however, promptly betrays Franklin's confidence by revealing the idea to Samuel Keimer and assisting with Keimer's short-lived management of the *Pennsylvania Gazette*.

The other founding members of the Junto whom Franklin names are, on the whole, better prepared to fulfill the conditions that he drew up to structure the club's activities. Each member was responsible for framing discussion questions for their Friday evening meetings and pledged, once every three months, to "produce and read an Essay of his own Writing on any Subject he pleased" (A, 117). The meetings were moderated by a president who enforced standards of dispassionate inquiry and civility with small fines against members who grew too heated during debate. Franklin may have been thinking of the clashes between Osborne and Ralph when he formed these rules, but he was also clearly determined to give this larger group of friends a degree of institutional stability that might protect the Junto against the disintegrative forces that threaten any human bonds.

Even so the brittle glazier, Thomas Godfrey, Franklin's tenant and a gifted mathematician, soon left the group. He "was not a pleasing Companion," Franklin recalled, "as like most Great Mathematicians I have met with, he expected unusual Precision in every thing said, or was forever denying or distinguishing upon Trifles, to the Disturbance of all Conversation." Uncompromising greatness of this sort proved incompatible with the more pliant traits of Franklin's other ingenious friends: Joseph Breintnall, "a good-natur'd friendly middle-ag'd Man, a great Lover of Poetry, reading all he could meet with, and writing some that was tolerable; very ingenious in many little Nicknackeries, and of sensible Conversation"; Nicholas Scull, "a Surveyor, afterwards Surveyor-General, Who lov'd Books, and sometimes made a few Verses"; William Parsons, "a Shoemaker, but loving Reading, had acquir'd a considerable Share of Mathematics, which he first studied with a View to Astrology that he afterwards laught at"; William Maugridge, "a Joiner, a most exquisite Mechanic and a solid sensible Man"; Robert Grace, "generous, lively and witty, a Lover of Punning and of his Friends"; and William Coleman, "who had the coolest clearest Head, the best Heart, and the exactest Morals, of almost any Man I ever met with. He became afterwards a Merchant of great Note, and one of our Provincial Judges: Our

Friendship continued without Interruption to his Death upwards of 40 Years" (A, 117–18).

Each of these figures receives a biographical caption in the memoir incorporating a measure of the same complexity that Franklin builds into the precepts for his thirteen virtues, exemplifying the interplay between inner and outer spheres of awareness that thoughtful self-government requires. The Junto and its membership "joins together" in more senses than one, becoming in the process the chief institutional counterweight in Franklin's narrative to the fragmenting energies symbolically represented by the segmented snake of his political cartoon. Like his friendship with William Coleman, the Junto itself proved extraordinarily durable, in large part because of the psychological checks and balances built into its members: generosity moderating wit; solid skills balancing exquisite ones; ingenuity channeled through a good-natured aptitude for nicknackeries; a shoemaker able to laugh at his astrological infatuation; a provincial judge distinguished for the blend of head, heart, and morals in his makeup. This group formed a living laboratory in which Franklin could test the practicality of his many public projects. At the same time it provided a contrasting model for the larger and far less stable patterns of human association that Franklin first describes, for his own benefit, in a digest of conclusions from his reading that he drafts in the Junto library in May 1731.

The first three parts of Franklin's memoir are divided by the seventeen years of tumultuous experience that break up the thread of its composition. But they are also closely knit together by the introduction of the Junto; by the formation of its library; by the role that it plays in the growth of Franklin's ambitions; and by the truly arduous enterprise in social engineering that he originally envisions, when he is twenty-five years old, as a response to the cyclical disorders that have plagued all recorded efforts to govern human affairs for the good. Franklin accomplishes this feat of integration not by drawing the parts of the narrative more closely together but by taking them apart and allowing two surrogate "readers" to play key roles in highlighting this emerging sense of purpose. The memoir describes one Junto and dramatizes another in the collaborative form that Franklin ultimately adopts to address the compositional disorders of his book. By introducing into his story two letters, a few pages of notes, and a "little Paper" of semiprivate reflections by an obscure young printer, he hints at a sense of narrative significance that far exceeds the limited promise of the biographical sketch that he thought he could complete, on a brief country holiday, in 1771.[1]

As Franklin's lifelong effort to shape his character had taught him, however, bold and arduous enterprises of all kinds are prone to collapse. His memoir is full of broken promises. Charles Osborne's failure to keep his pledge and acquaint his surviving friend with the state of the afterlife is a whimsical version of a pattern that Franklin first introduces into his story when he breaks the indentures he had signed committing him to work for his brother until he was twenty-one. He was seventeen at the time and remembers this act as "the first Errata of my Life" (A, 70). James Franklin set the original example of evading commitments by replacing the indentures that his brother had agreed to five years earlier with a secret instrument allowing him to comply with an order of the Massachusetts court to cease printing the *New England Courant* under his own name. James arranged to keep that promise, Franklin noted, but only by means of a very "flimsy Scheme." He decided to print the paper under Benjamin's name, write out a "full Discharge" of the old indenture for occasional display, but keep legal control of his brother's time and labor with a new, private agreement. James remained physically abusive, however, and with their very next argument Franklin simply walks out on this little subterfuge. Shortly afterward, he slips out of Boston entirely by deceiving a shipmaster into thinking that he has to evade yet another entangling set of promises to a pregnant lover and her marriage-minded relatives, imaginary domestic authorities who might force him to keep his word.[2]

William Keith and James Ralph each soon display an indifference to promises involving some serious cost to Franklin himself, as well as to the wife and child whom Ralph coolly abandons in Philadelphia. When Franklin, in turn, breaks off his relationship with Deborah Read, she finds herself married to a man for whom vows appear nearly meaningless, a bigamist and a debtor who soon leaves her ensnared in a web of broken obligations. A freethinking surgeon in London promises to introduce the star-struck young Franklin to Sir Isaac Newton but never makes good on the offer. Death prevents Thomas Denham from carrying out his promise to help establish Franklin in the West India trade, and his executors apparently did not feel constrained in any way by oral understandings between Denham and his newly hired clerk or by the affection that the two clearly had for one another.

Denham himself took a far different view of promises, even when he was not legally bound to do so. "I must record one trait of this good Man's character," Franklin explains as he prepares to portray, for the benefit of his son, an exemplary instance of transatlantic financial dealings. This brief record, too, is a political lesson that royal governors and English ministers would do well to heed, when comparing the difference between coercive policies and generous ones. On Denham's advice, Franklin took advantage of the predicament in which William Keith had placed him by improving his skills in the London printshops, while Denham himself hosted a group of his former creditors at a dinner with which he proposed to thank them for the favorable settlement terms that they had granted him after a previous business failure. "When they expected nothing but the Treat," Franklin recalled, Denham surprised them by honoring the balance of his obligations: "every Man at the first Remove, found under his Plate an Order on a Banker for the full Amount of the unpaid remainder with Interest" (A, 105). In paying tribute to Denham's integrity, Franklin is also illustrating the kind of friendly reciprocity that he envisions sustaining the English colonial system at large.[3]

Thomas Denham is a short-lived exception to the memoir's pattern of neglected commitments, broken contracts, or snapped "connections," as Franklin terms them, when he abruptly (and temporarily) ends his employment agreement with Samuel Keimer over a trivial outburst of temper. At these moments Franklin dramatizes the latent discontinuity of human purpose underlying the figure of the segmented snake that presides over so much of his experience. When his program of private devotion and the pursuit of moral perfection comes to a gradual end under the pressure of affairs, it joins a long list of obligations in default with which Franklin's story is filled. Abel James and Benjamin Vaughan, the authors of the two letters with which Franklin introduces the memoir's second section, are determined that the memoir itself, along with Franklin's commentary on "The Art of Virtue," escape a similar premature end. Vaughan in particular makes clear his conviction that the stakes of this final default would entail a drastic breakdown in the architecture of human associations upon which civilization depends.[4]

Small promises and momentous ones mingle in Franklin's pages, all participating to different degrees in the struggle to maintain the texture of private and public covenants upon which human happiness rests. The third fragment of his narrative is a survey of these covenants on every conceivable scale and at every stage of their evolution, from a casual agreement between two individuals on the best method for teaching each other Italian, to formal legal bonds that engage to supply a British army in the Pennsylvania wilderness. In each instance the promises involved are subject to pressures that expose the inherent fragility of human commitments, as well as the range of tactics required to establish and sustain them, regardless of how urgent or how trivial the commitments themselves prove to be. One motive that may have influenced Franklin's determination to preserve the fractures in his manuscript is to keep this interplay between joining together and breaking apart in the forefront of the reader's mind. The James and Vaughan letters with which he begins the 1784 segment of his story explicitly address the mixture of frustration and enticement built into his method. Each of these brief preambles awakens and disappoints the reader's hopes, but each is also a reminder that failure is as intrinsic to the significance of Franklin's experience as success.

THE PAGES OF THE MEMOIR bring success and failure into an uneasy but pervasive balance, the implications of which become much clearer when the reader glimpses them through contemporary eyes. Both of the friends who write Franklin near the end of his long diplomatic mission to France, urging him to resume work on his book, disguise significant anxieties behind the lighthearted pose that each adopts in addressing his famous correspondent. Abel James teases Franklin with a reference to "busy-Body" printers that alludes to the "Busy-Body" letters Franklin had written half a century earlier to build up the circulation of Andrew Bradford's Philadelphia newspaper at the expense of Samuel Keimer's newly founded competitor. Franklin describes this episode in the fragment of the memoir that James has in his possession when he reminds Franklin that printers can't be trusted with secrets, as Keimer had proved when he hurried his own newspaper into production in an effort to preempt the plan of his former employee.

Benjamin Vaughan is similarly facetious when he parodies Franklin's modesty in the opening sentences of the letter that he writes from Paris in 1783 to reinforce the view that Abel James had taken of the memoir's importance. "Various concerns have for some time past prevented this letter being written," Vaughan explains, " and I do not know whether it was worth any expectation: happening to be at leisure however at present, I shall by writing at least interest and instruct myself" (A, 135). These words echo the self-characterization that Franklin offers in the 1771 fragment of the memoir so closely and so subtly as to suggest that Franklin himself may have written them. Vaughan had seen none of the actual draft that Abel James retained in Philadelphia when he wrote to urge Franklin to finish his book, and Vaughan's manuscript letter does not survive. The friendly mimicry it displays, however, amounts to an adaptation of the tactics that Franklin had used to teach himself how to write by mimicking Joseph Addison's style, or of James Ralph's impressive mimicry of the eighteenth psalm. Language and character alike build upon models that one remembers and imitates—a conviction that both Abel James and Benjamin Vaughan stress in their appeals to Franklin's sense of his duty to the future.

Both of these supportive friends make clear that Franklin's memoir as it stands represents an unfulfilled promise of the utmost significance. "What will the world say," James complains, "if kind, humane, and benevolent Ben Franklin should leave his Friends and the World deprived of so pleasing and profitable a Work"? He is convinced that the memoir, once completed and published, will have an insensible influence on youthful minds, prompting them "to become as good and as eminent as the Journalist." The industry, frugality, and temperance that the author exemplifies are "of such vast Importance," James insists, that they eclipse all the other benefits that might arise from an attentive study of Franklin's life. Benjamin Vaughan's letter elaborates on the curious urgency behind James's plea. Vaughan was a thirty-two-year-old British diplomat assisting at the Paris peace negotiations when he wrote Franklin, in late January 1783, urging him to take Abel James's advice.[5] In doing so, he hints at a grim vision of the future that he hopes Franklin's example might be able to mitigate. The memoir, in his eyes, is a comprehensive antidote to an emerging cultural crisis. Contemporary education is informed by "false principles," Vaughan believes, and directed at a "false mark." Franklin's model of self-instruction is superior, an indication both to children and to parents that it is possible to prepare for "a reasonable course in life" without relying on any resources other than one's "private power."

The formation of character is Vaughan's chief concern in urging Franklin to finish his story, much as it was for Abel James, but Vaughan sketches out the public repercussions of the state of private character on a far more extensive scale than James does:

> It is in *youth* that we plant our chief habits and prejudices; it is in youth that we take our party as to profession, pursuits, and matrimony. In youth therefore the turn is given; in youth the education even of the next generation is given; in youth the private and public character is determined. . . . But your Biography will not merely teach self-education, but the education of *a wise man*; and the wisest man will receive lights and improve his progress, by seeing detailed the conduct of another wise man. And why are weaker men to be deprived of such helps, when we see our race has been blundering on in the dark, almost without

a guide in this particular, from the farthest trace of time? Shew then, Sir, how much is to be done, *both to sons and fathers*; and invite all wise men to become like yourself; and other men to become wise. (A, 136)

Vaughan's emphasis suggests his determination to underscore the value that Abel James attached to Franklin's little family anecdotes. These are exactly the materials that secure the story's importance, in Vaughan's view, making it accessible to weaker readers as well as to wise ones, to the young as much as to the old, just as John Bunyan had insisted that his own simple allegories were intended to do.

A blind and blundering history, marked by what Vaughan bluntly terms the cruelty of "statesmen and warriors," as well as the absurdity of superficially "distinguished men," characterizes the present course of the human race. Franklin's experience points the way to a less destructive path: "Some men have been virtuous blindly," Vaughan continues, "others have speculated fantastically, and others have been shrewd to bad purposes; but you, Sir, I am sure, will give under your hand, nothing but what is at the same moment, wise, practical and good." As the memoir will clearly demonstrate, privileged origins count for nothing in the pursuit of "happiness, virtue, or greatness," the attributes that Franklin exemplifies in Vaughan's eyes. Frame a plan of life like the one the memoir endorses, Vaughan insists, and anyone may hope to become "considerable."[6] The quality of "the whole of a life" and not the contingencies of the passing moment ought to guide our conduct. The ability to wait for advancement, to take comfort in the present, and to moderate one's hopes and regrets, rather than be crippled by them, distinguishes Franklin's temper from those "of various public cutthroats and intriguers" whose biographies Vaughan dismisses with particular scorn. The success of Franklin's mission to France clearly influenced Vaughan's view of his example. That enterprise was, above all, an exercise in a politic form of waiting, conducted amid a variety of intriguers whose mastery of their passions and desires was far less complete than Franklin's own.

But what Vaughan calls "the immense revolution of the present period" was by no means concluded as of January 1783, when his own letter was dated. The Peace of Paris was yet to be signed and the structure of America's postcolonial world had yet to be determined. Even by 1784, when Franklin finally responded to the pleas of his two friends and began to write, he could only do so provisionally. Abel James had not sent him a copy of the 1771 fragment upon which to build, only the string of mnemonic cues that Franklin had prepared twelve years earlier to help him carry the narrative past 1730. And these notes, placed where Franklin had indicated that he wanted them in the sequence of pieces that compose the memoir, would have offered a startling contrast to the grand hopes expressed in the James and Vaughan letters:

> Marry. Library erected. Manner of conducting the Project. Its plan and Utility. Children. Almanack. the Use I made of it. Great Industry. Constant Study. Fathers Remark and Advice upon Diligence. Carolina Partnership. Learn French and German. Journey to Boston after 10 years. Affection of my Brother. His Death and leaving me his Son. Art of Virtue. Occasion. City Watch. amended. Post Office. Spotswood. Bradfords Behavior. Clerk of Assembly. Lose one of my Sons. Project of subordinate Junto's. Write occasionally in the papers. Success in Business. Fire Companys. Engines. Go again to Boston in 1743. See Dr. Spence. Whitefield. My Connection with him. His Generosity to me. my returns. Church Differences. My part in them. Propose a College. not then prosecuted. Propose and establish a Philosophical Society. War. Electricity. (A, 269)

Franklin's personal papers were all in America, making it impossible to confirm key dates and details in this intriguing but wildly uneven flow of topics and memories. The necessary elaboration, correction, and revision, Franklin recognizes, can take place once he gets home, striking out any awkward repetition but leaving in place the two letters and the jumble of notes, along with the opening sentences of the 1784 fragment that Franklin had labeled "Continuation of the Account of my Life. Begun at Passy 1784." Conclusions, continuations, and beginnings overlap in the form that Franklin imposes on this portion of his story, a version of the orderly disorder that he will extend to the balance of the surviving memoir.[7]

In his response to the urging of his two friends, Franklin stresses that he too is writing in the dark, a state of blindness that corresponds perfectly to the ominous cultural darkness that Vaughan himself most fears as he concludes his appeal for the completion of Franklin's manuscript:

> For the furtherance of human happiness, I have always maintained that it is necessary to prove that man is not even at present a vicious and detestable animal; and still more to prove that good management may greatly amend him; and it is for much the same reason, that I am anxious to see the opinion established, that there are fair characters existing among the individuals of the race; for the

moment that all men, without exception, shall be conceived abandoned, good people will cease efforts deemed to be hopeless, and perhaps think of taking their share in the scramble of life, or at least of making it comfortable principally for themselves. (A, 139)

Prove to us that man may be amended, Vaughan pleads, and even if you fail, "you will at least have framed pieces to interest the human mind" and mixed some innocent pleasure with the anxiety and pain of the present.

These words take for granted the likelihood of failure in the vast redemptive task that Vaughan associates with Franklin's example, but he suggests at the same time a pair of propositions that closely resemble suitable topics for a Junto debate. Are human beings irredeemably vicious or subject to the influence of good management? Must we reconcile ourselves to a selfish scramble for individual comfort amid the chaos of history, or does life offer some encouragement for the efforts of fair characters to shape a communal future? Growing as it does directly out of the Junto's early years, Franklin's project for establishing a subscription library in Philadelphia begins the process of addressing Vaughan's anxieties with a case study in good management, gradually adapted to the weaknesses of human nature. The sequence of steps that leads to the founding of the Library Company dramatizes the counterpoise between joining together and breaking apart that will come to shape the longest portion of Franklin's narrative. This "first Project of a public Nature," in a lifetime of such projects, provided the place and the occasion in which Franklin formulated his own "great and extensive" plan for the furtherance of human happiness.

Early in the Junto's existence, Franklin had proposed that the members "club" their books together, as well as themselves, so that they could have access to a handy reference collection during weekly meetings and debates. The idea "was lik'd and agreed to" but apparently with some unspoken reservations, the seeds of a separation that quickly follows. The members contributed to the joint collection only "such Books as we could best spare," and even these appeared to suffer a degree of rough treatment while they were stored in the Junto's meeting room. Ultimately "each took his Books home again," presumably a bit disgruntled by the failed experiment. When Franklin adapted the "clubbing" plan to create a subscription library, he took care to remove the element of private ownership, and with it the possibility of private dissatisfaction. The first part of the memoir describes this second phase of the project very briefly, stressing its political impact on the "common Tradesmen and Farmers" of America who were challenging Parliament's authority. When Franklin begins writing the second part of his book in 1784, after "the Affairs of the Revolution" had come to an end, he expands his account, dramatizing the moment when the Library Company officially comes to life, and elaborating on the hints of resistance that the first version of the story barely addresses.

"Finding the advantage of this little Collection," Franklin recalled of the Junto's original effort, "I propos'd to render the Benefit from Books more common by commencing a Public Subscription Library":

> I drew a Sketch of the Plan and Rules that would be necessary, and got a skilful Conveyancer, Mr. Charles Brockden to put the whole in Form of Articles of Agreement to be subscribed; by which each Subscriber engag'd to pay a certain Sum down for the first Purchase of Books and an annual Contribution for encreasing them. So few were the Readers at that time in Philadelphia, and the Majority of us so poor, that I was not able with great Industry to find more than Fifty Persons, mostly young Tradesmen, willing to pay down for this purpose Forty shillings each, and Ten Shillings per annum. On this little Fund we began. (A, 142)

In addition to the membership fees and the annual purchase subscription, each subscriber signed a "promissory Note" to pay to the company double a book's value if the borrower failed to return it. The effect of these comparatively stern Articles of Agreement is to reverse completely the disintegrative outcome of the Junto's original book club. The subscription library thrives, and other towns throughout the colonies soon imitate the arrangement as its advantages become clear. "Reading became fashionable," Franklin drily observes, perhaps because even the metropolis of Philadelphia was discouragingly short on alternative forms of public amusement. Visitors took note of the beneficial results, an outcome that the memoir links explicitly to the class stereotypes that Franklin might have expected an English reader to bring to his story: the city's population seemed "better instructed and more intelligent than People of the same Rank generally are in other Countries" (A, 142).

Eventually a government charter gave "Perpetuity" to the Library Company, ensuring that it would fulfill Charles Brockden's prediction, as the original articles were being signed, that the institution would outlive all of its founders: "You are young Men," Franklin remembered Brockden observing, "but it is scarce probable that any of you will live to see the Expiration of the Term fix'd in this Instrument." Franklin's plan amounted to a momentous promissory note that committed the library's members, along with their heirs, to fifty years of support for the company. Despite Brockden's prediction, Franklin and several others did survive the expiration of this half-century term, a significant (if only partial) triumph over the influences of jealousy and vanity that had prompted the breakup of the Junto's first book club. These durable flaws in human character tested the Library Company as well. When Franklin first began to canvas his acquaintances for potential subscribers, he met with "Objections and Reluctances" that he traced to "the Impropriety of presenting one's self as the Proposer of any useful Project that might be suppos'd to raise one's Reputation in the smallest degree above that of one's Neighbours."

Disguised as the "Scheme of a *Number of Friends*" who had asked Franklin to play a minor role in carrying out their plan, the library proved an easier sale. This tactic is the first of several strategies that the memoir recommends for sidestepping the effects of jealousy rather than directly opposing them. "The present little Sacrifice of your Vanity," Franklin observes, "will afterwards be amply repaid. If it remains a while uncertain to whom the Merit belongs, some one more vain than yourself will be encourag'd to claim it, and then even Envy will be dispos'd to do you Justice, by plucking those assum'd Feathers, and restoring them to their right Owner" (A, 143). Franklin viewed the Junto as "the best School of Philosophy, Morals and Politics that then existed in the Province," not because its members had conquered self-interest but because they understood its stubborn nature and tried to harness it, just as Franklin had done with the process of gaining library subscribers. The Junto's weekly meetings helped sharpen its members' reading and speaking habits as they tried to influence the thinking of their friends, on the various subjects they addressed, without "disgusting" one another through displays of arrogance or temper. Persuasion and restraint were always on the agenda together precisely because vanity and envy, merit and justice, maintained such a precarious balance in human character.[8]

A similar counterpoise between individual and public interests shapes the Junto's more practical benefits as well. Its members routinely referred customers to one another's businesses, a practice that gives Franklin a chance to dramatize his own industry at a crucial early stage in his career. One printing job in particular that Joseph Breintnall had steered his way prompts Franklin and his partner Hugh Meredith to work "exceeding hard" for the apparently paradoxical reason that "the Price was low." The job was a commission to print forty folio sheets of the Quakers' official history, "Pro Patria Size, in Pica with Long Primer Notes," a complicated assignment that Franklin clearly hoped would demonstrate to these influential (if tight-fisted) clients the superiority of his workmanship, even when its economic returns were small:

> I compos'd of it a Sheet a Day, and Meredith work'd it off at Press. It was often 11 at Night and sometimes later, before I had finish'd my Distribution for the next days Work: For the little Jobbs sent in by our other Friends now and then put us back. But so determin'd I was to continue doing a Sheet a day of the Folio, that one Night when having impos'd my Forms, I thought my Days Work over, one of them by accident was broken and two Pages reduc'd to Pie, I immediately distributed and compos'd it over again before I went to bed. (A, 118–19)

A prominent Philadelphia surgeon, Patrick Baird, walking home "from Club" (as the memoir puts it) notices Franklin's late hours, comments among friends on this exemplary industry, and Franklin's business begins to thrive. The passage as a whole is an emblem in several carefully contrasted parts: exceeding hard work for low pay; a sheet a day of the prestigious Quaker history, interrupted by various "little Jobbs" for friends; two elaborate folio pages broken into "pie" and carefully reset out of a young tradesman's stubborn determination to stick to his plan; a single observant neighbor and an expanding reputation. This system of weights and counterweights ultimately neutralizes life's disruptive accidents. In the end, the competing circumstances of the passage advance a larger whole, much like the untoward events that initially "put back" the formation of a common library ultimately result in a more stable outcome than the Junto had been able to achieve on its own.

On one critical occasion that the memoir gratefully records, William Coleman and Robert Grace, two of Franklin's favorite Junto colleagues, help him redeem his commercial promises in the face of what seems, at first, to be a fatal setback in Franklin's career. A merchant who had helped Hugh Meredith's father to finance Franklin's printing business abruptly called in his loan. Without another hundred pounds to pay off this creditor, the press would have to be sold. Both Grace and Coleman independently offer to loan Franklin the money to pay off this debt, but their generosity is not without conditions. Each insists that Franklin buy out Meredith's share of the partnership. Meredith too was a Junto member, but Coleman and Grace thought his drinking and "playing at low Games in Alehouses" discredited the business. At first Franklin demurs, citing the "great Obligations" he felt toward the Merediths for their original support, but after "the matter rested for some time," he changed his mind. Conditions of rest seldom last long in Franklin's mutable world (A, 122).

The memoir's detailed account of these events makes clear that Franklin hid the offers of help from Coleman and Grace when he sounded out Meredith on his father's intentions, offering (sincerely or not) to leave the partnership himself rather than allow the business to fail. The result is an immediate counterproposal that frees Franklin to run the press alone, assists Meredith's father with his financial difficulties, and gives Meredith himself a new start in North Carolina (A, 123). Their severance agreement "was drawn up in Writing, sign'd and seal'd immediately," Franklin reports, acknowledging a degree of haste that suggests an eagerness to close the agreement before Meredith or his father could have second thoughts. Philosophy, morals, and politics—the key features of the Junto's informal curriculum—collaborate in a less-than-savory manner throughout this episode. Though the former partners appear to have remained friends, this stage in Franklin's career underscores the uneasy equilibrium between candor and secrecy, self-interest and selflessness, that dictate the making and breaking of promises throughout the narrative.

The evolution of the Library Company, the friction within the Junto, and the manipulations that lay behind Franklin's independent start in business make plain that the bonds fusing his closest acquaintances into a "joint" community of ingenious young men were clearly mixed, from the outset, with solvents capable of dissolving their union. When several members of the club eventually propose to introduce some of their friends to the group, Franklin is among those who object to this expansion out of motives that, again, seem far from pure: "We had from the Beginning made it a Rule to keep our Institution a Secret, which was pretty well observ'd. The Intention was, to avoid Applications of improper Persons for Admittance, some of whom perhaps we might find it difficult to refuse" (A, 170). Squeezing out Hugh Meredith is one thing; excluding a prominent lawyer or wealthy merchant is quite another.

Join and die—an inversion of the snake cartoon motto—is the outcome that Franklin apparently fears from this suggestion, but his response is a counterproposal that all the Junto members form "subordinate" clubs in which these new applicants could be introduced to the Junto's rules, and used to promote the Junto's interests, but "without informing them of the Connexion" with the Junto itself: a single serpent, in effect, that would be oblivious to its separate parts. In the end, only a handful of these subordinate clubs ultimately thrive under their various optimistic names, "the Vine, the Union, the Band, &c," a failure rate that seems to confirm Franklin's original misgivings. But his truncation of the list of club names is telling. "They were useful to themselves," he continues in this coolly dismissive passage, "and afforded us a good deal of Amusement, Information, and Instruction, besides answering in some considerable Degree our views of influencing the public Opinion on particular Occasions" (A, 171).

Franklin reports this episode in the third part of the memoir, the longest uninterrupted portion of the surviving manuscript and the first time in seventeen years in which he is able to continue working on his book with all of its earlier pieces available to him: the original 1771 fragment, the 1775 voyage letter, and the brief discussion of the thirteen virtues that he had composed at Passy in 1784 in response to the James and Vaughan appeals. Looking back at his 1771 boast that the Junto was the best school of philosophy, morals, and politics in Pennsylvania, Franklin could scarcely avoid noting the contrast between those earnest educational or ethical ends and the comparatively shallow benefits of Amusement, Information, and Instruction that his friends derive from observing the subordinate clubs.

But this portion of the memoir, too, is the first that Franklin writes with the express purpose of exploring the obstacles that have thwarted the operations of benevolence throughout history: the interplay between selfish and selfless motives that lies behind all the "great Affairs of the World." As Franklin presents it, the Junto is only a single, inconspicuous expression of a widespread human propensity for pursuing the noble goal of some "general Design" through collective means that ultimately end in confusion, like the meaningless "pie" of jumbled type that results when a printer's form breaks apart. Franklin outlines this repetitive cultural pattern in a "little Paper" of conclusions that he drew from the reading that he did in the Junto's first informal reference collection: "Observations on my Reading History in Library, May 9. 1731." The formation of the Library Company lay several months in the future when Franklin drafted and signed this provocative document, the first indication of an ambitious personal resolution that he was never able to carry out.

As Franklin sat down to work on his book in the late summer of 1788, he could glance at the close of the 1784 Passy fragment and pick up the broken thread of his discussion, elaborating on "a *great and extensive Project*" that he had mentioned only in passing four years earlier. The project itself was linked to his system of moral self-discipline and to his unwritten "Art of Virtue," but its scope does not become clear until he incorporates the 1731 library memo-random into the third section of his story. That memorandum, in turn, is yet another promissory note to himself, "accidently preserved" among his surviving papers through all the disruptions of the American Revolution. Franklin was clearly experimenting with the language of formal "articles" several months before asking Charles Brockden for help in framing the legal documents that created the Library Company. He begins this "little Paper" with a series of clauses that summarize his grasp of the historical process:

> OBSERVATIONS on my Reading History in Library, May 9. 1731.
>
> "That the great Affairs of the World, the Wars, Revolutions, &c. are carried on and effected by Parties.
>
> "That the View of these Parties is their present general Interest, or what they take to be such.
>
> "That the different Views of these different Parties, occasion all Confusion.
>
> "That while a Party is carrying on a general Design, each Man has his particular private Interest in View.
>
> "That as soon as a Party has gain'd its general Point, each Member becomes Intent upon his particular Interest, which thwarting others, breaks that Party into Divisions, and occasions more Confusion.
>
> "That few in Public Affairs act from a meer View of the Good of their Country, whatever they may pretend; and tho' their Actings bring real Good to their Country, yet Men primarily consider'd that their own and their Country's Interest was united, and did not act from a Principle of Benevolence.
>
> "That fewer still in public Affairs act with a view to the Good of Mankind.
>
> (A, 161)

The skeptical view of human nature that these preparatory observations reflect is scarcely original with Franklin, and like much of the skepticism pervading his culture, its roots are religious. When Ignorance falls in with Christian and Hopeful near the conclusion of *The Pilgrim's Progress* and blithely lays claim to a purity of heart that has freed him from all selfish desire, Christian bluntly asserts that he who trusts his own heart is a fool: "The imagination of man's heart is evil from his youth" (PP, 138). Youth though he was, in 1731, Franklin too recognized that the principle of benevolence was largely a pretense, in associations as well as in individuals. But he stops short of Christian's categorical extremes. The trajectory that Franklin's document describes, from the great affairs invoked by its introductory clause to the virtuous "few" implicit in its last, points to an elite ethical remnant capable of setting aside "particular Interest" in favor of "the Good of Mankind."[9]

Once Franklin arrives at these promising few, his notes shift their focus to a tentative proposal for action. This library memorandum too is a type of scale in which the counterweights of self-interest and benevolence seek out a viable equilibrium:

> "There seems to me at present to be great Occasion for raising an united Party for Virtue, by forming the Virtuous and good Men of all Nations into a regular Body, to be govern'd by suitable good and wise Rules, which good and wise Men may probably be more unanimous in their Obedience to, than common People are to common Laws.
>
> "I at present think, that whoever attempts this aright, and is well qualified, cannot fail of pleasing God, and of meeting with Success.   B.F." (A, 161–62)

As was the case with the half-century commitment of the Library Company articles, Franklin drafts this instrument too for a modest signing ceremony, though the obligation is nonbinding and only one set of initials follows its hopeful conclusion. The enterprise that this passage envisions cannot fail, Franklin grandly claims, while implying that failure will surely greet whoever neglects to adopt the right tactics to achieve it or who is ill-prepared to carry out the plan.

"From time to time," Franklin recalls in the memoir, he jotted down some ideas concerning those tactics and preparations on scattered "Pieces of Paper" that unlike the 1731 "Observations" themselves are now lost.[10] But the memoir records a few of the original elements that he had considered necessary for addressing this great occasion: the draft of a universal religious creed; the sketch of a "Sect" whose members would assent to the creed and adopt Franklin's regimen of the thirteen virtues; a cautious growth strategy for this little association, as well as a catchy name: "the Society of the Free and Easy." But like the sect that Franklin and Samuel Keimer had toyed with forming a few years earlier, these proposals ultimately come to nothing. Postponement followed postponement, Franklin noted, until he was finally too old to make an attempt. "I was not discourag'd by the seeming Magnitude of the Undertaking," he added in the memoir, "as I have always thought that one Man of tolerable Abilities may work great Changes, and accomplish great Affairs among Mankind, if he first forms a good Plan, and, cutting off all Amusements or other Employments that would divert his Attention, makes the Execution of that same Plan his sole Study and Business" (A, 163).

The third section of the memoir, in fact, is an extensive record of the great changes that Franklin actually is able to execute, even without the assistance of the Society of the Free and Easy: the wide-ranging impact of his almanac and his newspaper, the establishment of several of his journeymen in printing businesses throughout the colonies, his improvements in the colonial mail system and the Philadelphia night watch, the founding of the Union Fire Company, the organization and arming of a militia for the defense of the city, the invention of an efficient stove, the founding of a college. Each of these familiar entries on the resume of Benjamin Franklin is embedded, directly or indirectly, in experiences that partly neutralize its impact or expose once more the pervasive forces of division that attempt to dismantle whatever others strive to build.

The almanac is perhaps the most unqualified success of Franklin's career, ultimately selling nearly ten thousand copies annually during the twenty-five years that Franklin personally produced it. Its reach extended throughout the colonies, making it "a proper Vehicle for conveying Instruction among the common People, who bought scarce any other Books" (A, 164). Each issue of *Poor Richard* was a compact library of aphorisms and information that Franklin compressed still further in "The Way to Wealth," the preface to the 1758 edition in which Father Abraham—"a plain clean old Man, with white Locks"— joined together a quarter century of *Poor Richard*'s ethical advice in an effort to convince his neighbors not to squander their hard-earned money on a lavish sale of merchant's goods. "The bringing all these scatter'd Counsels thus into a Focus," the memoir recalls, "enabled them to make a greater Impression" (A, 164). But the almanac itself records a less favorable result. Father Abraham's famous experiment in segmented form is a famous failure. The people listened politely to the old man's advice, "approved the Doctrine, and immediately practiced the contrary, just as if it had been a common Sermon."[11]

The *Pennsylvania Gazette*, in Franklin's hands, was yet another avenue for public instruction, but the memoir makes clear that Franklin's journalistic principles clashed with the attitude of many of his competitors, who allowed their papers to inflame rather than inform their readers, "gratifying the Malice of Individuals by false Accusations of the fairest Characters among ourselves," printing "scurrilous Reflections on the Government of neighboring States, and even on the Conduct of our best national Allies, which may be attended with the most pernicious Consequences" (A, 165). One would-be contributor whose opinions Franklin declined to publish compared the *Gazette* to a stagecoach "in which anyone who would pay had a Right to a Place." A newspaper could magnify the impact of good management in amending destructive behavior, but it could also vilify the same exemplary traits of character to which Abel James and Benjamin Vaughan had attached their hopes for the future.

The Philadelphia city watch, when Franklin first arrived there, was operated by ward constables who charged each household—rich and poor alike—a flat fee for services that often involved little more than paying a handful of "Ragamuffins" to spend the night drinking in a tavern instead of walking rounds, while the constable pocketed a nice profit. In the memoir Franklin rather mildly describes these abuses as "Irregularities," in response to which he drafts a Junto paper suggesting two simple changes: the levying of city watch fees proportioned to the value of a householder's property and the hiring of regular watchmen "to serve constantly in the Business." The new law had to wait, however, until the Junto's members "were grown into more influence." Clearly the city's wealthiest citizens balked at paying a fair share of the cost to secure their shops and homes. By contrast, the same "Men of Property" were quick to adopt the plan for a fire company that the memoir describes in its very next paragraph. The implication of this juxtaposition of anecdotes in Franklin's story is that selfishness is a stubborn opponent that only equally elemental motives can overcome. Fire is a terrifying equalizer. All of these episodes depict the same moral: good doctrine and good policy are invariably held hostage to the irrational dictates of "particular private Interest."[12]

Franklin's proposal for an academy in Philadelphia, like his plan for reforming the city watch, has to remain "dormant" for a time in deference to the desires of a colleague, Richard Peters, who Franklin had hoped might direct the school, but "having more profitable Views in the service of the Proprietors," Peters backed out of the project (A, 182). The formation of a philosophical society goes much more smoothly, but the memoir mentions that institution only in passing. The explosive response to Franklin's plan for a militia association, by contrast, takes him almost completely by surprise—another instance of the efficacy of fear in suppressing selfishness. At a single public meeting twelve hundred hands signed Franklin's instrument of association in Philadelphia alone, without "the least Objection being made," more than ten thousand in the Province as a whole:

> These all furnish'd themselves as soon as they could with Arms; form'd themselves into Companies, and Regiments, chose their own Officers, and met every Week to be instructed in the manual Exercise, and other parts of military Discipline. The Women, by Subscriptions among themselves, provided Silk Colours, which they presented to the Companies, painted with different Devices and Mottos which I supplied. The Officers of the Companies composing the Philadelphia Regiment, being met, chose me for their Colonel; but conceiving myself unfit, I declin'd that Station, and recommended Mr. Lawrence, a fine Person and Man of Influence, who was accordingly appointed. (A, 183)

This elaborate social organism, as the memoir presents it, seems to evolve almost on its own into a network of "Associators" that cuts across rank and gender. Franklin's pamphlet, *Plain Truth*, is the spark that kindles this blaze, but the men and women of the province are only too ready to catch fire, despite Quaker resistance. "War. Electricity," Franklin had tersely written in the notes that Abel James sent to him in 1784, urging him to finish his book. The two phenomena have a primal relationship to one another that is both exhilarating and disturbing, a vivid illustration of the volatile world that Benjamin Vaughan hoped to contain and that Franklin himself had recognized in the cyclical pattern of wars, revolutions, and confusion that the 1731 library memorandum describes.[13]

In the memoir Franklin relishes discussing the cat-and-mouse game that he plays with Quaker purists, who were determined to keep the colony free of any involvement in warfare. At the end of these exchanges, he reports a conversation with the founder of the Dunkers, Michael Welfare, whose approach to the dilemmas of sectarian life served as a counterweight to the doctrinaire thinking that paralyzed many of Franklin's Quaker friends. The Dunkers were reluctant to tie themselves to a printed confession of faith for fear of stifling the evolution of their spiritual knowledge, a rare instance of "Modesty in a Sect" (the memoir declares) during a time when most others complacently assume themselves to be "in Possession of all Truth." The Quakers, in an effort to preserve this delusion, gradually withdrew from service in the Pennsylvania Assembly, "chusing rather to quit their Power than their Principle" that "no kind of War was lawful" (A, 190). Throughout this portion of the story, Franklin takes particular delight in the subterfuges that the Quakers find themselves forced to adopt to avoid blocking the efforts of their neighbors to defend the city without compromising their pacifist creed.

But Franklin is driven to adopt his own subterfuges as the militia association struggles to equip its defensive battery for the city in spite of the uncooperative behavior of some of the neighboring colonies. Franklin's lottery had funded the construction of the battery itself, as well as the purchase of "some old cannon from Boston"—presumably the only sort of cannon that the Massachusetts Assembly would part with—but it would be some time before new ones could arrive from England:

> Mean while Colonel Lawrence, William Allen, Abraham Taylor, Esquires, and myself were sent to New York by the Associators, commission'd to borrow some Cannon of Governor Clinton. He at first refus'd us peremptorily: but at a Dinner with his Council where there was great Drinking of Madeira wine, as the Custom at that Place then was, he soften'd by degrees, and said he would lend us Six. After a few more Bumpers he advanc'd to Ten. And at length he very good-naturedly conceded Eighteen. They were fine Cannon, 18 pounders, with their Carriages, which we soon transported and mounted on our battery, where the Associators kept a nightly Guard while the War lasted: And among the rest I regularly took my Turn of Duty there as a common Soldier. (A, 184)

This apparently convivial drinking bout accomplishes the Associators' goals, but Franklin's account clearly points to the invidious distinctions, both between governments and individuals, that often thwart collective efforts toward beneficial ends. Governor Clinton's good nature is a transient condition, no more stable than any other drunken promise. Franklin's self-effacing sentry duty, in turn, highlights the stubborn social divisions that persist between "Esquires" such as Lawrence, Allen, or Taylor and ordinary people like himself. The memoir ultimately softens this harsh lesson, much as the wine softens the peremptory selfishness of Governor Clinton, but it does not ignore its presence.

Franklin mutes his criticism of the Quakers, as well, when he likens their erratic behavior to the confusion of men traveling in a moral fog. Common dangers ultimately call for sacrifices in "common," regardless of social class or religious conviction. In the last analysis, however, as Michael Welfare's Dunkers had recognized, we are all living in a fog that reason alone is seldom adequate to address. The third part of Franklin's narrative repeatedly invokes the "common" plight of mankind as yet another counterweight to the episodic discontinuity that marks the segmented serpent of his civic life, but common perils or predicaments frequently awaken common failings as well as joint resolve. The 1731 library memorandum had summarized the circumstances that demanded from good and wise men a far greater consistency of purpose than "common People" were ordinarily able to provide in their obedience to "common Laws." Franklin's almanac seemed to him "a proper Vehicle for conveying Instruction among the common People, who bought scarce any other Books" (A, 164). The articles that he drafted for the Library Company strove to make the benefits of books more "common" in Pennsylvania. During his early years as a businessman, he reports that he tinkered with the "common Mode of teaching Languages" in the hope of accelerating his ability to read the books of other nations as well as English ones, and he puts together a creed for his new sect that strives to include "the Essentials of every known Religion" in search of common ground among the professors of various faiths.

Poor Richard affirms that "Common Sermons" are no more effectual at changing behavior than Father Abraham's litany of sage advice, though the memoir also describes the inspiration that Franklin briefly derived from the sermons of the Irish Presbyterian itinerant, Samuel Hemphill, whose Philadelphia ministry (in Franklin's view) temporarily eclipsed the "Practice of our common Teachers." The word "common," in all its varied meanings, circulates through the initial pages of the 1788 fragment of Franklin's narrative like the bipolar energies of his electric "fluid," maintaining a subtle state of equilibrium between the affirmative appeal of hope and Franklin's equally acute awareness of the profound limitations of human effort. It leaves its mark on the most painful of the failures that this portion of the book records:

> In 1736 I lost one of my Sons, a fine Boy of 4 Years old, by the Small Pox taken in the common way. I long regretted bitterly and still regret that I had not given it to him by Inoculation; This I mention for the Sake of Parents, who omit that Operation on the Supposition that they should never forgive themselves if a Child died under it; my example showing that the Regret may be the same either way, and that therefore the safer should be chosen. (A, 170)

Francis Folger Franklin, or Frankie as his parents often called him, had been weakened by a long bout with "flux" when smallpox broke out in Philadelphia in the fall of 1736. Before the little boy was strong enough to be inoculated— the procedure was arduous and risky—he died from the disease. Franklin explained these circumstances in the *Pennsylvania Gazette* shortly after Frankie's death, hoping to dispel rumors that his son had died as a result of a controversial medical advance that many of his contemporaries feared and opposed.[14]

But the account in the memoir suppresses the details that explain why Benjamin and Deborah Franklin had not chosen to inoculate their child before he became infected. The result is a record of private grief all the more powerful for its indirection, its brevity, and its resistance to time. The bitterness of the immediate loss may have dissipated in the decades since his child's death, the memoir implies, but Franklin makes clear that lingering guilt, along with the unfulfilled promise of "a fine boy" who never grows up, are sources of lasting sorrow. If he looked back at Benjamin Vaughan's 1783 letter as he drafted this passage, he surely recognized that its words offer little of the self-assured guidance that Vaughan had envisioned the memoir conveying to the post-Revolutionary world. Even the safer of two frightening alternatives, Franklin admits, may be fraught with lasting regret. Some sides of life are irrevocably darkened by a pain that no human tactics can amend.

FRANKLIN WROTE THE SECOND AND THIRD PARTS of his memoir during periods of leisure that followed remarkable accomplishments: the conclusion of the Peace of Paris, formally ending the American Revolution, and the ratification of the United States Constitution that Franklin had helped draft in the late summer of 1787. The memorandum opening the fragment of his book that Franklin wrote at Passy in 1784 calls attention to some aspects of time and place that bring special pressures to bear upon his writing. He is much less explicit about his personal circumstances in August 1788, when he begins the third section of his manuscript, though the 1731 library paper inevitably invites comparison to the recent attempt of the Constitutional Convention to compose a set of good and wise rules to replace the haphazard Articles of Confederation, just as a youthful Franklin had envisioned that his United Party for Virtue might do for mankind as a whole. The memoir clearly invites its readers to approach these portions of Franklin's story, at least in part, in the spirit that Benjamin Vaughan anticipated when he looked forward to reading the complete autobiographical legacy of the author of an "immense revolution."

As the inclusion of the fragmentary "Notes of my Life" in the body of the memoir suggests, Franklin himself is careful to discourage such triumphal expectations, to qualify his successes, and to dramatize—sometimes at significant emotional cost—his lifelong disappointments. But no portion of his story is so relentless in its depiction of failure and frustration as the section traditionally excluded from all modern editions of Franklin's book: the letter that he addressed to his son William on March 22, 1775, as he was sailing back to America, describing the breakdown of an elaborate sequence of last-minute efforts to mediate between the English Ministry and the American colonies. Unless Franklin undertook to tell this complex story twice after he was past seventy, during some of the busiest years of his life, these are the same pages that he offered to Thomas Jefferson, in 1790, as a sample of what his finished memoir would contain. They treat, in some detail, a topic that he had added to the copy of his working notes that Abel James had sent to him in France: "Negociation to prevent the War." Franklin did not initiate these negotiations, but between late November 1774 and late March 1775, he quickly became their central player as he responded to an assortment of direct and indirect overtures from English moderates who hoped to broker some kind of an agreement that would defuse an increasingly tense standoff.

In the 1775 voyage letter, Franklin devotes an extraordinary amount of energy to depicting the events of these four months, perhaps in part as a final effort to explain his motives and his feelings, at this critical juncture in his life, to the royal governor who was his only surviving son. Deborah Franklin had died in December 1774, and the news of her death had reached Franklin himself only in late February 1775, less than a month before he set sail for home. Under these circumstances, it is understandable that he would take pains to restore his fraying ties with his oldest child, as the 1771 portion of the memoir had in part set out to do. But during the four intervening years, a group of Boston protestors had destroyed a valuable cargo of English tea, and Franklin had been publicly abused before the Privy Council for his role in the publication of some letters from Thomas Hutchinson, the royal governor of Massachusetts, that exposed Hutchinson's loyalist sympathies. Parliament had endorsed the military occupation of Boston and the closing of its port. The First Continental Congress had met to organize American resistance and petition for redress. The chasm between the colonial governments and London had probably grown too wide to close, and would grow wider still while Franklin was at sea with the outbreak of fighting at Lexington and Concord. In the voyage letter he orchestrates a final breach of his own, as he retraces the serpentine sequence of exchanges that precedes his departure for America.[15]

Between the time that he sailed from Portsmouth, near the end of March 1775, and early May when his ship docked at Philadelphia, Franklin employed the weeks at sea preparing a dense narrative matrix for twenty-four docu-

Franklin's letter to his son, March 22, 1775, from "On board the Pennsylvania Packet." Reproduced from microfilm of the original manuscript in the collections of the Library of Congress. See *Benjamin Franklin: A Register and Index of his Papers in the Library of Congress* (Washington, DC: Library of Congress, 1973) under "Franklin, Benjamin—London Negotiations" Series 1, Vol. 14.

mentary insertions that chart a mix of secretive meetings, evolving proposals, intractable disagreements, parliamentary motions, and ministerial bribes, collectively illustrating how even the best-disposed public figures in England utterly failed to grasp the urgency and the determination fueling American resentment. Franklin opens the letter by describing how he had held himself aloof from public business for nearly seven months after "the Affront" he had received at the Privy Council meeting of January 1774, nursing his resentments but noting at the same time the first tentative overtures from English opponents of the Ministry's coercive American policy. Suddenly in late summer, two intermediaries arranged a surprise meeting between Franklin and William Pitt, now the Earl of Chatham, two years younger than Franklin himself but increasingly hobbled by bad health and for many years "an Inaccessible" when Franklin had tried to see him to discuss colonial affairs.

Out of the blue, the inaccessible Pitt—a national hero who had been elevated to the House of Lords for his leadership during the Seven Years' War—now sought to meet Franklin, both to express his sympathy for the beleaguered people of Massachusetts and to sound Franklin out on American resolve. "He mention'd an Opinion prevailing here that America aim'd at setting up for itself as an independent State; or at least to get rid of the Navigation Acts," Franklin wrote. "I assur'd him, that having more than once travell'd almost from one end of the Continent to the other and kept a great Variety of Company, eating drinking and conversing with them freely, I had never heard in any Conversation from any Person drunk or sober, the least Expression of a Wish for a Separation, or Hint that such a Thing would be advantageous to America" (P, 21.549). Franklin protests much too colorfully here, perhaps, but this dramatically scripted reassurance is aimed at the memoir's American audience at large rather than at William Pitt or William Franklin. It had been nearly a decade since Franklin himself had set foot anywhere in the colonies when he makes this sweeping claim, but his purpose is to establish for the readers of his letter that the Revolution first began in English suspicions, not in American plots.

Two months later, the probing of Franklin's opinions that the March 22 narrative records begins in earnest through an odd invitation that he receives to play chess with Caroline Howe, sister of the British naval hero Viscount Richard Howe, and a member of an aristocratic family with long-standing colonial ties. In quick succession, two of Franklin's old Quaker friends—David Barclay and John Fothergill—ask to meet with him to discuss the most effective way to prevent the "Calamity" of civil war in America. Franklin realizes only much later that the Howes and his Quaker colleagues were comparing the results of the series of meetings that ensues. To his delightful chess partner, Lady Howe, he blithely suggests that the quarrel between the Ministry and the colonies was "a matter of Punctilio, which Two or three reasonable People might settle in half an Hour," but the conversations he has with Barclay and Fothergill tell a much different story. Together, Franklin and these two "reasonable" friends wrangle at length over a list of seventeen proposals that Franklin drew up at their request and titled "Hints for *Conversation* upon the Subject of Terms that might probably produce a durable Union between Britain and the Colonies" (P, 21.366).

Years of practice framing tactful discussion questions for Junto meetings have their influence on Franklin's unassuming title for this document, but his proposals themselves are at once specific, direct, and wide-ranging, making short work of the most immediate grievances ("The Tea destroy'd to be paid for") but asserting unequivocal opposition to English intimidation ("No Troops to enter and quarter in any Colony but with the Consent of its Legislature"). These were the first and the eighth of Franklin's seventeen hints. In between them he conceded support for the Navigation Acts by which England monopolized American commerce and collected duties on all American shipping, but insisted that the revenue from the acts remain in America to meet American needs, not be siphoned into the English treasury. Franklin added detailed hints on how the colonies would support the central government through wartime requisitions, but he required in turn that the British restore to Massachusetts the control of Castle William in Boston Harbor, that Parliament reinstate the Massachusetts Charter, and that it grant "a free Government" to Canada. Franklin's conversational "hints," in other words, like his 1731 library "Observations," are far more imposing than his modest title implies.

On the question of Canadian sovereignty, Franklin explained to his astonished English friends that Americans did not like the idea of "Establishing an arbitrary Government on the back of our Settlements" where it could serve as a "Foundation for future Slavery laid in America." American soldiers had helped to conquer Canada from the French during the Seven Years' War, he pointed out, and as a consequence the American colonies had a right to some voice in how it was to be administered; "loving Liberty ourselves," he somewhat grandly asserted, "we wish't it to be extended among Mankind" (P, 21. 560). Barclay and Fothergill reluctantly bowed to Franklin's insistence on this unexpected demand. Americans "must risque Life and everything," Frank-

Hints for Conversation upon the Subject of Terms that might probably produce a durable Union between Britain and the Colonies.

1. The Tea destroy'd to be paid for.
2. The Tea-Duty Act to be repeal'd, and all the Duties that have been receiv'd upon it to be repaid into the Treasuries of the several Provinces from which they have been collected.
3. The Acts of Navigation to be all re-enacted in the Colonies.
4. A Naval Officer appointed by the Crown to reside in each Colony, to see that those Acts are observed.
5. All the Acts restraining Manufactures in the Colonies to be reconsider'd.
6. All Duties arising on the Acts for regulating Trade with the Colonies, to be for the public Use of the respective Colonies, and paid into their Treasuries. The Collectors and Custom house Officers to be appointed by each Governor, and not sent from England.
7. In Consideration of the Americans maintaining their own Peace Establishment, and the Monopoly Britain

The first sheet of Franklin's "Hints for *Conversation*" inserted into Franklin's letter to his son, March 22, 1775. Reproduced from microfilm of the original manuscript in the collections of the Library of Congress. See *Benjamin Franklin: A Register and Index of his Papers in the Library of Congress* (Washington, DC: Library of Congress, 1973).

lin claimed, rather than tolerate the arbitrary rule of Parliament anywhere in North America. But they struck out of the list entirely one of Franklin's hints, got him to modify another, expressed skepticism over the political viability of several others, and promised to circulate the revised document among influential friends "as the Sentiments of considerate Persons" rather than the product of Franklin's pen. All three agreed that it was best to keep Franklin's involvement in these preliminary conversations a "deep secret," to avoid offending the many members of the government who despised him, but only Franklin observed these conditions.

These hints are the first extensive insertion in the March 22 letter, and Franklin devotes many pages to his defense of their terms against Barclay's and Fothergill's objections. Even two moderate Quakers anxious to prevent "the Mischiefs" brewing between England and America were confident that the king would never accept limits on his ability to quarter troops wherever he chose to do so, and neither man approved of Franklin's obstinacy on this point. But how (Franklin wondered in return) could Americans negotiate in good faith over terms of accommodation with England while the implicit threat of force was always at hand in the form of General Gage's regulars, who were currently occupying Boston? In a later conversation with William Pitt that Franklin adds to the March 1775 letter, he elaborates on both the practical and the principled reasons for this demand:

> I mentioned to him the very hazardous State I conceiv'd we were in by the Continuance of the Army in Boston; that whatever Disposition there might be in the Inhabitants to give no just Cause of Offence to the Troops, or in the General to preserve Order among them, an unpremeditated unforeseen Quarrel might happen between perhaps a drunken Porter and a Soldier, that might bring on a Riot, Tumult and Bloodshed, and in its Consequences produce a Breach impossible to be healed: that the Army could not possibly answer any good purpose there, and might be infinitely mischievous: that no Accommodation could properly be propos'd and entred into by the Americans while the Bayonet was at their Breasts: that to have any Agreement binding all Force should be withdrawn. His Lordship seem'd to think these Sentiments had something in them that was reasonable. (P, 21.570)

Franklin's reading of Pitt's reaction to his impassioned appeal echoes the mixed portrait of reason and inference that he had explored throughout the 1771 fragment of the memoir. The strategic discovery he claimed to have made, in 1723, that big fish eat little fish, leads to the realization that "reasonable" creatures have a limitless capacity to justify acting on their desires. "Something that pretended to be reason," Franklin would write in the memoir's second part, ultimately convinced him to abandon his pursuit of moral perfection. That William Pitt "seem'd" to find "something" reasonable in Franklin's sentiments is both a reassuring and an unsettling detail: both a promising concession and a worrisome extension of the pattern of equivocation that Franklin's experience had taught him to expect in human affairs.

Near the end of January 1775, Pitt responds to Franklin's fears when he offers a motion in the House of Lords to carry out Franklin's recommendation for a troop withdrawal. The carefully worded proposal that Pitt presents to his colleagues is the tenth of Franklin's documentary insertions in the March 22 letter and indicates how cautiously even a distinguished national hero has to tread when indirectly addressing the king, biggest fish of all, through his paid retainers in Parliament:

Lord Chatham's Motion, Jan. 20. 1775.

That an humble Address be presented to his Majesty, most humbly to advise and beseech his Majesty, that, in order to open the Way towards an happy Settlement of the dangerous Troubles in America, by beginning to allay Ferments and soften Animosities there; and above all, for preventing in the mean time any sudden and fatal Catastrophe at Boston, now suffering under the daily Irritation of an Army before their Eyes, posted in their Town, it may graciously please his Majesty that immediate Orders may be dispatched to General Gage for removing his Majesty's Forces from the Town of Boston, as soon as the Rigour of the Season and other Circumstances indispensable to the Safety and Accommodation of the said Troops may render the same practicable. (P, 21.577)

Pitt made an impressive speech when he introduced this motion on the floor of the House, with Franklin in the gallery as his guest. Lord Camden, "another wonderfully good Speaker and clear close Reasoner," Franklin wrote, supported the resolution, along with "several other Lords who spoke excellently well." But eloquence and reason had little softening effect. "The Motion was rejected," Franklin curtly noted: "Sixteen Scotch Peers, and twenty four Bishops, with all the Lords in Possession or Expectation of Places when they vote together unanimously as they generally do for Ministerial Measures, make a dead Majority that renders all Debating ridiculous in itself, since it can answer no End" (P, 21.577). The upper house of the most venerable legislative body in the world could not do what the Junto had done, on a weekly basis, for most of Franklin's life: read, listen, and speak "to the purpose" in a "sincere Spirit of Enquiry after Truth" (A, 117). This is the first of three occasions in the voyage letter when Franklin asserts the venality of the English government, particularly the House of Lords, though the Commons (he hastened to add) was no better.

Meanwhile, Franklin's hints continued to circulate among the English opposition through the offices of David Barclay and John Fothergill, and the Howes renewed their chess initiative, with Lady Howe now introducing her brother to the conversation. After apologizing for Franklin's treatment before the Privy Council nearly a year earlier, Lord Howe, disingenuously, asked Franklin to prepare some "Propositions" for restoring peace between England and America, though Franklin would learn before long that Howe had already seen the suggestions he had drawn up and discussed with Barclay and Fothergill. Indeed, at their very next meeting a few days later, Howe produced a copy of the hints "in D. Barclay's Hand" and summarily brushed them aside as unacceptable, suggesting at the same time that Franklin might expect "any Reward in the Power of the Government to bestow" if he would reconsider his position and offer a plan more acceptable to the "dead Majority," which Franklin would soon have a chance to observe firsthand as it rejected Pitt's humble petition. "This to me was what the French call *Spitting in the Soup*," Franklin wrote of Howe's thinly veiled attempt to buy his complicity in a political understanding more favorable to English than to American interests (P, 21.572).

Howe would spit in the soup at least once more before Franklin left England, at a meeting on February 18, 1775, in which he asked Franklin to join him as part of a peace commission to America, offering "a proper Consideration" for Franklin's services, as well as "a firm Promise of subsequent Rewards" after an agreement was reached. Franklin bluntly explained to Howe that any ministerial favors to him, at such a crucial juncture in colonial affairs, "would be considered as so many Bribes to betray the Interest of my Country" (P, 21.590). Fair terms were all that Franklin strove to secure from the government, but he left England fully convinced by these exchanges that even the most fair-minded members of Parliament understood bribery better than they did the motives behind the American resistance.

As the 1775 voyage letter slowly unfolds, the futility of Franklin's efforts becomes plain. The scramble of life that Benjamin Vaughan came to fear was clearly in the ascendant in English political circles over these last months before open revolution in America. Place seekers made debate useless in the House of Lords, where the members attended to their private material comfort rather than the well-being of the greater nation. Among influential public figures in London, everyone is assumed to have a price. As Franklin's frustrations increase, his anger once more begins to smolder, as it did during and after the Privy Council attack. This emotional shift in the March 22 letter begins, oddly, with an extraordinary act of deference by William Pitt, who visits Franklin at his Craven Street residence to deliver the text of a parliamentary act that Pitt had drafted in order to settle all the differences with the colonies, "requesting me to consider it carefully and communicate to him such Remarks upon it as should occur to me" (P, 21.579). Franklin's judgment was a "Regulator," Pitt said, by which other men might set their watches.

But when Franklin returns the visit two days later to give Pitt his thoughts, the great man simply does not listen. His own eloquence completely engrosses him. "He is not easily interrupted," Franklin drily observed in the letter, "and I had such Pleasure in hearing him that I found little Inclination to interrupt him." In this account, Pitt's intelligence resembles a ticking watch more closely than he imagined. Franklin consoled himself with the thought that floor debate would alter the language of any proposed act so completely, and give so many chances to improve it, that there was little point in urging preliminary modifications. But he had briefly (and astutely, from the point of view of narrative impact) forgotten the lesson of his first encounter with the dead majority in the House of Lords.

When Pitt presented his act to the English peers, Lord Dartmouth seemed initially inclined to accept it for consideration by the Ministry, but very quickly a groundswell of opposition grew. Lord Sandwich implied that Franklin, not Pitt, was the act's actual author and maligned Franklin from the House floor as "one of the bitterest and most mischievous Enemies this country had ever known." Once again, Franklin notes, he was in the gallery, keeping his face "as immovable as if my Features had been made of Wood," but other "Lords of the Administration" joined Sandwich's assault. Under pressure, Dartmouth backpedaled, and, in spite of a final appeal from Pitt asserting his own authorship of the act while praising Franklin to the point of embarrassment as "an Honour not to the English Nation only but to Human Nature," the act was rejected out of hand. This outcome elicits a summation from Franklin that is less spontaneous in its disgust than it seems:

To hear so many of these *Hereditary* Legislators declaiming so vehemently against, not the Adopting merely, but even the *Consideration* of a Proposal so important in its Nature, offered by a Person of so weighty a Character, one of the first Statesmen of the Age, who had taken up this Country when in the lowest Despondency, and conducted it to Victory and Glory thro' a War with two of the mightiest Kingdoms in Europe; to hear them censuring his Plan not only for their own Misunderstandings of what was in it, but for their Imaginations of what was not in it, which they would not give themselves an Opportunity of rectifying by a second Reading; to perceive the total Ignorance of the Subject in some, the Prejudice and Passion of others, and the wilful Perversion of Plain Truth in several of the Ministers; and upon the whole to see it so ignominiously rejected by so great a Majority, and so hastily too, in Breach of all Decency and prudent Regard to the Character and Dignity of their Body as a third Part of the National Legislature, gave me an exceeding mean Opinion of their Abilities, and made their Claim of Sovereignty over three Millions of virtuous sensible People in America, seem the greatest of Absurdities, since they appear'd to have scarce Discretion enough to govern a Herd of Swine. (P, 21.582–83)

The idea of hereditary legislators, Franklin continues, insults the intelligence, but the elected members in the House of Commons were equally implicated in a system of bribery that bound together electors, representatives, and ministers in a corrupt and immovable alliance. This comprehensive dismissal of English institutions is clearly framed for public delivery, a foretaste of the message that Franklin would shortly begin to deliver to his colleagues in the Second Continental Congress.

A few days after the failure of Pitt's draft act, Barclay and Fothergill make a final overture to Franklin in an attempt to repair the damage that the House of Lords had inflicted. The outcome only makes matters worse. During a meeting of the three men at Fothergill's residence, they produce an annotated copy of Franklin's original hints, incorporating additional objections that they had collected from their influential friends and hinting, in turn, that America needed to resolve these disputes peacefully and quickly, "since it was so easy for Britain to burn all our Sea Port Towns" (P, 21.584). This language from two affluent and intelligent Quakers, committed in principle at least to pacifism, was too much for Franklin to bear: "I grew warm, said that the chief Part of my little Property consisted of Houses in those Towns; that they might make Bonfires of them whenever they pleased; that the Fear of losing them would never alter my

Franklin concludes Parliament had "scarce Discretion enough to govern a Herd of Swine," excerpt from his letter to his son, March 22, 1775. Reproduced from microfilm of the original manuscript in the collections of the Library of Congress. See *Benjamin Franklin: A Register and Index of his Papers in the Library of Congress* (Washington, DC: Library of Congress, 1973).

Resolution to resist to the last the Claim of Parliament; and that it behov'd this Country to take Care what Mischief it did us, for that sooner or later it would certainly be obliged to make good all Damages with Interest" (P, 21.584).

This splendid outburst at once echoes, amplifies, and inverts William Denham's stylish gesture, much earlier in the memoir, of repaying the balance of his financial obligations to his English creditors with interest and without any threat of legal compulsion. But the scales of Atlantic relations have shifted dramatically in the fifty years since Denham's dinner. Franklin bluntly refuses to barter principle for property. Fothergill smiles at his forceful words, "with some Approbation" Franklin hopes, and promises to pass on his response to Dartmouth, but at this point in the voyage letter it is difficult for both its author and its reader to know whether these old friends have simply been testing Franklin or if they, like Lord Howe, are given to spitting in the soup.

Ultimately Franklin agrees to endorse the idea of a high-ranking peace commissioner to be sent to America to negotiate the terms of a reconciliation treaty and drafts a series of papers to that end, both for the other colonial agents in the city to sign and for Barclay and Fothergill to use in further discussions with their government contacts. Franklin collects all these papers too for insertion into the voyage letter, but a tepid and very limited resolution from Lord North on the collection of American revenue is the only outcome of this final flurry of activity. "After a good deal of wild debate," Franklin notes, North's proposal passes the House of Lords by a strong majority, but in a later conversation with Lord Hyde, another ministerial intermediary, Franklin compares North's empty gesture to the act of a "Highway-man who presents his Pistol and Hat at a Coach-Window, demanding no specific Sum, but if you will give all your Money or what he is pleas'd to think sufficient, he will civilly omit putting his own Hand into your Pockets. If not, there is his Pistol" (P, 21.595). The matter of punctilio that Franklin had minimized during his first chess matches with Caroline Howe has escalated into a menacing parliamentary farce.

The final two documents that Franklin includes in the 1775 voyage letter elaborate on this grim turn of events. They consist of the draft of an angry memorial to Lord Dartmouth that Franklin prepares within a few days of his departure for America, followed by a soothing note from an old English friend: another instance of the temperamental counterpoises that shape the memoir's portrait of human behavior. In the draft memorial Franklin bluntly demands "Satisfaction" from the government for the injuries it has inflicted on the colonies and protests against yet another punitive measure "now under Consideration in Parliament" and "likely to give such Umbrage to *all the Colonies*, that in no future War, wherein other Conquests may be meditated, either a Man or a Shilling will be obtained from any of them to aid such Conquests, till full Satisfaction be made as aforesaid" (P, 21.528). A brief but firm admonishment from Thomas Walpole to whom Franklin had shown the draft, convinces him that its intemperate language could have "dangerous consequences to your person" (P, 21.529). The Dartmouth memorial is never sent. But in pocketing these last two pieces of paper, as Franklin does so many of the records embedded in this remarkable narrative, he both suppresses and preserves them. They capture in concentrated form the interplay of passion and principle that lay behind the collapse of his most ambitious civic design.

CHAPTER FOUR

Litera Scripta Manet

In the fall of 1773, Franklin contributed to the *Public Advertiser* the last of his efforts to influence English colonial policy through the London press, including two of his most celebrated satires: "Rules by Which a Great Empire May be Reduced to a Small One" and "An Edict by the King of Prussia." After the news arrived in January 1774 of the destruction of the tea in Boston Harbor, followed by Franklin's excruciating experience before the Privy Council the same month, he abandoned all attempts to shape English opinion, in print, through the formidable blend of reason and wit that had become his trademark.[1] This decision is part of the sullen silence that he maintains, as the British Ministry marshals its Coercive Acts, early in 1774, to punish the people of Massachusetts. After August, Franklin's silence breaks, not through a renewal of his print campaign but through the intense and complex series of verbal exchanges depicted in the 1775 voyage letter.

Other parts of the memoir use documentary insertions, in a very limited way, to illustrate Franklin's life story: Uncle Benjamin's poems, a sample page from Franklin's ivory booklet of the thirteen virtues, the 1731 library "Observations," or the advertisement that Franklin prepared in 1755 to assist the Braddock expedition. But the voyage letter greatly expands the role that such exhibits play in the book. It is an archive as well as a narrative, a drama in paper and on paper at the same time, setting a wide variety of formal and informal records in motion, in draft and in print, triggering an equally wide range of public and private responses. Twice late in the letter Franklin pulls written memoranda out of his pocket in order to correct misunderstandings or willful distortions of his own thoughts or those of others. During one of his last meetings with Richard Howe, for instance, he is able to prove very quickly that he has not tried to impose unacceptable negotiating conditions on the Ministry by appealing directly to his written proposals, "having a Copy of that Paper in my Pocket" (P, 21.594). A day or two later, when Lord Hyde suggests that Franklin has misread the implications of Lord North's revenue measure in Parliament, Franklin takes out a copy of the recently passed act and reads it, whereupon Hyde "wav'd that Point."

The "Hints for *Conversation*" that Franklin prepares for Barclay and Fothergill, late in 1774, are the focus of at least one actual, extended conversation that Franklin compresses in the voyage letter, as well as several other implicit ones that take the form of the annotations that Barclay and Fothergill add to the original paper. Franklin prepares his own annotations to William Pitt's proposed act for reconciling differences with the colonies and includes them among his voyage letter insertions, but when the two men meet so that Franklin can present his suggestions, Pitt can scarcely bring himself to listen to Franklin's points in his fervor to defend his draft.[2] Howe appears, at least, to have read Franklin's "Hints," though he uses them chiefly as a dramatic prop in his efforts to buy Franklin's loyalty, while Franklin in turn captures the dysfunctional state of Parliament as a whole both by recording what its members say, in the course of "wild Debate," and by dramatizing what they refuse to read.

Words and ideas take on a number of permanent and impermanent forms as the voyage letter documents this crucial stage in the disintegration of the glorious transatlantic political fabric that Franklin had hoped to preserve. Even during his extended hiatus from printing, in the months before he leaves England, he is immersed in the circulation of manuscripts that invite the participation of many "hands" in their evolution toward laws that might be enacted or treaties that could be signed in the hope of stabilizing the diplomatic flux. In falling short of this goal, however, the effort is not a complete failure. The voyage letter highlights the versatility of the written word as a vehicle that may or may not always arrive at a fixed destination, that can both advance and retard the process of compromise, harden or soften animosity, restrain or amplify the explosive passions of speech.[3]

Early in the memoir, Franklin apologizes to his son for the "rambling Digressions" into which he found his letter drifting. "I us'd to write more methodically," he confesses, "But one does not dress for private Company as for a public Ball" (A, 57). One does, however, dress for both—as Franklin's simple but graceful metaphor implies—along with the countless other public and private occasions that fall somewhere on the spectrum lying between these complementary social spheres. The 1775 voyage letter incorporates many of these manifestations of verbal life across the full range of settings available for human performance, as if Franklin intended to create an anthology, within an archive, within a letter, within a book. In this sense, too, the March 22, 1775, narrative is perfectly consistent with the rest of the memoir.

Each of the book's sections is a study in the capacity of words to shuttle back and forth between the fixity of an epitaph in stone, at one extreme, and the ephemeral atmosphere of unspoken thought and imperfect memory at the other.[4] Some degree of written permanence is vital, in human affairs, both as an organizational resource and as a barrier to forgetfulness. Unrecorded promises or commitments are all too easily left unrecognized and unfulfilled. But speech as an experimental verbal medium, hospitable to the rambling or exploratory propensities of the mind, is equally important to the subtle operations of language that Franklin's story ultimately celebrates. The memoir's formal solution to these expressive demands is an episodic continuum, inscribed across space and time, like the curvilinear serpent that Franklin hoped would convey to his fellow colonists their participation in a social whole.

THE OPENING SENTENCES of Franklin's book position its reader in the midst of a complex transmission process, beginning with his report to his son on the outcome of a collecting expedition. He and William had visited Ecton and Banbury to interview distant relatives, consult parish registers, and compile Franklin's own recollections together with his Uncle Benjamin's notes into a preliminary family history before its oral roots could be entirely lost. "Some old people at Ecton," in the course of sharing their memories, convinced William that the oldest of his father's uncles, Thomas Franklin, was an uncanny forerunner of his father, a first edition perhaps. "He died in 1702, Jan. 6, old Stile," Franklin wrote, "just 4 years to a Day before I was born," but the resemblance between the two men's lives struck William with special force: "Had he died on the same Day, you said one might have suppos'd a Transmigration" (A, 48).

In fact, Franklin has a variety of transmigrations in mind as he begins these pages. He has set out to compile written records of various sorts, along with private memories and family anecdotes, in an effort to establish a continuous lineage capable of bridging the emotional and ideological divisions that the old style–new style calendar disjunction implicitly depicts: a barrier dividing him both from his son and from his past. The Ecton church records confirm the intriguing genealogical fact that Benjamin Franklin was the youngest son of a youngest son for five successive generations, a discouraging heritage of hierarchical subordination that is wonderfully neutralized by the mysterious affinity of character linking Franklin to his father's gifted and successful oldest brother.[5] Other forms of transmission throughout the memoir take equally unusual but far less mystical paths. The course of conversation at Josiah Franklin's dinner table, for instance, was a tactic for transmitting immaterial forms of nourishment across the generational gap. When his father sought to prevent Franklin from running away to sea to escape the tallow chandler's trade, he tried to do so by transmitting his wishes through similarly indirect means:

> He therefore sometimes took me to walk with him, and see Joiners, Bricklayers, Turners, Braziers, &c. at their Work, that he might observe my Inclination, and endeavour to fix it on some Trade or other on Land. It has ever since been a Pleasure to me to see good Workmen handle their Tools; and it has been useful to me, having learnt so much by it, as to be able to do little Jobs my self in my House, when a Workman could not readily be got; and to construct little Machines for my Experiments while the Intention of making the Experiment was fresh and warm in my Mind. My Father at last fix'd upon the Cutler's Trade, and my Uncle Benjamin's Son Samuel who was bred to that Business in London being about that time establish'd in Boston, I was sent to be with him some time on liking. But his Expectations of a Fee with me displeasing my Father, I was taken home again. (A, 57)

For the time being Josiah's parental goals are frustrated, but his efforts have an unexpected impact on his son's life, as well as a far-reaching influence on the memoir in which Franklin describes them. Transmission can take on a life of its own. Joining, bricklaying, turning wood, and shaping metal attract Franklin's eye during these instructive walks, drawing it to processes rather than products, as he notes with delight how skilled workmen handle their tools and give form to their hidden intentions. Franklin implies that he is already responding, at an early age, to the interplay between the fleeting warmth of an idea and the little machines best suited to explore its possibilities.

More than one form of fixing is underway in this passage, blunting the keen effects of the cutler's trade on Josiah's relationship with his brother's family. More than one form of joining is underway as well. Particularly in this portion of his story, Franklin takes a playful interest in workshop puns, noting a sentence or two after expressing his admiration for joiners and turners that Cotton Mather's *Essays to Do Good* "gave me a Turn of Thinking" toward public service. Puns too are a form of joining, one that highlights the fluidity of meaning that words frequently exploit in the course of performing very much like little machines that Franklin is able to call upon throughout his life to address his civic and literary experiments. Long familiarity with a composing stick, setting lines of text, assembling pages and forms, casting fresh type in lead matrices, mixing ink, or engraving ornaments had steeped him in the tactile life of language, in the remarkable malleability that enabled writing to capture meaning without confining it: to impose a highly adaptable "fixity" on the volatile energies of existence.

The memoir addresses this feature of Franklin's life by dramatizing repeatedly, in its earliest episodes, the interaction between the mobile intelligence of a reader and the superficial immobility of the written or the printed page. Franklin illustrates this phenomenon to memorable effect in his description of how he taught himself to write. Delighted with the "Manner" of the *Spectator* essays that he had encountered in a random volume from his brother's extensive printing house collection, Franklin set out to explore the way in which the essayist had handled his tools in the hope of learning how he achieved his effects. The outcome of the intense, physical process that he promptly applied to these printed pages, like the result of Josiah Franklin's instructive strolls, took a direction that the *Spectator* authors could scarcely have envisioned.[6]

Franklin describes how he read the book "over and over," with inexhaustible pleasure, until he decided to try to "imitate" its effects. The result of this decision, however, is anything but imitative. He proceeds not by mirroring the book's style but by rebuilding it from scratch, recast in his own idiom, working initially from "short Hints of the Sentiment in each Sentence" that he would put aside for several days to further distance them from their model before recreating an entire essay "in any suitable Words, that should come to hand" (A, 62). He then mixed the hints and rearranged them in different sequences, turning some of the essays from prose to verse and back to prose again, at each stage comparing the transmuted result to the original from which he had begun. Sentiments and sentences, in this method, are as "movable" as lead type, and as capable of endless change. Franklin was teaching himself that the power of a printed or a written page to delight its reader depends upon a sophisticated appreciation for the infinite verbal mobility that lies behind it.

The epistolary debates that he held with John Collins called for maintaining a similar degree of agility and attentiveness. Unable to finish one of their combative verbal exchanges, Franklin sent Collins some additional "Arguments" in writing, keeping his drafts for reference while the conversation unfolded through "three or four Letters of a Side" (A, 61). When Josiah Franklin finds these records among his son's "Papers," he in turn uses them as a means of critiquing the performance of both boys: "Without entring into the Discussion, he took occasion to talk to me about the Manner of my Writing, observ'd that tho' I had the Advantage of my Antagonist in correct Spelling and pointing (which I ow'd to the Printing House) I fell far short in elegance of Expression, in Method and in Perspicuity, of which he convinc'd me by several Instances." Franklin's drafts offered his father a convenient opportunity to talk, rather than scold or prescribe, and to suggest places where Franklin's use of words might have been improved. Instead of simply asserting his parental authority, he models the comparative process (and the interest in "manner") that Franklin adapts in the memoir's following paragraph to a systematic study of the *Spectator*'s prose.

In these early portions of Franklin's story, books and papers mingle with their readers in casual or accidental ways, transmitting their contents almost surreptitiously. Franklin originally "caught" his disputatious habits of speech and his love of argument from Josiah's infectious library of theological polemic. Matthew Adams, an "ingenious Tradesman" in Boston, takes a liking to Franklin and gives him the run of his "pretty Collection of Books," without imposing his judgment or his taste further than to lend Franklin "such Books as I chose to read" (A, 59). The outcome of this seductive experience is Franklin's short-lived passion for poetry. When James Franklin found that his precocious brother had "made some little Pieces" of verse on his own, he saw a chance to exploit a popular market "and put me on composing two occasional Ballads" that Franklin later peddled around town. "The first sold wonderfully," he recalled, the triple drowning it lamented "having made a great Noise," but Josiah's subsequent ridicule squelches Franklin's poetic career. He was not quite thirteen years old, however, when this first experience with the capacity of writing to manipulate the "great Noise" of recent events into memorable form awakens a lifelong ambition.

During these same years Franklin reports that he stumbled on a book of advice by Thomas Tryon and "determin'd to go into it," adopting Tryon's vegetarian diet with the same zeal that he brought to poetry and to argument. He "took" to Edward Cocker's "Book of Arithmetic" with a similar degree of determination and "went thro' the whole by my self with great Ease" to compensate for his early removal from school. Two Socratic dialogues in the back of a grammar textbook exert a similar physical charm on Franklin. Among the very few books that he indicates he merely "read," in this portion of the memoir, are "Locke on Human Understanding, and the Art of Thinking by Messrs. du Port Royal" (A, 64). Neither of these prestigious studies of consciousness or reflective method seems to seize on Franklin's imagination or excite his energies like the incitements to action or to movement that he finds in Xenophon, Shaftesbury, Tryon, or Bunyan.

Reading and writing are to a great extent contemplative activities, calling for the kind of quiet and privacy that Franklin secures when he negotiates a new boarding arrangement with his brother in order to free long lunch hours for study. He often spends "the greatest Part of the Night" reading a book that one of his fellow apprentices had "borrowed" for him "lest it should be missed or wanted" the following morning by the master printer or bookseller who owned it. But even these details suggest the extent to which Franklin's inner and outer lives are interleaved with one another in the memoir's pages. Collaboration, not competition, shape their relationship, even before Franklin himself had begun to write. Like the tools he had learned to study on his Boston walks, a book requires a workman who knows how to handle it. Accordingly Franklin often depicts himself catching knowledge on the fly, meeting with odd volumes by happenstance and finding uses for them, or intercepting unexpected opportunities to exercise his gifts and his interests. His first published work is an outgrowth of just such opportunism.

Two or three years after Franklin had begun his apprenticeship, his brother decided to start a newspaper, putting the now fairly experienced Franklin to work on every phase of production and distribution, composing, printing, and delivering the finished product to subscribers:

He had some ingenious Men among his Friends who amus'd themselves by writing little Pieces for this Paper, which gain'd it Credit, and made it more in Demand; and these Gentlemen often visited us. Hearing their Conversations, and their Accounts of the Approbation their Papers were receiv'd with, I was excited to try my Hand among them. But being still a Boy, and suspecting that my Brother would object to printing any Thing of mine in his Paper if he knew it to be mine, I contriv'd to disguise my Hand, and writing an anonymous Paper I put it in at night under the Door of the Printing House. It was found in the Morning and communicated to his Writing Friends when they call'd in as usual. They read it, commented on it in my Hearing, and I had the exquisite Pleasure, of finding it met with their Approbation, and that in their different Guesses at the Author none were named but Men of some Character among us for Learning and Ingenuity (A, 67–68)

The printing house was James Franklin's workplace but it doubled as a social center where his "Writing Friends" could regularly meet to talk over the impact of their work. Hearing these conversations prompts Franklin to try his luck at joining them without his brother's permission—to try his "hand" by disguising it—ultimately exacerbating the friction between the two but also equipping Franklin with the confidence to defend James in print when the Massachusetts Assembly had him briefly jailed for refusing to name the author of an article in the paper that had offended Boston's political leaders. Franklin "made bold to give our Rulers some Rubs" in the paper's pages that partly compensated James for the difficulty his talented and temperamental younger brother frequently caused.

A few pages later, the memoir introduces another printing house that is indirectly responsible for a still bolder venture with words in Franklin's early years. During the few months that he spent at Palmer's "famous Printing House in Bartholomew Close" while he was in London in 1725, he overheard another sort of conversation that he decided to join. While composing pages for a new edition of a book by William Wollaston, Franklin found himself quarreling with some of the author's "Reasonings" as he set them in type, slipping into the kind of private give-and-take with the printed page that is second nature to an avid reader. The result (the memoir reports) was "a little metaphysical Piece, in which I made Remarks on them," a modest description that implies Franklin's remarks were little more than glorified marginalia on portions of Wollaston's book.

In fact Franklin's younger self had given his pamphlet a far more ambitious title, *A Dissertation on Liberty and Necessity, Pleasure and Pain*, and gave little indication in its pages that he was simply responding to Wollaston's treatise. The permission to use Palmer's types, press, and paper to produce this piece had to come from Palmer himself, who like Matthew Adams a few years earlier in Boston apparently enjoyed and appreciated Franklin's intelligence enough to trust him with the resources of his business and the reputation of his house, "tho' he seriously expostulated with me upon the Principles of my Pamphlet which to him appear'd abominable" (A, 96). "My printing this Pamphlet was another Erratum," Franklin dutifully records in his book, but by including the anecdote he stresses once more the intimate collaboration among his reading, writing, and working lives.[7]

This episode, too, is one of the earliest instances in which the memoir illustrates the transformative impact that print can have on otherwise sharp personal differences. As long as Franklin and Collins were exchanging arguments in the letters that Josiah Franklin critiqued, their friendship remained firm. Their tempers ultimately flare, and the relationship ends over an impulsive dispute in a rowboat. Franklin's father almost certainly saw evidence of his son's emerging disdain for received opinion in the pages of his correspondence with Collins, but he responded to their shared appreciation for the accuracy, elegance, and "perspicuity" of good writing, rather than to any growing differences of belief between them. By contrast, Mr. Palmer tackles these differences directly, and though he vigorously disapproves of Franklin's Deist convictions, and could easily have intervened to keep the pamphlet from appearing at all, he maintains a high regard for its author "as a young Man of some Ingenuity." On several occasions in his book, Franklin will revisit this paradoxical capacity of a lettered culture to accommodate stark oppositions within a cohesive verbal frame.

Franklin's errant metaphysical pamphlet finds admirers who behave, on the whole, with less generosity than its most visible critic. Like his disputatious correspondence with John Collins, the *Dissertation on Liberty and Necessity* has a mobility of its own that carries its author along in its wake:

> My Pamphlet by some means falling into the Hands of one Lyons, a Surgeon, Author of a Book entitled *The Infallibility of Human Judgment*, it occasioned an Acquaintance between us; he took great Notice of me, call'd on me often, to converse on those Subjects, carried me to the Horns a pale Ale-House in [blank]

Lane, Cheapside, and introduc'd me to Dr. Mandevile, Author of the Fable of the Bees who had a Club there, of which he was the Soul, being a most facetious entertaining Companion. Lyons too introduc'd me, to Dr. Pemberton, at Batson's Coffee house, who promis'd to give me an Opportunity some time or other of seeing Sir Isaac Newton, of which I was extreamly desirous; but this never happened. (A, 97)

Franklin falls into the hands of this trio of freethinking doctors as casually as his pamphlet does, but they appear to drop their young protégé just as quickly. In preserving the title of Lyons's book, however, the memoir offers a whirlwind exposure to the sweeping intellectual ambitions of London's coffeehouse culture, a dizzying blend of the facetious and the infallible, of great "Notice" and abrupt neglect. By contrast, the preceding paragraph of Franklin's narrative describes a much more fruitful bookish relationship that marked his months in London: the friendly arrangement that he is able to work out with a neighboring bookseller, allowing him to borrow volumes "on certain reasonable Terms" from the shop's "immense Collection of second-hand Books" whenever he chose. Franklin is able to enjoy the advantages of this impromptu library through much of his stay in the city, a privilege that is completely independent of the capricious promises of coffeehouse wits (A, 97).

The varieties of textual and human movement portrayed in these adjacent anecdotes depict the double-edged nature of print as both a durable and a fleeting medium of human exchange, not so different from the porous memory that it serves. Franklin can recall a specific tavern or coffeehouse, at a distance of over four decades, but not the first names of the surgeon who befriended him or the bookseller, "one Wilcox," whose generous lending terms have also slipped his mind. As with other social overtures, authors could not always count on being able to lay lasting claim to a reader's attention or control the value a given audience would attach to their work. Secondhand books like those which composed Wilcox's immense collection were, presumably, in search of new owners who might regard their contents more highly than the original purchasers, but in the meantime they waited in relative neglect on a bookseller's overstocked shelves, emblems of the transient nature of literary reputation. In this context, the title of Dr. Lyons's work, *The Infallibility of Human Judgment*, is an invitation to ridicule rather than admiration or acquisition. Franklin records it in implicit mockery of the abominable folly of his own pamphlet and of the social channels into which it had led him.

When he in turn tries to wean James Ralph from his infatuation with poetry, he copies and sends to him "a great Part" of one of Edward Young's recently published satires on fame that fails completely in its purposes. Ralph ignores the advice and persists in sending back for Franklin's review "large Specimens of an Epic Poem" that he was convinced would ultimately rescue him from the dishonorable profession of country schoolmaster. Even a famous poet's indictment of poetic fame, painstakingly copied out by a thoughtful friend, might as easily confirm one's fantasies as cure them. Franklin himself had first been attracted to the ideas of the Deists by reading anti-Deist tracts:

> It happened that they wrought an Effect on me quite contrary to what was intended by them: For the Arguments of the Deists which were quoted to be refuted, appeared to me much stronger than the Refutations. In short, I soon became a thorough Deist. My Arguments perverted some others, particularly Collins and Ralph: but each of them having afterwards wrong'd me greatly without the least Compunction and recollecting Keith's Conduct towards me, (who was another Freethinker) and my own towards Vernon and Miss Read which at Times gave me great Trouble, I began to suspect that this Doctrine tho' it might be true, was not very useful. (A, 114)

Two stages of untoward transmission in this passage ultimately convince Franklin that the ambitious Deist pamphlet he had printed on Palmer's press was not "so clever a Performance as I once thought." Though its contents might well be sound, Franklin suspected, some error had "insinuated itself unperceiv'd into my Argument," slipping invisibly between the lines of type that the author had written, set, and printed himself, in an effort to exert the maximum amount of control over words that still succeeded in having their own way.[8]

"Written Resolutions" of the kind that Franklin soon adds to his 1726 voyage journal remain the best hope one has for controlling or for navigating the ceaseless flow of events and feelings that make up our existence. In the 1771 fragment of the memoir, Franklin directs his son's attention to this manuscript record "for the Incidents of the Voyage" and for the particulars of the plan "which I formed at sea, for regulating my future Conduct in Life" (A, 106). Ocean voyages, in fact, repeatedly prompt Franklin's instincts for stabilizing experience in written form, for drawing conclusions, or for drafting documents, as he does when he watches the crew of a coastal vessel catching fish on an early trip from Boston to New York, or in the 1775 voyage letter, which he uses as an opportunity to impose a measure of order on his last troubled months in England. Franklin was at home amid fluid media in several senses of the term: in the boats or canoes that his boyhood friends usually allowed him to "govern," in the swimming skills that he had originally mastered by adding his own "graceful and easy" variations to strokes he had learned from a book, on the sailing vessels that enforced an interval of confinement and reflection in between periods of urgent terrestrial business, and amid the written records that are invariably caught up in the flow of events. The written or the printed word, too, takes for granted its immersion in unpredictable currents. It only seems to stand still, even when its human agents adopt extraordinary measures to fix its nature and its social role.

Such measures take a particularly revealing form in Franklin's life on the occasions when he is called upon to print paper money. These jobs demanded a unique degree of public supervision in the printing house to ensure that the currency designs were sufficiently complicated to thwart counterfeiting, that the number of paper bills produced did not exceed a legally fixed amount, and that the plates necessary to produce them were promptly destroyed so that the printer could not manufacture extra money at will. The skills Franklin had acquired in the sophisticated printshops of London made him especially well suited to these tasks once he had returned home. He had become "quite a Factotum" in Samuel Keimer's printing business in part because he had learned how to contrive letter molds, how to improvise puncheons out of old type to create fresh letters, and how to do the kind of simple engraving that helped make paper currency difficult to forge. But as Keimer's cheaper apprentices grew more skilled under Franklin's expert supervision, Franklin's higher wages had become a burden to his employer, who "grew by degrees less civil, put on more of the Master, frequently found Fault, was captious and seem'd ready for an Out-breaking" (A, 110).

Franklin's presence in Keimer's printing house both stabilizes and destabilizes the business, shifting its nature "by degrees" in opposite directions. The more effective he is at transmitting his skills to Keimer's inept "hands," the more Keimer himself chafes to break through the limits of the agreement that he and Franklin had reached when they resumed working together. "At length," Franklin writes, "a Trifle snapt our Connexion," like a broken form that scatters its carefully set type on the floor:

For a great Noise happening near the Courthouse, I put my Head out of the Window to see what was the Matter. Keimer being in the Street look'd up and saw me, call'd out to me in a loud Voice and angry Tone to mind my Business, adding some reproachful Words, that nettled me the more for their Publicity, all the Neighbours who were looking out on the same Occasion being Witnesses how I was treated. He came up immediately into the Printing-House, continu'd the Quarrel, high Words pass'd on both Sides, he gave me the Quarter's Warning we had stipulated, expressing a Wish that he had not been oblig'd to so long a Warning: I told him his Wish was unnecessary for I would leave him that Instant; and so taking my Hat walk'd out of Doors; desiring Meredith whom I saw below to take care of some Things I left, and bring them to my Lodging. (A, 110–11)

Though the passions that this passage depicts are explosive, they are also carefully choreographed, the synchronized movements of the principals functioning with the rhythmic efficiency of a skilled factotum in a pressroom. A restless but orderly sequence of prepositions—out, up, out, and up once again—culminates in the "high Words" that precipitate Franklin's abrupt descent and departure. Both men seem genuinely "nettled," but at the same time each is acutely aware of the publicity of his movements and his words, generating the theatrical potential of their great scene. Franklin structures the exchange in the memoir with a degree of skill that only the retrospective control of writing can confer.

Meredith manages to soothe Franklin's temper, in part by proposing their secret business partnership, and Keimer soon apologizes out of similar ulterior motives. A lucrative contract to print paper money for New Jersey requires Franklin's special skills, and Keimer wants to keep the benefit of his services. "The New Jersey Jobb was obtain'd," Franklin wrote: "I contriv'd a Copper-Plate Press for it, the first that had been seen in the Country. I cut several Ornaments and Checks for the Bills. We went together to Burlington, where I executed the Whole to Satisfaction, and he received so large a Sum for the Work, as to be enabled thereby to keep his Head much longer above Water" (A, 112). The train of events that begins with Franklin putting his head out a window closes with Keimer's head barely above water, a simple narrative "ornament" that gives this episode its own singular imprint, like a piece of currency stamped from a copperplate. The ulterior motives that both parties share contribute to the coherence of the design, as do the paired groups of witnesses at either end of the transaction: Keimer's curious neighbors who observe Franklin's original mistreatment and the committee charged by the New Jersey Assembly to "attend the Press" and make sure that its instructions on the size of the currency issue were followed.

As was the case with James Franklin and his Boston friends, during the early years of the *New England Courant*, this episode captures another instance of unexpected social outcomes unfolding in a crowded printing house. The New Jersey committee members find a way to mix business with pleasure as their duty to oversee the printing of the bills requires their presence at the press:

> They were therefore by Turns constantly with us, and generally he who attended brought with a him a Friend or two for Company. My Mind having been much more improv'd by Reading than Keimer's, I suppose it was for that Reason my Conversation seem'd to be more valued. They had me to their Houses, introduc'd me to their Friends and show'd me much Civility, while he, tho' the Master, was a little neglected. In truth he was an odd Fish, ignorant of common Life, fond of rudely opposing receiv'd Opinions, slovenly to extream dirtiness, enthusiastic in some Points of Religion, and a little Knavish withal. We continu'd there near 3 Months, and by that time I could reckon among my acquired Friends, Judge Allen, Samuel Bustill, the Secretary of the Province, Isaac Pearson, Joseph Cooper and several of the Smiths, Members of Assembly, and Isaac Decow the Surveyor General. (A, 113)

The spontaneous outburst of high words in Keimer's Philadelphia printing house and this gratifying professional triumph in Burlington form a suggestive, figurative contrast between the counterfeit and the genuine in human relations as well as in paper money. Like a badly printed bill (Franklin implies), Keimer is slovenly, rude, and a little knavish. The "civil Message" with which he reestablished good relations with Franklin—"old Friends should not part for a few Words, the Effect of sudden Passion"—is sound enough on its surface but without any durable basis to underwrite its value. By contrast, Franklin's improved mind, copperplate press, and careful craftsmanship lead to a well-connected array of "acquired Friends," as Franklin calls them, both to underscore the economic analogy and to contrast the upward trajectory of his own life with Keimer's downward spiral, reversing the pattern of their original quarrel.[9]

Franklin clearly meant the subtle interplay between these episodes to be unobtrusive but distinct, not unlike the ornaments and "checks" that a careful engraver will build into a plate that is not meant for easy replication. But one of the New Jersey committee members, old Isaac Decow, is an attentive reader of character:

> The latter was a shrewd sagacious old Man, who told me that he began for himself when young by wheeling Clay for the Brickmakers, learnt to write after he was of Age, carry'd the Chain for Surveyors, who taught him Surveying, and he had now by his Industry acquir'd a good Estate; and says he, I foresee, that you will soon work this Man out of his Business and make a Fortune in it at Philadelphia. He had not the least Intimation of my Intention to set up there or any where. These Friends were afterwards of great Use to me, as I occasionally was to some of them. They all continued their Regard for me as long as they lived. (A, 113)

Friendly regard and mutual interest reinforce one another in this array of relationships, much as shrewdness and sagacity do in the character of Isaac Decow. Franklin's abilities make it a simple matter for New Jersey's wily surveyor general to take the measure of his young acquaintance, at the same time that he acknowledges a biographical bond between them that enables him to foretell Franklin's future. The passage as a whole resembles a composite plate of meticulously interwoven episodes and words, a form of paper currency cast as a story.

A second experience with producing paper money leads to the third piece of published writing in Franklin's career, *The Nature and Necessity of a Paper Currency*. He distributes this pamphlet as a way of supporting and channeling "a Cry among the People for more Paper-Money" that results when an earlier issue of Pennsylvania notes was about to be "sunk," or redeemed, and removed from circulation. As with the discussion of the profitable New Jersey job, this passage too begins with a collision between popular feeling and the jealousy of a class of "masters," represented on this occasion not the by the "great Noise" near City Hall that triggered Franklin's quarrel with Samuel Keimer but by an articulate public outcry arousing fears among Philadelphia's "wealthy Inhabitants" that a new currency issue would prove harmful to their interests as creditors.

Franklin thinks otherwise, recurring not to his New Jersey experience or to his memories of the use of paper bills in New England but to the observational strolls that he had taken around Philadelphia in recent years, supplemented by Junto meetings that had addressed the pros and cons of expanding the amount of paper money in circulation:

We had discuss'd this Point in our Junto, where I was on the Side of an Addition, being persuaded that the first small Sum struck in 1723 had done much good, by increasing the Trade Employment, and Number of Inhabitants in the Province, since I now saw all the old Houses inhabited, and many new ones building, where as I remember'd well, that when I first walk'd about the Streets of Philadelphia, eating my Roll, I saw most of the Houses in Walnut street between Second and Front streets with Bills on their Doors, to be let; and many likewise in Chesnut Street, and other Streets; which made me then think the Inhabitants of the City were one after another deserting it. (A, 124)

The Junto debates convinced Franklin to write his pamphlet, but the memoir portrays this publishing decision less as a catalyst than as a collaborative engagement with an already lively atmosphere of discussion around the city, a great noise arising from the shifting material circumstances and class divisions among its citizens. *The Nature and Necessity of a Paper Currency* is another little machine that captures the adaptation of Franklin's thought to the shifting currents of his world.

A few pages earlier he had included in the memoir the gloomy predictions of Samuel Mickle, a neighborhood "croaker" who dropped by Franklin's newly opened printing business in 1728 specifically to tell him that his expensive investment was doomed. "Philadelphia was a sinking Place," Mickle insisted: "And he gave me such a Detail of Misfortunes, now existing or that were soon to exist, that he left me half-melancholy" (A, 116). But paper money had helped to make the city buoyant again, despite the fears of wealthy creditors, and Franklin's pamphlet in turn buoyed up the currency advocates, "for it increas'd and strengthen'd the Clamour for more Money," a surge of public feeling that the measure's wealthy opponents could not stem, "they happening to have no Writers among them that were able to answer it." Talent is certainly one ingredient in this outcome, but Franklin makes clear that "our Debates" in the Junto had given impetus to his writing abilities, and the political representatives of "the common People in general" had engineered a favorable result. Ultimately Franklin got the currency printing contract, along with the gratitude of the Assembly members, and over the years (he notes) paper money helped finance the costs of the Seven Years' War as well as the growth of the province.

The memoir's account of this episode concludes by recording a private doubt on Franklin's part about an unqualified reliance on paper bills—"I now think there are Limits beyond which the Quantity may be hurtful" (A, 125)—closing a series of events that had begun with a public "Cry" by recording Franklin's silent reservations about the urgent "necessity" that his pamphlet had embraced. In the course of telling the whole story, however, Franklin situates his pamphlet title in the midst of an extraordinary range of verbal and nonverbal display: the original clamor of popular opinion, the Junto discussions that fuel his decision to write, the resentful silence of the wealthy, and the victorious Assembly majority that ultimately "carried" the point in its votes. The incidents give Franklin a chance to revisit his initial tour of Philadelphia's streets, long before he began to influence its affairs, and to link these early lessons to the geopolitical issues dominating his life in 1771, as he drafts the first portion of his memoir. "My being able to Write," Franklin concludes, was a great advantage in bringing about this prudent public measure, and so it was. But while writing and printing have a unique capacity to impose concrete form on vocal energies, to focus and to amplify thought, they depend in turn on forms of verbal currency that thrive on constant movement.

The written word as the memoir presents it is part of an elaborate social performance that the name of James Franklin's newspaper, the *New England Courant*, implicitly celebrates. The term *courant* or courier had come to mean, literally, a newspaper by Franklin's day, but the same word referred to the movement of flowing water, as well as to a lively dance more akin to popular jigs than to a courtly minuet. In an age that loved puns, the multiple references would have seemed obvious and delightful. The social energies of the printing house itself dramatize the analogy, presenting Franklin's adolescent debut in the *Courant*'s pages, for instance, as if the "anonymous Paper" that he had slipped beneath his brother's shop door were a mysterious guest at a masked ball whose striking appearance had the other maskers offering "their different Guesses" at the identity of their new partner. Even half a century afterward, Franklin records in the memoir his "exquisite Pleasure" at the sensation he had caused.

When in his turn, Franklin begins publishing the *Pennsylvania Gazette*, he describes its impact too as a grand entrance into Philadelphia's social and political scene:

> Our first Papers made a quite different Appearance from any before in the Province, a better Type and better printed: but some spirited Remarks of my Writing on the Dispute then going on between Govr. Burnet and the Massachusetts

Assembly, struck the principal People, occasion'd the Paper and the Manager of it to be much talk'd of, and in a few Weeks brought them all to be our Subscribers. Their Example was follow'd by many, and our Number went on growing continually. This was one of the first good Effects of my having learnt a little to scribble. Another was, that the leading Men, seeing a News Paper now in the hands of one who could also handle a Pen, thought it convenient to oblige and encourage me. Bradford still printed the Votes and Laws and other Publick Business. He had printed an Address of the House to the Governor in a coarse blundering manner; We reprinted it elegantly and correctly, and sent one to every Member. They were sensible of the Difference, it strengthen'd the Hands of our Friends in the House, and they voted us their Printers for the Year ensuing. (A, 121)

Stylish appearance and a "spirited" manner single out the *Gazette* from its lumbering competition, quickly making this new presence the talk of the town. Elsewhere in the memoir Franklin disparages the mistaken emphases of women's education on the superficial attainments of music and dancing, favoring the practical benefits of accounting instead, but the exhilarating atmosphere of a public ball shapes the remarkable range of verbal display that marks this passage: an eye for good type and skillful printing, the taste for elegance and perspicuity of expression that Josiah Franklin had originally encouraged in his son, the diffusive and formative power of talk as well as print, the literal and figurative interplay of "hands" and "handling" that captures the limitless malleability of words. This first key step on Franklin's journey from private tradesman to steward of the "Publick Business" is not the by-product of a single skill alone but the outcome of a sensory complex to which the enduring and the ephemeral aspects of his verbal world both contribute.[10]

WHEN FRANKLIN ULTIMATELY INVOKES the Latin proverb *litera scripta manet* in his memoir, he points first of all toward the fixity and durability of writing or printing, in contrast to the fleeting influences of speech, stressing the advantages and disadvantages that accrue to each. The permanence of the written word gives it a lasting influence but also exposes it to the meticulous scrutiny of critics. Oral misstatements or errors might be "afterwards explain'd, or qualify'd," he notes, but oral brilliance, though powerful, is also difficult for the memory of one's hearers to reconstruct (A, 180). Franklin's close identification with printing would appear to align him with only one of these verbal worlds, but the story of his lifelong engagement with language presents a more complicated picture, one in which movement and change play roles that are every bit as crucial as the capacity of the letter to remain.

Litera scripta movet is an indispensable companion to the original truism that Franklin cites. A writer, in the pages of the memoir, is primarily a collector and arranger who is able to harness the variety of forms that words can take to advance existing processes of social aggregation or individual growth. Franklin's description of the success of the *Pennsylvania Gazette* puts all these verbal energies in play, beginning with the stable and visible properties of better type and better printing, but quickly shifting focus to an "ongoing" political dispute that prompts Franklin's own spirited participation in the pages of his paper, igniting in turn so much talk among Philadelphia's influential citizens as to dramatically increase the *Gazette*'s subscription list. The ability to handle a pen sets many other hands in motion, culminating in the active hands of political supporters in the Assembly who are "sensible" of Franklin's skills. The audible, social, and vocal aptitudes of hearing and feeling are as critical to this response as the elegant visual effects with which the *Gazette*'s swift rise begins. Its audience is initially "struck" as well as persuaded by Franklin's words.

A collection of newspaper subscribers is only one illustration of the aggregative force of the written word depicted in the memoir. Franklin's paper currency pamphlet involved, in its formative stages, the collective energies of the Junto before expanding to help structure the popular urban movement that had brought it into being. His *Dissertation on Liberty and Necessity* drew both admirers and critics into Franklin's circle of London acquaintances. The almanac, like the *Gazette*, was by design a collection zone where Franklin could showcase the aphorisms that he gathered from his reading, just as the 1731 library memorandum was a digest of research conclusions, as well as an endorsement of the collecting impulse itself, when Franklin outlines his interest in assembling a set of "suitable good and wise Rules" as a nucleus for his "united Party for Virtue." The organizational Articles of the Library Company become the template for a number of written commitments that Franklin will ultimately peddle around Philadelphia, as he once peddled ballads in the streets of Boston, shaping varieties of social noise toward beneficial ends.

The memoir repeatedly places this informal oral and written collection process in the foreground of Franklin's story: gathering little family anecdotes with his son, recording scattered ideas for an ethical guidebook on loose slips of paper, arranging a list of virtues and devising a way to record lapses in personal behavior, drafting and numbering a handful of "hints" to initiate an unofficial diplomatic exchange. Franklin's book as a whole seems more at ease with these provisional phases of composition—hints, conversations, or fleeting notes to oneself—than with the attainment of final form. Like the Dunker leader Michael Welfare, Franklin recognized both the uses and the risks of hardening one's convictions in print, as well as the advantages of speech as an impermanent forum for exploring controversial ideas. Though admittedly a poor speaker himself, he seizes every opportunity that the memoir provides to admire the dramatic impact and versatility of oral gifts as a complement to the writing and printing with which he is most closely linked. The two chief purposes of speech that Franklin identified early in his book—the transmission of information and the giving of pleasure—require both the ephemeral and the fixed word to realize their ends.[11]

The memoir records a number of fleeting remarks that preserve the rich oral world through which Franklin moved and bring the book's various characters to life: William Franklin's wry comment on the transmigration of his father's soul; old William Bradford's wily approach to the gullible and glib Samuel Keimer; Charles Osborne's effusive excitement at Franklin's stunning performance of James Ralph's psalm. But the portions of the story that touch directly on preaching give Franklin a sustained opportunity to stress the balanced relationship between the fixed and ephemeral verbal worlds that shaped his career. In the first of these episodes, an evocative but enigmatic verse from Philippians leads Franklin to imagine a sermon from his Presbyterian minister that will enlarge on the implications of the printed text, inspiring its audience to pursue moral excellence rather than inflicting a series of stagnant doctrines on a passive congregation. The result is a deep disappointment: a dry rehearsal of sectarian platitudes that drives Franklin out of the church altogether, in despair and disgust, sending him back to the *Articles of Belief and Acts of Religion* that he had prepared a few years earlier as "a little Liturgy or Form of Prayer for my own private Use" (A, 148).

The memoir does not reproduce the *Articles* themselves in its pages, perhaps because Franklin is writing this portion of the book in France, sometime in 1784, thousands of miles away from his personal papers. His portable ivory memorandum booklet is at hand, allowing him to transcribe his thirteen virtues and their descriptive precepts into this section of the story. But the more elaborate liturgical script of the *Articles of Belief* is in Philadelphia. "I return'd to the Use of this," Franklin writes as he explains his disappointment with Presbyterian preaching, "and went no more to the public Assemblies. My conduct might be blameable, but I leave it without attempting farther to excuse it, my present purpose being to relate Facts, and not to make Apologies for them" (A, 148). In leaving this anecdote to speak for itself, however, Franklin quietly underscores the natural reciprocity between written records and their spoken accompaniments, between a biblical text and the sermon that brings it to life, between the fixity of "fact" and the explanatory impulses that facts customarily trigger. If the contents of Franklin's personal liturgy were inserted into his book, then the text itself would inevitably engross the reader's attention. Instead, its title alone highlights the interaction between two forms of verbal experience: the written "articles" and the living "acts" that, in turn, give dramatic substance to the stationary letter. Franklin returned to the "use," not to the doctrinal content, of his scheme of private worship. It is a verbal structure that requires an active inhabitant, a voice, to give it efficacy.

His categorical claim that "I went no more to the public Assemblies" after his disappointment with the Philippians sermon is a calculated overstatement. The third portion of the memoir records two periods in Franklin's life, after this apparently decisive break, when he did attend public religious assemblies that took place outside the auspices of a church. Both occasions explore the rich cross-fertilization of speech and print that Franklin's story repeatedly exemplifies. The first involves two forms of verbal misrepresentation in direct collision with the desire of Philadelphia's Presbyterian synod to control the inherent disorders of speech. Heterodox and orthodox utterance, print and performance, durable and ephemeral language are all parties to the concise account Franklin offers of Samuel Hemphill's brief career in Philadelphia:

> About the year 1734 there arrived among us from Ireland, a young Presbyterian Preacher named Hemphill, who delivered with a good Voice, and apparently extempore, most excellent Discourses, which drew together considerable Numbers of different Persuasions, who join'd in admiring them. Among the rest I became one of his constant Hearers, his Sermons pleasing me, as they had little of the dogmatical kind, but inculcated strongly the Practice of Virtue, or what in the religious Stile are called Good Works. Those however, of our Congregation, who considered themselves as orthodox Presbyterians, disapprov'd his Doctrine, and were join'd by most of the old Clergy, who arraign'd him of Heterodoxy before the Synod, in order to have him silenc'd. (A, 167)

The memoir makes plain that the mutual antagonism between youth and age partly fuels this dispute. Franklin is only twenty-eight years old in 1734, *Poor Richard's Almanac* has appeared only twice at this point in his life, and the *Pennsylvania Gazette* is barely five when Hemphill arrives in the city, a newcomer who is in all likelihood quite close to Franklin's age, preaching sermons that offend "the old Clergy" and its allies.

As with the discussion of the *Spectator* essays in the book's opening pages, this passage stresses Hemphill's manner as much as his message. His discourses are "most excellent" in Franklin's view both because they urge the practice of virtue on their audiences and because they do so in dramatically memorable fashion, in a good voice that seems to emerge directly from the speaker's physical being rather than from a written text. Franklin becomes one of Hemphill's "constant Hearers" out of pleasure in a performance that differs sharply in "stile" as well as in substance from the sectarian terminology of the day. The Synod, in seeking to silence this dissident voice, at first only magnifies its impact by driving the conflict into print, where Franklin's skills can take up Hemphill's cause:

> I became his zealous Partisan, and contributed all I could to raise a Party in his Favour; and we combated for him a while with some Hopes of Success. There was much Scribbling pro and con upon the Occasion; and finding that tho' an elegant Preacher he was but a poor Writer, I lent him my Pen and wrote for him two or three Pamphlets, and one Piece in the Gazette of April 1735. Those Pamphlets, as is generally the Case with controversial Writings, tho' eagerly read at the time, were soon out of Vogue, and I question whether a single Copy of them now exists. (A, 167)

This episode compresses into a few sentences a series of striking verbal contrasts, from the emergence of Hemphill's magnetic voice to the extinction of the vocal controversy that surrounded him, a different order of "silence" from the sectarian censorship that the Synod sought to impose, one rooted in the transient nature of controversy itself. Writing that falls "out of Vogue" has none of the residual energy of a passionate speaker who has been forced, by unsympathetic authorities, to hold his peace. Moreover, Hemphill, for his part, is a puzzling blend of the elegant and the inept: an articulate and powerful preacher whose powers mysteriously desert him when he tries to write.

Franklin fills this strange silence himself by adopting Hemphill's "voice" when he writes in his defense, a kind of rehearsal for the remarkable feat of ventriloquism that is ultimately responsible for driving Hemphill from the city. These decisive events too turn upon the mutually reinforcing worlds of the fixed and the ephemeral word, both of which figure in the detection of Hemphill's fraud at the height of the zealous pamphlet combat that Franklin was organizing on his behalf:

> During the Contest an unlucky Occurrence hurt his Cause exceedingly. One of our Adversaries having heard him preach a Sermon that was much admired, thought he had somewhere read that Sermon before, or a least a part of it. On Search he found that Part quoted at length in one of the British Reviews, from a Discourse of Dr. Foster's. This Detection gave many of our Party Disgust, who accordingly abandoned his Cause, and occasion'd our more speedy Discomfiture in the Synod. I stuck by him however, as I rather approv'd his giving us good Sermons compos'd by others, than bad ones of his own Manufacture; tho' the latter was the Practice of our common Teachers. He afterwards acknowledg'd to me that none of those he preach'd were his own; adding that his Memory was such as enabled him to retain and repeat any Sermon after one Reading only. On our Defeat he left us, in search elsewhere of better Fortune, and I quitted the Congregation, never joining it after, tho' I continu'd many Years my Subscription for the Support of its Ministers. (A, 168)

Hemphill's powers of attraction apparently extended, in some measure, to his adversaries as well as to his partisans. At least one of these opponents listened with sufficient care to a particularly effective sermon to detect an echo of the printed page. The memoir does not elaborate on the motives that influenced one of Hemphill's enemies to join an audience of his admirers, but Franklin clearly appreciates the subtle stages of recognition that lie behind this damaging discovery: the disconcertingly vague feeling that "somewhere" in one's reading one has encountered "some part" of a cluster of memorable words before, followed by the triumphant but still largely intuitive search that uncovers the source. The perfunctory disgust of Hemphill's allies, while an understandable reaction, is also a superficial one, at least to the extent that it ignores the array of verbal gifts on display in these incidents: the complementary abilities of these human antagonists to integrate what they hear or speak with what they read.

In Hemphill's case the gift is particularly seamless, a memory that requires only a single reading to absorb an entire sermon and equip its possessor to deliver the words by heart as a talented actor might deliver a complex monologue from the stage. By contrast, Franklin's combative scribbling and printing evaporates with the "vogue" of the controversy, almost as swiftly as Hemphill himself disappears from the scene. These linked disappearances, in turn, are comprehensive forms of silence that disclose a latent futility in all aspects of speech. Franklin's apparently cheerful embrace of plagiarism, in this anecdote, points to the vanity that underlies all claims to original utterance. The "Practice of our common Teachers," he implies in a deft echo of Ecclesiastes, is to overvalue their "own" words over the "good" ones that their listeners most need to hear, and which those listeners embraced "in considerable Numbers" when Samuel Hemphill offered them.

Franklin concludes his account of these events by describing the peculiar state of semi-alienation that he maintained from Philadelphia's Presbyterian church in the aftermath of Hemphill's departure: a "subscriber" who refuses to attend services, substituting an attenuated form of written presence for his living engagement with the congregation. In making this gesture Franklin stresses the sense in which written commitments, though fixed in place, can in some circumstances be more superficial than unwritten actions. The record that "remains"—Franklin's name on a register of church members—is shallow in contrast to the less durable but more substantive forms of expression and endorsement that led him to prize Hemphill's undoctrinaire discourses. These sermons had converted him into a constant hearer; the Synod's triumph puts an end to this constancy. But the nominal commitment of "subscription" makes it possible for Franklin to sustain at least some ties to the religious tradition in which he had been raised.

Defeat, discomfiture, and disgust, in this passage, coexist with several instances of the instinct to stick by ideas, institutions, or people one admires, even when that admiration is compromised by unlucky occurrences or unexpected flaws. The energies released by controversy and combat largely evaporate, from individuals as well as from the print record, leaving undisturbed the memorable—and, to a significant degree, invisible—verbal fabric that had made possible both Hemphill's rapid success and his rapid disgrace. The interplay between reading and speaking, print and memory, in this brief episode is anything but straightforward. In the memoir's final and most extensive treatment of preaching, Franklin draws speech and print together in equally complex ways, highlighting the subtle inversions that come into play as durable and ephemeral expressive media exchange roles.

Franklin situates his acquaintance with George Whitefield in the loosely sequential chronology of the memoir's third fragment, noting the famous preacher's first appearance in Philadelphia five years after the Hemphill fiasco. But the pages that Franklin devotes to their friendship range across the three decades that they knew one another, ending in London in the last years of Whitefield's life, when the two men were still discussing the charitable interests that they had in common.[12] Like Hemphill before him, Whitefield quickly antagonizes Philadelphia's religious establishment, but he attracts Franklin's interest and, finally, his loyalty not for the doctrinal reasons that Hemphill did but for psychological or tactical ones. Whitefield had an unparalleled ability to transmit his fervor to others, to draw people together and to change their behavior in tangible and audible ways. Franklin is, at first, struck by this phenomenon, examining it very much in the spirit of a natural philosopher:

> In 1739 arriv'd among us from England the Rev. Mr. Whitefield, who had made himself remarkable there as an itinerant Preacher. He was at first permitted to preach in some of our Churches; but the Clergy taking a Dislike to him, soon refus'd him their Pulpits and he was oblig'd to preach in the Fields. The Multitudes of all Sects and Denominations that attended his Sermons were enormous, and it was matter of Speculation to me who was one of the Number, to observe the extraordinary Influence of his Oratory on his Hearers, and how much they admir'd and respected him, notwithstanding his common Abuse of them, by assuring them they were naturally *half Beasts and half Devils*. (A, 175)

Some of the parallels between Whitefield's appearance and Hemphill's original impact are immediately clear, but the memoir adopts a much more reserved approach to this second charismatic figure. Hemphill's "extempore" manner was an important part of his attraction for Franklin. By contrast, the memoir warily notes, Whitefield had "made himself remarkable" in England before coming to America—by implication a much less extemporaneous achievement—and Franklin's own presence at his sermons is not that of a constant hearer but a student of other "Hearers," a speculator or an observer rather than a listener.

Whitefield's grim view of human nature is a drastic extension of Benjamin Vaughan's stark vision of the scramble of life as a struggle among vicious and detestable animals, but its cathartic effect on Philadelphia's sectarian population prompts Franklin to his own oratorical excesses as he passes from skeptical observer to civic enthusiast, admiring the social energies that the revival is able to arouse, while briefly forgetting the entrenched doctrinal differences that lie beneath its spiritual euphoria:

> It was wonderful to see the Change soon made in the Manners of our Inhabitants; from being thoughtless or indifferent about Religion, it seem'd as if all the World were growing Religious; so that one could not walk thro' the Town in an Evening without Hearing Psalms sung in different Families of every Street. And it being found inconvenient to assemble in the open Air, subject to its Inclemencies, the Building of a House to meet in was no sooner propos'd and Persons appointed to receive Contributions, but sufficient Sums were soon receiv'd to procure the Ground and erect the Building which was 100 feet long and 70 broad, about the Size of Westminster-hall; and the Work was carried on with such Spirit as to be finished in a much shorter time than could have been expected. Both House and Ground were vested in Trustees, expressly for the Use of any Preacher of any religious Persuasion who might desire to say something to the People of Philadelphia, the Design in building not being to accommodate any particular Sect, but the Inhabitants in general, so that even if the Mufti of Constantinople were to send a Missionary to preach Mahometanism to us, he would find a Pulpit at his Service. (A, 176)

This last claim seems expressly calculated to illustrate the kind of exhilaration that Whitefield was able to awaken. In Franklin's initial draft of this passage, he dampens its enthusiasm almost as soon as the memoir gives into it by noting that the trustees in charge of managing the meetinghouse that Whitefield's supporters had built were drawn from all of the city's various sectarian communities in order to avoid giving a "Predominancy" to any single group. Generosity and jealousy are inextricably joined in this single structure. Franklin subsequently strikes out this reference to the dangers of competitive predominancy and moves it to another portion of the manuscript, but its original placement is telling: a signal that Franklin is only too aware of how far he has allowed himself to be carried away in his fanciful reception of Islamic missionaries in Philadelphia.[13]

Revisions and all, these sentences enact the ambivalence that Franklin never entirely disavows in the face of Whitefield's influence. "Ours was a mere civil Friendship," he writes elsewhere in this portion of his story. But it was "sincere on both sides, and lasted to his Death" (A, 178). Mere civility, however, is a bland term for the intensity of their interactions and for the dramatic detail with which Franklin invests them in the memoir's pages. The two men first disagree over the strategy that Whitefield proposes for dealing with the large number of orphans that he found during a preaching tour of Georgia. Whitefield determined to build an orphanage in that colony so that these neglected children could be cared for and came north to raise the necessary funds. Franklin advised him to build the orphanage in Philadelphia, where workmen and materials were easy to obtain, and bring the orphans to it rather than vice versa, "but he was resolute in his first Project," the memoir records, and Franklin was equally resolute in his decision to withhold his support unless Whitefield agreed to take his advice.

Ultimately Whitefield's eloquence wins this contest, when Franklin decides to attend one of his fund-raising sermons, "silently resolved" to resist any appeals, but gives in to the force of words:

> I had in my Pocket a Handful of Copper Money, three or four silver Dollars, and five Pistoles in Gold. As he proceeded I began to soften, and concluded to give the Coppers. Another Stroke of his Oratory made me asham'd of that, and determin'd me to give the Silver; and he finish'd so admirably, that I empty'd my Pocket wholly into the Collector's Dish, Gold and all. At this Sermon there was also one of our Club, who being of my Sentiments respecting the Building in Georgia, and suspecting a Collection might be intended, had by Precaution emptied his Pockets before he came from home; towards the Conclusion of the Discourse however, he felt a strong Desire to give, and apply'd to a Neighbour who stood near him to borrow some Money for the Purpose. The Application was unfortunately to perhaps the only Man in the Company who had the firmness not to be affected by the Preacher. His Answer was, *At any other time, Friend Hopkinson, I would lend to thee freely; but not now; for thee seems to be out of thy right Senses.* (A, 178)

Unlike his fellow Junto member, Thomas Hopkinson, Franklin only recognized that a collection was about to take place after the sermon was underway—or so the memoir leads its reader to believe—but he acknowledges carrying with him a surprisingly large amount of money, in nicely graduated categories of value, as if he were in fact preparing a kind of experimental machine to measure Whitefield's verbal potency. The wording of the passage implies that, unlike Hopkinson, Franklin keeps his senses at least partly under control, rewarding by scrupulous increments an admirable performance rather than surrendering his judgment entirely to his emotions.[14]

Spontaneity and design play complementary roles in the thinking of each of this episode's chief participants, all of whom deliberately set out to test the impact of ephemeral feelings against fixed resolution. Even the anonymous Quaker speaker who refuses Hopkinson's plea apparently went to the sermon with Hopkinson's same cautious instincts in mind. Firmness completely triumphs over strong desire in one of the three listeners that this passage describes. It completely succumbs in a second and achieves a kind of compromise in the third. A similar fluid negotiation between these mental antagonists structures nearly every passage in the memoir that depicts Franklin's relations with George Whitefield. Despite their differences over the orphanage project and the merely "civil" footing of their friendship, the two remained close enough for Franklin to host Whitefield on one of his visits to Philadelphia when another old acquaintance with whom Whitefield often stayed had since left the city. In the memoir, Franklin transcribes part of the correspondence that ensues when Franklin steps in to fill the gap, signaling both the warmth of the invitation and the ideological reserve that makes the Franklin household (in contrast to others in Whitefield's intimate circle) a relatively "scanty" refuge. These words too mix firmness with strong desire: "You know my House," Franklin wrote Whitefield, "if you can make shift with its scanty Accommodations you will be most heartily welcome" (A, 178).

The preacher replies with a clerical formula that Franklin brushes aside, insisting that he made his offer for Whitefield's sake, not for Christ's sake, thus fixing the social "Obligation" on Earth, as one of Franklin's friends jokingly observes. The single-sentence paragraph that immediately follows, however, stresses the fragility of all earthly obligations: "The last time I saw Mr. Whitefield was in London," Franklin wrote, "when he consulted me about his Orphan House Concern, and his Purpose of appropriating it to the Establishment of a College" (A, 179). This final encounter finds Whitefield once more adjusting intentions to possibilities as a seasoned itinerant evangelist would, even at the very end of his life. Benevolent purposes, the memoir implies, ultimately resist our best efforts to realize them. Many of life's obligations inevitably remain unpaid.

In Franklin's earlier response to Whitefield's lodging needs, he had written that his friend was heartily welcome to make shift with Franklin's hospitality when he next visited Philadelphia. As the surrounding incidents quickly begin to demonstrate, Franklin's casual expression is more substantive than it seems. A necessity to make shift—to adapt to the instability that is an irreducible fact of existence—reflects the implicit embrace of the ephemeral that the memoir as a whole acknowledges in its opening paragraph, when Franklin declares that the comparative durability of writing is simply the best that we can do with the fleeting nature of memory, since the "Repetition" and perfection of life itself are "not to be expected" (A, 44). By contrast, words can be repeated and perfected most easily in the medium of which Whitefield is master: itinerant preaching. Written work has the advantage of durability but the disadvantage of rigidity; it cannot respond, in the moment, to the feelings of an audience whose murmurs and movements might signal how a writer's words are being received. An alert speaker could do just that, and a traveling minister, with a stock of sermons at hand, could accumulate a body of experience that would permit him to perfect his performance as he moved from place to place. Franklin appreciated the care with which Whitefield exploited these opportunities:

> By hearing him often I came to distinguish easily between Sermons newly compos'd, and those which he had often preach'd in the Course of his Travels. His Delivery of the latter was so improv'd by frequent Repetitions, that every Accent, every Emphasis, every Modulation of Voice, was so perfectly well turn'd and well plac'd, that without being interested in the Subject, one could not help being pleas'd with the Discourse, a Pleasure of much the same kind with that receiv'd from an excellent Piece of Musick. This is an Advantage itinerant Preachers have over those who are stationary: as the latter cannot well improve their Delivery of a Sermon by so many Rehearsals. (A, 180)

This regimen of rehearsals permits Whitefield to "place" his oral effects as carefully as a writer or a printer sets words in place on paper, an analogy the memoir quietly invites its reader to draw. In this passage Franklin's own wording is a particularly careful exercise in placement. Its repetitions and modulations—every accent, every emphasis, "well turn'd and well plac'd," being interested, "being pleas'd" and receiving Pleasure— mimic Whitefield's artistry, at the same time that Franklin implicitly distinguishes between the formal polish of a careful performance and the unguarded spontaneity that itinerant preachers strove to imitate and to elicit from their hearers. Hemphill's career remains a sobering reminder, however, that even "extempore" brilliance is not always what it seems.

Without the support of Whitefield's considerable vocal skills, the memoir reports, his writing sometimes fell short of expectations. His printed sermons sometimes elicited violent attacks from critics who succeeded in diminishing his influence. *Litera scripta manet,* Franklin sagely observes. Had Whitefield never written out his discourses, his impact might have been more lasting: "And his Reputation might in that case have been still growing, even after his Death; as there being nothing of his Writing on which to found a censure; and give him a lower Character, his Proselites would be left at liberty to feign for him as great a Variety of Excellencies, as their enthusiastic Admiration might wish him to have possessed" (A, 180). Fittingly enough, this observation is the memoir's last word on Whitefield, but it is hardly so conclusive as it seems. Two competing forms of expressive energy remain actively engaged with one another in this assessment: the incontrovertible power of writing as a check on unreflective enthusiasm, and the determination of the imagination to exercise its formidable liberty of invention. Each is in some degree permanent and in some degree ephemeral.[15]

A few sentences before offering this summary dismissal of Whitefield as a writer, Franklin had carefully measured his potency as a speaker, using Philadelphia itself as a calibrated scientific tool. Like Hemphill, Whitefield had an extraordinary voice: loud, clear, and so authoritative in tone (Franklin recalled) that his audiences "observ'd the most exact Silence" under its influence. One of his open-air sermons gives Franklin a chance to calculate how far-reaching that influence might be:

> He preach'd one Evening from the Top of the Court House Steps, which are in the Middle of Market Street, and on the West Side of Second Street which crosses it at right angles. Both Streets were fill'd with his Hearers to a considerable Distance. Being among the hindmost in Market Street, I had the Curiosity to learn how far he could be heard, by retiring backwards down the Street towards the River, and I found his Voice distinct till I came near Front-Street, when some Noise in that Street, obscur'd it. Imagining then a Semi-Circle, of which my Distance should be the Radius, and that it were fill'd with Auditors, to each of whom I allow'd two square feet, I computed that he might well be heard by more than Thirty-Thousand. This reconcil'd me to the Newspaper Accounts of his having preach'd to 25000 People in the Fields, and to the antient Histories of Generals haranguing whole Armies, of which I had sometimes doubted. (A, 179)

This passage too is a subtle exercise in various forms of placement, locating Whitefield and Franklin on the physical grid of the city's streets much as type is carefully set in the grid of a printer's form. Franklin may even intend to stress the implicit analogy by allotting an improbably small space of two square feet to each of Whitefield's imaginary listeners—an estimate that treats bodies like closely packed lead letters in preparation for printing, allowing scarcely enough room for plausible human beings to stand or breathe, let alone for one among them to drift slowly backward, as Franklin does, through the shifting vacancies of an actual crowd until the "noise" of life once more interrupts the "exact" silence of the printed word. Franklin reconciles more than one sort of account in this anecdote, vindicating the historical status of ancient manuscripts and the complementary vitality of the written and the spoken words that structure his story.

CHAPTER FIVE

Some Uses of Cunning

From the moment that Franklin begins writing his memoir, he conceives of it as a record of excuses. The book as a whole, he insists, is an indulgence of an old man's natural inclination to reminisce about his past. Franklin apologizes for doing so, in the memoir's opening sentences, but vanity entices him to continue, consoled by the thought that readers (unlike listeners) need not pretend to be a polite audience. This convenient by-product of writing is also the writer's most comprehensive excuse. Tabulating personal "errata" as Franklin does in the first section of his story is one way of apologizing for them, at the same time that it offers him a chance to explain and sometimes to excuse his behavior. He took unfair advantage of his brother's conflict with the Massachusetts Assembly to evade the terms of his secret apprenticeship, Franklin admits, but his brother's hot temper and tyrannical behavior were too much to bear. James "was otherwise not an ill-natur'd Man," Franklin concedes, before taking some of the blame for their quarrels upon himself: "Perhaps I was too saucy and provoking" (A, 70).

After his Boston companion, John Collins, decides to join Franklin in Philadelphia, Collins's drinking debts tempt Franklin to commit "one of the first great Errata of my Life": loaning Collins money that he was supposed to be holding in trust. This lapse, Franklin notes, confirms his father's judgment that, at eighteen, he was "too young to manage Business of Importance" (A, 86). But an inability to say no to a desperate friend is at least some excuse, particularly at Franklin's age. More substantial excuses account for the broken structure of the memoir itself. "The Affairs of the Revolution," Franklin explained, were responsible for the first and longest interruption in his draft, the thirteen years that separate the book's first and second sections. And his great distance from home, as he wrote at Passy in 1784, would force him to rely on an imperfect memory as he continued his narrative.

Four years later, Franklin once again called attention to the handicaps he faced, explaining that the war had resulted in the loss of many of the records that he had hoped to use, now that he was home, to help organize the extensive section of the memoir he began writing in August 1788. Only a single "little Paper" survives as a starting point, the 1731 memorandum of "Observations on my Reading History" that in itself is both a call to action and an excuse for not acting. The "great Occasion" that the "Observations" identify for mitigating the partisan cycles of the past prompts Franklin's encouragement for "whoever" decides to take up the cause, but Franklin himself is careful to withhold a wholehearted personal commitment to the attempt, at least in so many words. Ultimately, circumstances interfere with his plans—the demands of the printing business, "my multifarious Occupations public and private"—time goes by, and the opportunity to please God by forming a United Party for Virtue is gone.

As Franklin begins to itemize what he actually did accomplish during the years when he was postponing his great and extensive project for worldwide reform, he often finds it necessary to continue making excuses for tactics that he suspects some readers might deem questionable. The establishment of Philadelphia's hospital is a case in point. Franklin's "particular" friend Thomas Bond had initiated the project in 1751 but ran into difficulty acquiring subscriptions to support it:

> At length he came to me, with the Compliment that he found there was no such thing as carrying a public Spirited Project through, without my being concern'd in it; "for, says he, I am often ask'd by those to whom I propose Subscribing, Have you consulted Franklin upon this Business? and what does he think of it? And when I tell them that I have not, (supposing it rather out of your Line)

they do not subscribe, but say they will consider of it." I enquir'd into the Nature, and probable Utility of his Scheme, and receiving from him a very satisfactory Explanation, I not only subscrib'd to it myself, but engag'd heartily in the Design of Procuring Subscriptions from others. (A, 199–200)

This friendship was apparently particular in more senses than one. Once Franklin removes himself from consideration as a potential excuse for prospective donors—and once Bond makes his own excuses for failing to consult Franklin in the first place—the rate of subscriptions increases. But when the fund raising bogs down again, Franklin takes the idea to the Pennsylvania Assembly in the form of a bill designed to obviate objections from "Country Members" who believe the hospital will benefit Philadelphia more than the outlying districts of the province. A "conditional" clause in Franklin's proposal engages to tap public funds only after private subscribers have raised a significant amount of capital on their own, allowing reluctant members of the Assembly to justify an act of legislative charity that they believe will never cost them anything.

But Franklin's clause "work'd both ways," the memoir explains, securing enough votes for the bill to pass and giving a boost to private contributions at the same time, once people understood that "every Man's donation would be doubled" by the Assembly appropriation as soon as the private subscription figure had been met. "A convenient and handsome Building was soon erected," Franklin reports, "the Institution has by constant Experience been found useful, and flourishes to this Day. And I do not remember any of my political Manoeuvres, the Success of which gave me at the time more Pleasure. Or that in after-thinking of it, I more easily excus'd my-self for having made some Use of Cunning" (A, 201). Like the legislative tactic that it describes, this last excuse too works both ways: it is an apology for an infraction that, in this instance at least, Franklin has not really committed. Nothing in the bill that he proposes to support the hospital subscription is intended to fool the members who consider it. If anyone in this episode exercises cunning, in its least palatable form, it is the handful of assemblymen who vote to endorse an appropriation that they never expect to be asked to supply, trusting that private generosity would fall short of its goal.

But a misplaced excuse, in its turn, can be meaningful. In offering it, Franklin invites his readers to exercise their own cunning as they move through the dense, anecdotal fabric of this section of his narrative, marveling at the extraordinary diversity of the vocational "line" that he inscribes across the public affairs of his province. Like the passages portraying Franklin's relationship with George Whitefield, these pages too are full of incidents in which Franklin and others repeatedly make shift to address the mixed purposes of existence, devising tactics that invariably work both ways to accommodate, even if only in passing, the incompatible interests of a diverse and often fractured community. "Join, or Die," the caption of Franklin's serpent cartoon, implies a dramatic finality to the choice it depicts that experience does not always confirm. Collective interest and individual well-being repeatedly negotiate the terms of their coexistence in the longest, sustained section of Franklin's book.[1]

AT MANY POINTS IN HIS MEMOIR, Franklin clearly enjoys describing the clash of wits or interests that often elicits from him and from his various collaborators some decisive exercise of cunning. The verbal "Evasions" that Pennsylvania's Quaker assemblymen employ when they vote to appropriate money for military campaigns without openly violating their pacifist principles are too transparent to deceive anyone, but that transparency is in many respects their chief virtue. Granting funds "*for the King's Use*" without restricting those uses in any way is a means of signaling compliance with royal demands without taking direct responsibility for the consequences. An authorization directing the governor to buy "Bread, Flour, Wheat, *or other Grain*" for the public benefit prompts some of the governor's council to advise embarrassing the Quaker Assembly members who framed it by pretending not to recognize their calculated euphemism: "But he reply'd, 'I shall take the Money, for I understand very well their Meaning; *Other Grain*, is Gunpowder'; which he accordingly bought; and they never objected to it" (A, 189). Franklin briefly thinks of adopting similar tactics to accommodate the scruples of the Quaker majority in the Union Fire Company by first gaining its approval to spend money on a "fire engine" and then buying a "Great Gun" for the city battery with the proceeds. "I see," a friend remarks when Franklin explains this plan, "you have improv'd by being so long in the Assembly" (A, 190).

Cunning in this sense calls for an audience that is appreciative, and in some instances complicit, in order to register its success. The practical joke that Franklin and James Ralph pull off when Franklin presents Ralph's version of the eighteenth psalm as his own is not fully realized until the two confess their trick and expose Osborne's critical prejudices to the mild ridicule of a circle of young men who value their friendship more than their wit. Josiah Franklin puts cunning to a benign use when he takes his son on walks around Boston specifically to study the boy's inclinations toward various trades in the hope of using them to keep him close to home—a tactic that Franklin ultimately admires. By contrast, Franklin's first courtship, managed by his Philadelphia tenants the Godfreys, is an exercise in cunning gone awry when Franklin begins to suspect that the motives of his prospective in-laws are crudely manipulative.

Mrs. Godfrey had singled out the "very deserving" daughter of a relative as a good match for Franklin and "a serious Courtship on my Part ensu'd":

> The old Folks encourag'd me by continual Invitations to Supper, and by leaving us together, till at length it was time to explain. Mrs. Godfrey manag'd our little Treaty. I let her know that I expected as much Money with their Daughter as would pay off my Remaining Debt for the Printinghouse, which I believe was not then above a Hundred Pounds. She brought me Word they had no such Sum to spare. I said they might mortgage their House in the Loan Office. The Answer to this after some Days was, that they did not approve the Match; that on Enquiry of Bradford they had been inform'd the Printing Business was not a profitable one, the Types would soon be worn out and more wanted, that S. Keimer and D. Harry had fail'd one after the other, and I should probably soon follow them; and therefore I was forbidden the House, and the Daughter shut up. Whether this was a real Change of Sentiment, or only Artifice, on a Supposition of our being too far engag'd in Affection to retract, and therefore that we should steal a Marriage, which would leave them at Liberty to give or withhold what they pleas'd, I know not: But I suspected the latter, resented it, and went no more. Mrs. Godfrey brought me afterwards some more favourable Accounts of their Disposition, and would have drawn me on again: but I declared absolutely my Resolution to have nothing more to do with that Family. (A, 127–28)

These incidents depict a collision between passions and interests that a very young Franklin is not yet equipped to manage with the kind of skill that he brings to Thomas Bond's hospital project. The old folks misjudge the depth of Franklin's feelings, as well as the speed with which he was capable of moving from serious courtship to stubborn resentment. He in turn misreads an implicit offer to negotiate from one settlement "sum" to another—not an unusual step in contemporary marriage arrangements.

After some days of reflection and a visit with the wily Andrew Bradford—who may have sensed an opportunity to hamper the progress of a dangerous young competitor—the parents decide to try to undermine Franklin's confidence in his future as a means of chastening him. But Franklin responds by dismissing the whole family out of hand. The Godfreys in turn resent Franklin's behavior and move out of his house. "I resolv'd to take no more Inmates," Franklin writes, but the brief satisfactions of this good-riddance gesture quickly lead to a series of risky sexual "Intrigues" that make Mrs. Godfrey's solicitations seem trivial. The passions of youth are "hard-to-be-govern'd," Franklin famously concedes, but not all forms of self-government are equal. The instances of cunning that he most relishes, throughout his book, are those that, unlike "Artifice," enable the little treaties that are necessary among people without forcing the parties to swallow their pride, their principles, or their dignity.[2]

Cunning as a tool of accommodation—as a means of exerting influence by appearing to relinquish it—is a central feature of Franklin's public life, but its origins ultimately lie in the habits of private speech that he describes at some length twice in his book and dramatizes repeatedly as the 1788 fragment of the memoir unfolds. Early in the book's first section, Franklin explains how he gradually abandoned the "very artful and expert" tactics of argument that he had polished on John Collins or Samuel Keimer and learned to avoid using words "that give the Air of Positiveness to an Opinion" (A, 65). An opinionated manner, Franklin concludes, "seldom fails to disgust, tends to create Opposition, and to defeat every one of those Purposes for which Speech was given us":

> For if you would *inform*, a positive dogmatical Manner in advancing your Sentiments, may provoke Contradiction and prevent a candid Attention. If you wish Information and Improvement from the Knowledge of others and yet at the same time express your self as firmly fix'd in your present Opinions, modest sensible Men, who do not love Disputation, will probably leave you undisturb'd in the Possession of your Error; and by such a Manner you can seldom hope to recommend your self in *pleasing* your Hearers, or to persuade those whose Concurrence you desire. (A, 65)

Lovers of argument, Franklin suggests, tend to listen only for opportunities to argue, withholding the sort of "candid Attention" to the opinions of others that is necessary if people are to find grounds for agreement. Sensible listeners, by contrast, resist as best they can the allure of fixed opinions and withhold knowledge rather than plunge into disputes. Pleasure and persuasion are the natural casualties in contentious exchanges, much as they prove to be natural allies (in the memoir's pages) when modest, sensible habits prevail.

Throughout the third section of his book, Franklin sketches the personalities and policies of Pennsylvania's colonial governors with this account of the requirements of fruitful conversation in mind. The first of these officials with whom Franklin has public dealings, George Thomas, is the astute listener who accepts the flimsy euphemism of the Quaker assemblymen when he needs to purchase "other Grain" or gunpowder for the province's defense. After the Assembly balks at crafting a militia law, out of the same sectarian scruples, Governor Thomas shows his gratitude for Franklin's initiative in forming a private militia association by inviting him to meetings of his council and seizing on Franklin's suggestion that the governor proclaim a public fast "to promote Reformation, and implore the Blessing of Heaven on our Undertaking" (A, 184).

Deferring to Franklin's New England "Education," the province secretary leaves the wording of the proclamation to him: "I drew it in the accustomed Stile," Franklin wrote, and saw it properly "divulg'd" throughout the province: "This gave the Clergy of the different Sects an Opportunity of Influencing their Congregations to join the Association" (A, 185). Both Franklin and Governor Thomas clearly recognize that they are acting as much out of political opportunism as piety in taking this step, but the memoir implies that the province's clergymen too are searching for an excuse that the proclamation conveniently provides for exhorting their flocks to take up arms in their own defense. Franklin knows how to phrase this public appeal in such a way that all of Pennsylvania's contentious sects (except the Quakers) combine to support the militia association. "If the Peace had not soon interven'd," Franklin notes with mock regret, the militia would have been a near universal success.[3]

Governor Thomas was an equally enthusiastic proponent of Franklin's stove, offering him a patent on the design that Franklin declines out of the same principle of conversational generosity that influences his conception of the uses of speech. The memoir cites the complete title of Franklin's stove pamphlet as an instructive instance of modest self-assertion: *An Account of the New-Invented* PENNSYLVANIA FIRE PLACES: *Wherein their Construction and manner of Operation is particularly explained; their Advantages above every other Method of warming Rooms demonstrated; and all Objections that have been raised against the Use of them answered and obviated.* &c (A, 191). Franklin's Junto friend Robert Grace is able to profit from casting the plates for these stoves, and a London ironmonger plagiarizes the design and makes a fortune, but Franklin insists that "invention" is not a commodity and declares himself averse to patent or property disputes.

As the pamphlet's elaborate title implies, Franklin explains, demonstrates, answers, and obviates, all with a considerable degree of patience and restraint in what is clearly a quarrelsome, as well as a cold, climate, and all without naming the inventor of this newly invented device. The memoir introduces the stove episode just at the point where the Quaker dilemmas over purchasing gunpowder and financing fire engines become moot when peace is declared. But this final Pennsylvania "fire engine," too, seems as capable of heating the passions as of warming rooms. Franklin employs the events to underscore his stress on useful rather than explosive forms of energy, a cunning adaptation of the Promethean iconography that Turgot and many others had long attached to Franklin's image. By 1788 the master of lightning was ready to signal his interest not in harnessing or deflecting celestial power but in coaxing fire, along with water through the social offices of the Union Fire Company, to serve practical human needs.[4]

James Hamilton eventually succeeds George Thomas as Pennsylvania's governor and puts Franklin's talents to some of the same confidential uses as his predecessor did. It is Hamilton who names Franklin to two sensitive diplomatic commissions charged to negotiate with groups of native peoples during the first stages of the Seven Years' War. The second of these gives Franklin a chance to suggest a plan of political union to the colonial representatives gathered at Albany in 1754 to discuss mutual defense interests with the Iroquois. But Hamilton is nearly alone among Pennsylvania's governing officials in supporting Franklin's ambitious proposal. Worn out by this and other arguments with the Assembly arising from the Penn family's insistence that their personal estates be exempt from provincial taxation, Hamilton finally resigns his post (A, 212). Robert Hunter Morris takes Hamilton's place and quickly offers Franklin a chance to dramatize both the uses and abuses of speech in human affairs. This section of the story is cunning in ways that would have seemed particularly obvious to Franklin's contemporaries, who recognized the family tie between the Robert Hunter Morris of Franklin's book and his nephew, Gouverneur Morris, one of Pennsylvania's wealthiest and most outspoken delegates to the Constitutional Convention of 1787, which had completed its work in Philadelphia less than a year before Franklin resumed writing his book.

Franklin had known the elder Morris for some years before he succeeded Hamilton as Pennsylvania's governor. When the two first meet in their new relation as natural opponents in the proprietary government—Franklin as spokesman for the Assembly and Morris as the executive appointee of the

Penns—Morris makes clear that he is looking forward to the same intractable political clashes that had driven Hamilton to resign: "My dear Friend, says he, pleasantly," when he and Franklin meet in New York as Morris is traveling to his new post, "how can you advise my avoiding Disputes. You know I love disputing; it is one of my greatest Pleasures" (A, 212):

> He had some Reason for loving to dispute, being eloquent, an acute Sophister, and therefore generally successful in argumentative Conversation. He had been brought up to it from a Boy, his Father (as I have heard) accustoming his Children to dispute with one another for his Diversion while sitting at Table after Dinner. But I think the Practice was not wise, for in the Course of my Observation, these disputing, contradicting and confuting People are generally unfortunate in their Affairs. They get Victory sometimes, but they never get Good Will, which would be of more use to them. We parted, he going to Philadelphia, and I to Boston. In returning, I met at New York with the Votes of the Assembly, by which it appear'd that notwithstanding his Promise to me, he and the House were already in high Contention, and it was a continual Battle between them, as long as he retain'd the Government. (A, 212–13)

Franklin was a party to these battles, drafting Assembly responses to the governor and his English patrons in exchanges that, over time, grew "indecently abusive." The two men nevertheless remained on cordial terms. For Morris, dispute was largely a game that left his private friendships unaffected. But Franklin proves equally deft at exploiting the same boundary between public adversary and private companion, putting individual good nature to political use in another instance of the propensity to work both ways in this portion of Franklin's story. The memoir includes a deliberately provocative account of a social occasion involving Franklin and Morris that turns what had seemed to be a brief private respite from the province's growing level of political animosity into a complicated means of focusing and intensifying it, for Franklin's readers as well as for the participants in the anecdote.

On an impulse at another accidental meeting, this time in the streets of Philadelphia, Morris invited Franklin home for supper to join a group of the governor's friends. During the wine and "gay Conversation" that followed the meal, Morris joked about the advantages that Sancho Panza saw in having responsibility for "a Government of *Blacks*," since he could sell his people whenever they became uncooperative—a none-too-cunning introduction of *Don Quixote* into the after-dinner discussion that quickly leads to a breach in social decorum. Why don't you sell your troublesome Quaker colleagues in the Assembly? one of Morris's guests abruptly asks Franklin; "the Proprietor would give you a good Price." Franklin answers in a way that demonstrates how quickly these political quarrels could verge on indecency: "The governor, says I, has not yet black'd them enough" (A, 214). Indeed, the memoir continues, the members of the Assembly "wip'd off his Colouring as fast as he laid it on, and plac'd it in return thick upon his own Face; so that finding he was likely to be negrify'd himself, he as well as Mr. Hamilton, grew tir'd of the Contest, and quitted the Government."

At no other point in Franklin's book is today's reader more likely to cringe than at this example of crude racial humor. But in prompting such a visceral response, Franklin's language also dramatizes, with stunning immediacy, the destructive impact of speech that sacrifices good will in favor of victory. His portrait of this exchange enacts, as well as describes, the social and moral failures of Pennsylvania politics at the time. Indeed, the cunning in the passage runs deeper still, for Franklin's contemporaries in 1788 had just endured a bruising public debate on the relations of "blackness" to government as they tried to frame a federal system that would satisfy the demands of slaveholders without driving the increasingly adamant opponents of slavery out of the union. The notorious three-fifths clause in Article 1 of the Constitution that resulted from these efforts is an exercise in proportional "blackness" that has a suggestive affinity with Franklin's reply to the guest who invites him to sell out the rights of the Assembly to the interests of the Penns.

Franklin had been president of the Pennsylvania Society for Promoting the Abolition of Slavery for over a year when he reconstructed this long-ago supper party, resurrected its long-dead participants, and invited his reader to compare its casual racism to the views of Morris's nephew and of Franklin himself, as both men slowly outgrew the commonplace bigotry of their time. During a heated exchange on the floor of the Federal Convention, in the summer of 1787, Gouverneur Morris had attacked the three-fifths compromise with memorable force. James Madison took careful note of his words:

> The admission of slaves into the representation [Morris insisted] when fairly explained comes to this: that the inhabitant of Georgia and S.C. who goes to the Coast of Africa, and in defiance of the most sacred laws of humanity tears away his fellow creatures from their dearest connections & damns them to the most cruel bondage, shall have more votes in a Govt. instituted for protection of the

rights of mankind, than the Citizen of Pa or N. Jersey who views with a laudable horror, so nefarious a practice."[5]

Rather than "saddle posterity with such a Constitution," Morris continued, he would prefer to see the nation tax itself heavily enough to buy and emancipate all the slaves in the United States once and for all. Eventually Morris brought himself to accept the new Constitution, including the three-fifths clause, but the issue was only postponed, not resolved, a predicament that the Philadelphia Convention explicitly recognized by providing for an opportunity to outlaw American participation in the international slave trade—though not American slavery itself—twenty years after the Constitution's ratification. The memoir incorporates a cunning allusion directed at this intractable "contest," too, by depicting Robert Morris's weary withdrawal from the provincial government, immediately after describing his dinner party, a kind of secession that belies Morris's lifelong love of disputes.

No narrative necessity explains Franklin's decision to describe Morris's supper party in his memoir more than thirty years after it took place and more than a quarter century after Morris's death, but its presence indirectly crystallizes deep anxieties among Franklin's contemporaries in 1788, as well as among the parties to the United States Constitution over two centuries later. Long after the proprietary rights of the Penn family had ceased to be an issue, the racial mockery with which Robert Hunter Morris and Benjamin Franklin chose to illuminate their thoughts during a dinner party in 1755 evoked profound divisions over a far more explosive "proprietary" claim, one entailing bitter debates over how many congressional seats would be sufficient to satisfy slaveholders that their black population counted in the legislative scale. Was the Constitution's three-fifths provision adequate to acknowledge a slave's presence among the "people" without conceding rights to slaves? The memoir's wording applies a cunning twist to this painful question.

The replies that Franklin had drafted, on the Assembly's behalf, to Morris's combative messages reached the point where "one might have imagined that when we met we could hardly avoid cutting Throats" (A, 213). The cutting of throats over explosive differences remained a very real possibility among America's contending ideological camps in 1788, much as Benjamin Vaughan had feared a few years earlier when he urged Franklin to finish his book and as Franklin himself had discerned in 1731 when he took note of the hopeless confusion of history. This episode is the first of several in the longest section of Franklin's book that responds, with considerable subtlety, to the violent passions of his times. In doing so, it finds another means of working both ways by quietly inviting the reader to situate the events that the memoir describes in two contexts at once, looking back and looking forward, for hints at how best to address an uncertain future.[6]

The most extended of Franklin's many excuses in the 1788 section of his book is the apology that he offers for taxing the reader's patience with the description of such "trifling Matters" as paving, lighting, and sweeping city streets. This apology too is double-edged. Like the account of Robert Morris's supper party, it directs attention toward a number of different subjects and settings at once: the past and the present, London and Philadelphia, the privileged and the destitute, the blind and the farsighted. Beneath these comparatively innocuous passages, too, extraordinary forces are at work: an interplay of destructive and constructive energies that Franklin ultimately hopes his heirs will learn to manage.

Improvements in the quality of urban life were seldom far from Franklin's mind, an echo of his boyhood interest in the utility of stone wharves. The contrast between the "beautiful Regularity" of Philadelphia's street grid and "the Disgrace of suffering those Streets to remain long unpav'd" eventually prompted him to help pave a small area near the Jersey market to reduce the mud and dust that plagued pedestrians as well as the owners of the nearby shops and houses. The convenience of this arrangement, coupled with the labor of "a poor industrious Man" whom Franklin hired to sweep the paved area twice a week, convinced the citizens to accept a tax for paving the entire city. When the bill that Franklin drafted for this purpose came before the Assembly, the members added a provision for introducing street lights "with the Idea of enlightning all the City" at the same time, initially with "Globe Lamps" from London that quickly grew smoky, were prone to breaking, and hard to replace. Franklin improved the lamp design, using four flat panes of glass ventilated by a funnel to allow the smoke to escape:

> By this means they were kept clean, and did not grow dark in a few Hours as the London Lamps do, but continu'd bright till Morning; and an accidental Stroke would generally break but a single Pane, easily repair'd. I have sometimes wonder'd that the Londoners did not, from the Effect Holes in the Bottom of the Globe Lamps us'd at Vauxhall, have in keeping them clean, learn to have such Holes in their Street lamps. But those Holes being made for another purpose,

viz. to communicate Flame more suddenly to the Wick, by a little Flax hanging down thro' them, the other Use of letting in Air seems not to have been thought of. And therefor, after the Lamps have been lit a few Hours, the Streets of London are very poorly illuminated. (A, 204)

These trifling matters require only a few verbal adjustments on Franklin's part in order to form a little parable of the difference between Philadelphia's "enlightning" energies and London's perverse adherence to its murky "Globe." One city is systematically emerging from its urban "Quagmire," as Franklin calls it, tapping the labor of its poorest citizens as well as the taxable property of its most prosperous ones, whereas the other, for all its wealth and imperial reach, is inexplicably committed to darkness.

The memoir repeats the parable almost immediately, with intriguing modifications, by describing a proposal that Franklin once made to John Fothergill, "a great Promoter of useful Projects," for cleaning London's streets. This time the plan begins not with a clash between beautiful regularity and disgraceful filth but in an accidental encounter that Franklin describes with one of London's desperately poor scavengers. During his long periods of residence in the city between 1757 and 1775 as the agent for various colonial assemblies, an inefficient system for keeping its streets passable did exist, relying on "poor People with Brooms" to maintain temporary pathways through the muck until it was periodically shoveled into carts and hauled away. An intimate glimpse of this system in action awakens the latent civil engineer that Franklin often seems to resemble in this section of his book:

> I found at my Door in Craven Street one Morning a poor Woman sweeping my Pavement with a birch Broom. She appeared very pale and feeble as just come out of a Fit of Sickness. I ask'd who employ'd her to sweep there. She said, "Nobody; but I am very poor and in Distress, and I sweeps before Gentlefolkeses Doors, and hopes they will give me something." I bid her sweep the whole Street clean and I would give her a Shilling. This was at 9 a Clock. At 12 she came for the Shilling. From the slowness I saw at first in her Working, I could scarce believe that the Work was done so soon, and sent my Servant to examine it, who reported that the whole Street was swept perfectly clean, and all the Dust plac'd in the Gutter which was in the Middle. And the next Rain wash'd it quite away, so that the Pavement and even the Kennel were perfectly clean. I then judg'd that if that feeble Woman could sweep such a Street in 3 Hours, a strong active Man might have done it in half the time. (A, 205)

These sentences go out of their way to depict a collaborative exercise in urban cunning: a feeble scavenger who proves surprisingly skilled and energetic once the economic prospects are favorable, and an opportunistic colonial agent (equally dependent on the whims of "Gentlefolkeses") who is only too eager to demonstrate "how much Sweeping might be done in a little Time," as Franklin puts it, fully aware of the figurative history that John Bunyan too exploited when the Interpreter in *The Pilgrim's Progress* made "sweeping" a simple emblem for far-reaching spiritual purges.[7]

The plan that Franklin soon sends to Fothergill, based on the lessons of this experience, provides "for the more effectual cleaning and keeping clean the streets of London and Westminister," the commercial and the political "city," using watchmen to contract with scavengers and supply them with "Brooms and other proper Instruments" for the job. Equally effective diplomatic or political instruments for keeping Westminster's parliamentary chambers clean prove more elusive, as Franklin's bitter experiences with the British Ministry will ultimately show, though London's long summer days offer ample opportunity to accomplish the task: "For in Walking thro' the Strand and Fleetstreet one Morning at 7 a Clock I observ'd there was not one shop open tho' it had been Day-light and the Sun up above three Hours. The Inhabitants of London chusing voluntarily to live much by Candle Light, and sleep by Sunshine; and yet often complain a little absurdly, of the Duty on Candles and the high Price of Tallow" (A, 207). The tallow chandler's son from Boston must have enjoyed this opportunity to profit, even if only symbolically, over a people whose political system (as Franklin had experienced it) squandered natural light.

At this point, Franklin interrupts the narrative ostensibly to apologize for its trivial nature, but in doing so he adds to these first two political fables a third variation that carries a more ominous undercurrent:

> Some may think these trifling Matters not worth minding or relating. But when they consider, that tho' Dust blown into the Eyes of a single Person or into a single Shop on a windy Day, is but of small Importance, yet the great Number of the Instances in a populous City, and its frequent Repetitions give it Weight and Consequence; perhaps they will not censure very severely those who bestow some of Attention to Affairs of this seemingly low Nature. Human Felicity is produc'd not so much by great Pieces of good Fortune that seldom happen, as by little Advantages that occur every Day. Thus if you teach a poor young Man to shave himself and keep his Razor in order, you may contribute more to the Hap-

piness of his Life than in giving him a 1000 Guineas. . . . With these Sentiments I have hazarded the few preceding Pages, hoping they may afford Hints which some time or other may be useful to a City I love, having lived many Years in it very happily; and perhaps to some of our Towns in America. (A, 207–8)

Blindness in individuals is perhaps of negligible importance, Franklin admits, but blindness in entire cities or nations has potentially tragic consequences, as England's had at the beginning of the Revolution and as France's recent experience was beginning to illustrate for Franklin's contemporaries in 1789, the year during which he was writing these words. After Philadelphia's poor but industrious street sweeper and London's feeble scavenger, the third version of the neglected underclass that these successive paragraphs present is a young man with a razor, kept in good order, and more valuable to him in the long run than a thousand guineas. In significant respects, these details do indeed add up to hazardous sentiments, as Franklin implies, without abandoning his rhetorical guise as the giver of "hints," a variety of cunning that informs every instance of useful speech that his book depicts.[8]

ROBERT HUNTER MORRIS SOUGHT TO ENTANGLE Franklin in Pennsylvania's military affairs at least twice: first when he sent him to represent the province's interests to Edward Braddock, the British general who was festering in Maryland over the failure of the colonial governments to provide supply wagons for his campaign against the French, and once again after Braddock's stunning defeat in the wilderness near Fort Duquesne. Morris offered Franklin a general's commission to continue the abortive effort to drive the French out of the Ohio Valley, an opportunity Franklin prudently declined, though he did agree to help build some forts in the Pennsylvania backcountry to defend the civilian population against raids. During this brief stint as a militia officer, Franklin has occasion to solve a minor disciplinary problem with rum. In doing so, he draws together the crude and the sophisticated incentives to goodwill represented, throughout his book, by liquor and by cunning:

> We had for our Chaplain a zealous Presbyterian Minister, Mr. Beatty, who complain'd to me that the Men did not generally attend his Prayers and Exhortations. When they enlisted, they were promis'd, besides Pay and Provisions, a Gill of Rum a Day, which was punctually serv'd out to them half in the Morning and the other half in the Evening, and I observ'd they were as punctual in attending to receive it. Upon which I said to Mr. Beatty, "It is perhaps below the Dignity

of your Profession to act as Steward of the Rum. But if you were to deal it out, and only just after Prayers, you would have them all about you." He lik'd the Thought, undertook the Office, and with the help of a few hands to measure out the Liquor executed it to Satisfaction; and never were Prayers more generally and more punctually attended. So that I thought this Method preferable to the Punishments inflicted by some military Laws for Non-Attendance on Divine Service. (A, 235)

As with the Quaker euphemisms during Governor Thomas's administration, or the carefully crafted hospital legislation that Franklin had sponsored, this tactic too works both ways to accomplish its transparent goals. The conflation of "offices" that Franklin proposes meets the expectations of both the men and the minister, and achieves something more besides. The barrier between the chaplain and his congregation diminishes, once it becomes clear that Mr. Beatty's zeal is not above exploiting human nature as well as chastising it. He values an audience for his prayers above his clerical dignity. At the same time, Franklin is able to dramatize the superiority of ingenious tactics over the punitive practice of "military Laws," and the new system of daily liquor rations and prayers gives general "Satisfaction"—a term as evasive as any of the Quaker assemblymen's euphemisms in their appropriation bills, since it carefully skirts the question of whether the prayers, the exhortations, or the rum had the most impact on the inner lives of Franklin's men.

Assessing the inner thoughts of others is every bit as difficult as influencing them. Franklin understood the human propensity to resent instruction and resist change, instincts that are partly responsible for the silence of modest, sensible people when confronted by an argumentative dogmatist. Franklin, Mr. Beatty, and the militia are satisfied with the terms of an outward compliance that accepts the limitations of coercion, an extension of some "judicious" advice that Franklin had already quoted in his book. "Men should be taught as if you taught them not," Pope wrote in the *Essay on Criticism*, "And things unknown propos'd as things forgot." The memoir's first account of Franklin's efforts to cultivate habits of modest diffidence cites these lines to underscore his belief that argument is futile as a means of changing the convictions or securing the cooperation of others. When he returns to this subject near the end of the memoir's 1784 fragment, he stresses the limited success that an outward compliance with reasonable rules has on his own combative nature. In this second account of the restraints that he imposes on his speech, the behavioral transformation he describes is more abrupt and involves much more of a struggle on Franklin's part—details that may reflect the considerable strains of the eight years that he had just spent in France, coping with the clash of personalities and goals involved in orchestrating French support for the American Revolution.

Unlike the gradual and graceful process of verbal change, mediated by Pope's elegant couplets, that Franklin had portrayed in 1771, the second part of the memoir describes his concerted attack on a serious personal weakness. A Quaker friend, he remembered, "kindly informed me that I was generally thought proud," so much so that he often struck others as "overbearing and rather insolent" in conversation, vices that Franklin sets out to "cure" initially by adding "Humility" to his list of twelve virtues and "giving an extensive Meaning to the Word": "Imitate Jesus and Socrates" (A, 159). This precept is at best curious medicine for the sickness of pride, but it has a certain cunning in its design. To imitate is to concede important limitations in one's nature that preclude a close adherence to exalted models. Moreover, neither Jesus nor Socrates could finally offer much encouragement to a person hoping to please his hearers or prompt a measure of political concurrence among a group of savvy merchants, wily assemblymen, or seasoned European diplomats. For much of his public life, Franklin sought to make himself useful with the kind of audiences that preferred to martyr prophets and sages rather than honor them.[9]

Recognizing that his standards for achieving humility were out of reach, and probably poorly chosen as exemplars of modest diffidence, he took sterner measures by imposing rules and laws on his aggressive nature:

> I made it a Rule to forbear all direct Contradiction to the Sentiments of others, and all positive Assertion of my own. I even forbid myself agreable to the old Laws of our Junto, the Use of every Word or Expression in the Language that imported a fix'd Opinion; such as *certainly, undoubtedly*, &c. and I adopted instead of them *I conceive, I apprehend*, or *I imagine* a thing to be so or so, or it so appears to me at present. When another asserted something, that I thought an Error, I deny'd my self the Pleasure of contradicting him abruptly, and of showing immediately some Absurdity in his Proposition. . . . I soon found the Advantage of this Change in my Manners. The Conversations I engag'd in went on more pleasantly. The modest way in which I propos'd my Opinions, procur'd them a readier Reception and less Contradiction; I had less Mortification when I was found to be in the wrong, and I more easily prevail'd with others to give

up their Mistakes and join with me when I happen'd to be in the right. And this Mode, which I at first put on, with some violence to natural Inclination, became at length so easy and so habitual to me, that perhaps for these Fifty Years past no one has ever heard a dogmatical Expression escape me. (A, 159)

These words immediately precede Franklin's concession that pride is the most stubborn "of our natural Passions," finding ways to conceal and sustain itself even in the course of our efforts to achieve humility. But in declaring victory over dogmatical inclinations, Franklin slyly dramatizes their stubborn persistence: proclaiming an immodest absurdity virtually in the same breath that he asserts a half century of success at restraining his love of assertion. These words, too, are as carefully chosen as the verbal formulas that Franklin initially adopts to help change his confrontational habits. He is successful not at eliminating his aggressive instincts but at denying himself the pleasure of expressing them. The instincts themselves never cease their search for avenues of escape, just as pride strives to do, no matter how vigilantly an individual sets out to "struggle with it, beat it down, stifle it, mortify it as much as one pleases" (A, 160).

Franklin's passing reference in this passage to the Junto's "old Laws" is yet another cunning reminder of struggles within human nature that may not be susceptible to any tactics of containment. His original account of the Junto describes it as a school of philosophy, morals, and politics governed by "Rules" and "small pecuniary Penalties" if any member grew too impassioned during debate. At the time that he was adding humility to his list of virtues and suppressing his love of contradiction, these Junto practices were hardly old, nor did the members appear to view them in precisely the same light as "laws." But evoking the ethical clash between a punitive Old Law and its forgiving successor allows Franklin to signal his awareness that the traditional conception of "sin" (to which pride belongs) and the Enlightenment nomenclature of "natural Passions" have a stubborn and bitter kinship that John Bunyan and George Whitefield would have been quick to recognize. In making this latest excuse for the influence of pride in his personal "History," Franklin sets the stage for a study of the pervasive struggle with deep-seated prejudices that the third section of the memoir explores.

On a geopolitical level, this struggle takes the form of Franklin's involvement with Edward Braddock's military campaign. It is Braddock's "violent Prejudices" that Franklin is initially sent to soothe, when the general cannot collect enough wagons in the Maryland and Virginia countryside to carry his supplies. Braddock's presence in America, in turn, is an outgrowth of "Suspicions and Jealousies" in the British government aroused by the plan of colonial union that Franklin had proposed at Albany the year before Braddock's arrival—a plan that failed in part because of the mutual suspicions and jealousies of the colonies themselves. "History is full of the Errors of States and Princes," Franklin sententiously observes, as he reflects on the series of shortsighted acts that eventually led to the American Revolution (A, 211). But states and princes alone are not the only agents given to thwarting the general good on petty or personal grounds.

The third section of the memoir makes clear that Franklin's own experience with managing suspicions and jealousies begins on a much less ambitious scale, with the careful partnership contracts that he prepared when he established his former journeymen in their own printing businesses, first in South Carolina as early as 1733, when Franklin himself had been an independent printer for barely five years:

> Most of them did well, being enabled at the End of our Term, Six Years, to purchase the Types of me; and go on working for themselves, by which means several Families were raised. Partnerships often finish in Quarrels, but I was happy in this, that mine were all carry'd on and ended amicably; owing I think a good deal to the Precaution of having very explicitly settled in our Articles every thing to be done by or expected from each Partner, so that there was nothing to dispute, which Precaution I would therefore recommend to all who enter into Partnerships, for whatever Esteem Partners may have for and Confidence in each other at the time of the Contract, little Jealousies and Disgusts may arise, with Ideas of Inequality in the Care and Burthen of the Business, &c. which are attended often with Breach of Friendship and of the Connection, perhaps with Lawsuits and other Disagreable Consequences. (A, 181)

Unlike the disastrous courtship negotiation with the Godfreys, Franklin manages these little treaties with considerable success, but like that negotiation, these contracts too anticipate on a miniature scale the great breach between England and its colonies for which much of Franklin's early life is a rehearsal. His partnership experience makes him equally effective at mediating an agreement between two groups of trustees each of which hopes to control the use of the large meetinghouse that George Whitefield's followers had constructed

Some Uses of Cunning 169

but which they could not afford to maintain on their own. With Franklin's help, the parties agree to share the building, making it available "for occasional Preachers according to the original Intention" but allowing it to be modified to accommodate "a Free School for the Instruction of poor Children," which eventually develops into what Franklin knows as the University of Philadelphia (A, 195).

As the narrative continues to unfold, more formidable treaties prove much harder to manage and require more problematic excuses, as Franklin's public responsibilities grow. He abandons the role of justice of the peace when he finds that "attending a few Courts, and sitting on the Bench to hear Causes" requires more legal knowledge than he possesses. "I gradually withdrew from it," Franklin confesses, "excusing myself by my being oblig'd to attend the higher Dutys of a Legislator in the Assembly" (A, 197). The English Board of Trade and the various colonial assemblies can't agree on whether the plan of union Franklin proposed at the Albany conference contained too much royal prerogative or too much colonial democracy, and the idea falls by the wayside, in Pennsylvania at least because a cunning member of the Assembly arranges to have the plan rejected in Franklin's absence. Like the mediating role that Franklin had played in the founding of the Philadelphia Academy, his first participation in a negotiation with native peoples also revolves around a unique building in which the memoir stages a much darker blend of cunning and excuses.

In 1753, two years before Braddock's arrival in America, Franklin traveled at the Assembly's request to Carlisle, Pennsylvania, with Richard Peters and Isaac Norris to meet a delegation of Indians from several tribes who had requested reassurances of English support against the incursions of the French and their native allies from the North. The memoir glosses over these preliminary details, omitting the year, the political circumstances, and even the arduous, four-day journey that Franklin and his colleagues had to make on horseback to attend the Carlisle meeting. The account focuses instead on a vivid picture of violent passions that Franklin intends to set in the frame provided by the living quarters of the Indian delegates and their families. The scene itself recasts a number of instances throughout the book where ugly aspects of human nature find release through drinking. Robert Hunter Morris's supper rapidly deteriorates into racist banter as the guests linger over their wine. Hugh Meredith's drinking and John Collins's drunken outbursts played formative roles in the early stages of Franklin's Philadelphia career. The compositors and pressmen whom he met in London observed "a detestable Custom" of drinking throughout the workday and paying a substantial portion of their weekly wages to support their reliance on "muddling Liquor" (A, 100).

Governor Clinton grows progressively more generous with his cannon, under the influence of several "Bumpers" of Madeira wine, when Franklin and his Pennsylvania colleagues visit New York in the hope of borrowing some guns for the Philadelphia battery. Franklin himself keeps a wary distance from this picture of gentlemanly excess, though he is not above profiting from it, in the interests of his city's defense. William Denny, the last provincial governor of Pennsylvania to try to court Franklin's support, grows increasingly profuse with his "Solicitations and Promises" the more heavily he drinks, bribes to which the memoir responds with such an extensive list of sober and civil answers on Franklin's part that Denny abandons his drunken efforts (A, 247). Temperance heads Franklin's list of virtues, in part, because alcohol pervades his world, requiring considerable cunning in those who hope to avoid becoming its victims.

In order to keep the Carlisle treaty discussions as orderly as possible, the Pennsylvania delegates forbid the English traders who had come to the negotiations to sell any rum until the public business was done. Once the treaty was "concluded to mutual Satisfaction," Franklin wrote, the Indian delegates "claim'd and receiv'd the Rum" that they had been promised at the outset of the meeting:

> This was in the Afternoon. They were near 100 Men, Women and Children, and were lodg'd in temporary Cabins built in the Form of a Square just without the Town. In the Evening, hearing a great Noise among them, the Commissioners walk'd out to see what was the Matter. We found they had made a great Bonfire in the Middle of the Square. They were all drunk Men and Women, quarrelling and fighting. Their dark-colour'd Bodies, half naked, seen only by the gloomy Light of the Bonfire, running after and beating one another with Firebrands, accompanied by their horrid Yellings, form'd a Scene the most resembling our Ideas of Hell that could well be imagin'd. There was no appeasing the Tumult, and we retired to our Lodging. At Midnight a Number of them came thundering at our Door, demanding more Rum; of which we took no Notice. The next Day, sensible they had misbehav'd in giving us that Disturbance, they sent three of their old Counsellors to make their Apology. The Orator acknowledg'd the Fault, but laid it upon the Rum; and then endeavour'd to excuse the Rum, by

saying, "The great Spirit who made all things made every thing for some Use, and whatever Use he design'd any thing for, that Use it should always be put to; Now, when he made Rum, he said, LET THIS BE FOR INDIANS TO GET DRUNK WITH. And it must be so." (A, 198–99)

Like many of the excuses with which Franklin fills his narrative, this one too has a cunning capacity to work both ways. In making their apology, the three "old Counsellors" invoke the same criterion of "use" that Franklin repeatedly applies to various personal or social challenges in the course of his memoir, beginning with his struggle to restrict the use of assertive words and favor the use of modest ones in order to contain (or at least to disguise) his aggressive instincts. The appearance of the word in this painful setting suggests that the Indians too have invisible uses for behavior that outside observers can easily misconstrue. The many other instances of drunkenness in Franklin's book seem trivial by comparison with this melancholy acknowledgment of cultural destruction, but the native orator's words are coupled with an implicit assertion that rum has "uses" as well as frightening effects.

Oblivion is certainly one use: a temporary escape from despair or a release for feelings of impotent rage at the devastating changes that the presence of Europeans had imposed on their world. But Franklin's comments pointedly include the implicit "use" of rum as a tool of English policy in the observation with which he follows the orator's speech: "And indeed if it be the Design of Providence to extirpate these Savages in order to make room for Cultivators of the Earth," he writes, "it seems not improbable that Rum may be the appointed Means. It has already annihilated all the Tribes who formerly inhabited the Seacoast" (A, 199). Up to this point in the memoir's account, Franklin stresses the presence of families among the Indian delegation at Carlisle: men, women, and children gathered in a "Square" that invites comparison to the town squares of New England, the Court House square in Philadelphia where Whitefield preached his doctrine of natural depravity, or the city squares of London and Paris, some of which would shortly become revolutionary gathering places as Franklin wrote this portion of his story. His startling shift in scale, however, from domestic nightmare to the invidious clash between "Savages" and "Cultivators of the Earth" immediately underscores the adroit parody of providential design with which the old counsellors had initially excused the rum. Franklin's closing words make it only too plain that it is people, not Providence, who deploy the appointed means of annihilation.

In echoing the apology of the native orator, Franklin magnifies rather than diminishes the sense of mutual culpability that pervades their exchange. Both are careful to observe the memoir's criteria for choosing words that minimize confrontational certitude, making use of religious formulas that mimic the instrumental potency of rum. But each is equally careful to hint at a sense of suffering for which no excuse can be made. Franklin himself is the author of both statements, voicing in turn the complex confession of the Indian delegates and dramatizing the arrogant rigidity of European prejudice. Few instances of cunning in his book are more subtle and far-reaching than the picture of perverse concurrence that this episode entails: its insistence that human communities are ultimately responsible for determining what must be so.[10]

LIKE THE CULTURAL COLLISION depicted in the Carlisle negotiation, Franklin's relations with Edward Braddock, and the efforts that he makes to address the British general's needs while protecting the interests of colonial farmers and colonial assemblies, form a preamble in miniature to his long diplomatic engagement with centers of European power. These events provide Franklin's first direct encounter with English imperial policy, as well as with the attitudes and assumptions of its ministerial agents. In some respects they anticipate the role he would play in France as a procurer of supplies for the Continental army and a representative of American "simplicity" in the sophisticated political circles of London and Paris. The memoir enlarges on this portion of Franklin's story both because of its intrinsic historical and biographical importance and because it embraces many contexts and many subjects at once, through the verbal media that Franklin had made his lifelong study.

When the Pennsylvania Assembly first sent Franklin to Braddock's Frederic Town camp, he was acting "under the guise" of his role as postmaster general of the colonies, hoping to streamline the movement of military dispatches, but the Assembly also intended his visit to serve as a surreptitious gesture of goodwill. Over the course of several days and several dinners at the camp, Franklin was able to manage this double role effectively, but as he was on the point of returning to Philadelphia, a second opportunity arose to "work both ways" in a much more tangible fashion. In the course of scouring the Maryland and Virginia countryside, Braddock's officers had managed to collect only 25 of the roughly 150 wagons that the expedition would need to carry its supplies deep into the Ohio Valley to attack the French at Fort Duquesne. Franklin expressed sympathy with the general's dilemma and hinted at a solution that Braddock quickly seized:

> I happen'd to say, I thought it was pity they had not been landed rather in Pennsylvania, as in that Country almost every Farmer had his Waggon. The General eagerly laid hold of my Words, and said, "Then you, Sir, who are a Man of Interest there, can probably procure them for us; and I beg you will undertake it." I ask'd what Terms were to be offer'd the Owners of the Waggons; and I was desir'd to put on Paper the Terms that appear'd to me necessary. This I did, and they were agreed to, and a Commission and Instructions accordingly prepar'd immediately. What those Terms were will appear in the Advertisement I publish'd as soon as I arriv'd at Lancaster; which being, from the great and sudden Effect it produc'd, a Piece of some Curiosity, I shall insert at length, as follows. (A, 217)

The memoir as a whole refers to various examples of Franklin's writing that have great and sudden effects: the paper currency pamphlet that strengthens popular feeling and stifles its wealthy opponents, the "sudden and surprizing" impact of *Plain Truth* in forming a militia association, the astute incentives of the Assembly's hospital bill, and Father Abraham's proverbial "Harangue" that compressed twenty-five years of almanac advice into a single speech, widely reprinted on both sides of the Atlantic and translated twice into French.

But despite the willingness that Franklin displays in the 1775 voyage letter to fill out his narrative with illustrative documents, these contractual terms for supplying wagons to the British, along with their companion address to Pennsylvania's farmers, are the only instances of Franklin's previously published work that the surviving manuscript of the memoir includes—a fact sufficiently curious in itself. His presence in Braddock's camp at just this historical juncture is every bit as strategic as the appearance of a London scavenger at his Craven Street door. This and subsequent visits that Franklin made as Braddock prepared to march almost certainly resulted in Franklin's first acquaintance with George Washington, who commanded the Virginia militia attached to Braddock's force and who would distinguish himself during the fighting that covered the British retreat. The memoir, however, never mentions Washington's presence, a second curious feature of this episode, made all the more conspicuous by Washington's recent prominence as presiding officer at the Federal Convention that Franklin had attended less than a year before beginning the third portion of his book.

Braddock's eagerness to make use of Franklin's reputation (as the supporters of the Constitution sought to make use of Washington's) is more than matched by Franklin's own surprising readiness to draft, virtually on the spot, a complicated contract allowing for several farmers to spread the risk of this venture among themselves and share the profits of supporting the campaign. In attributing to Braddock the odd phrase "Man of Interest," rather than the more familiar label "Man of Influence," the memoir points to the balancing act that Franklin engages to perform among competing interests as he converts potential antagonists into allies. The contract terms that the memoir includes, in their entirety, encourage several farmers to collaborate on meeting the expedition's needs by combining teams, wagons, drivers, packhorses, packsaddles, and feed from different owners into the units that will form Braddock's baggage train.

Every piece of equipment and every animal, Franklin stipulated, would be "valu'd by indifferent Persons" at the time the arrangements were made, with the valuation to be paid to the suppliers in case of loss. The drivers were explicitly excused from doing "the Duty of Soldiers" (A, 218–19). Franklin and his son William, who had significant military experience, would replace Braddock's officers as agents authorized to negotiate on the army's behalf, and they divided the Pennsylvania counties between them when they set out to meet with interested parties who responded to Franklin's elaborate "Advertisement," a document of some cunning as well as curiosity. This address "To the Inhabitants of the Counties of Lancaster, York, and Cumberland" implies that Pennsylvania's internal "Dissensions," not the feeble response from Virginia and Maryland, had so exasperated Braddock and his staff that they were contemplating taking drastic measures to supply their expedition:

> It was proposed to send an armed Force immediately into these Counties, to seize as many of the best Carriages and Horses as should be wanted, and compel as many Persons into the Service as would be necessary to drive and take care of them.
>
> I apprehended that the Progress of a Body of Soldiers thro' these Counties on such an Occasion, especially considering the Temper they are in, and their Resentment against us, would be attended with many and great Inconveniencies to the Inhabitants; and therefore more willingly undertook the Trouble of trying first what might be done by fair and equitable Means. (A, 219–20)

This preamble, aimed at arousing the anxieties of Franklin's "Friends and Countrymen," rewrites the circumstances that precede its appearance in the narrative. The memoir in fact reports that Braddock had "declar'd the Expedition was then at an End" when his first efforts to collect wagons in Virginia and Maryland produced such a meager result. Moreover, by Franklin's original account, the general's frustrations were directed not at the colonists but at his superiors, the ministers in London who had sent his soldiers to fight in a country too poor to provide the support they needed. Understating the "great Inconveniencies" of military predation and exaggerating or distorting Braddock's intentions appear to play equally transparent roles in preparing for Franklin's presentation of the mutual interests at play in these circumstances.

The army's mission, Franklin suggests, will give the backcountry farmers a chance to profit from the war by dividing among themselves "upwards of Thirty thousand Pounds . . . in Silver and Gold of the King's Money" that their wagons and teams will earn from the campaign. The people of Lancaster, York, and Cumberland "have lately complained to the Assembly that a sufficient Currency was wanting," Franklin noted. Here was an opportunity to address that deficiency. The army, in turn, has an interest in protecting its supplies that will prompt the soldiers to keep the baggage train secure. And Pennsylvania as a whole, Franklin continues, has an interest in dramatizing its loyalty to the crown, while at the same time preventing an angry British general from seizing by force what he cannot procure with money. The only impartial party to these arrangements (the advertisement claims) is Franklin himself, who recognizes that "the King's Business must be done" under reasonable terms, if at all possible, but through "violent Measures" if necessary:

> I have no particular Interest in this Affair; as (except the Satisfaction of endeavouring to do Good and prevent Mischief) I shall have only my Labour for my Pains. If this Method of obtaining the Waggons and Horses is not like to succeed, I am oblig'd to send Word to the General in fourteen Days; and I suppose Sir John St. Clair the Hussar, with a Body of Soldiers, will immediately enter the Province, for the Purpose aforesaid, of which I shall be sorry to hear, because I am, very sincerely and truly your Friend and Well-wisher, B. Franklin (A, 221)

This blended posture of indifferent bystander and concerned neighbor was unlikely to have deceived anyone who read Franklin's flyer. His menacing supposition about the impending seizure of wagons and conscription of drivers, while not entirely implausible, is an equally transparent device.

In the end, the owners of the wagons and teams that Franklin assembled were less interested in his good wishes or in the advertisement's threats than in the personal bonds that Franklin provided as additional security for the army's official promise to pay for any animals and equipment lost or destroyed during the campaign. Ominous warnings about John St. Clair's Hussars did not keep these farmers from exercising a degree of cunning on their own behalf, which, in the event, came close to ruining Franklin when the British government proved slow in paying the claims that arose from Braddock's defeat. The aggrieved owners' demands "gave me a great deal of Trouble," Franklin confessed, and many of them sued to have him fulfill his bonds. Only the timely intervention of William Shirley, the governor of Massachusetts whose son had died with Braddock, rescued Franklin from financial ruin.[11]

Financial difficulties also threaten a number of Braddock's junior officers when they find they cannot afford to buy supplies for the upcoming expedition. With his son's help, and with Assembly funds, Franklin supplies twenty of these men with packhorses carrying parcels of food and drink for their private use during the march. In a final, curious gesture, the memoir carefully lists the contents of each parcel, nearly all of which wound up feeding the victorious French and their Indian allies or being destroyed after Braddock's death, when his second-in-command was frantically trying to speed up his retreat to Philadelphia (A, 226). Franklin itemizes these gifts, apparently from memory, as carefully as he preserves the contents of the 1731 library memorandum or the legal particulars of the wagon advertisement on which the security of his personal fortune depended.

Each officer received twelve pounds of sugar, half in white loaf and half unrefined brown "Muscovado"; one pound each of two varieties of tea; six pounds each of ground coffee, chocolate, rice, and raisins; fifty pounds "best white Biscuit"; two cured hams; half a dozen dried tongues; a twenty pound keg of butter; a "Gloucester" cheese; two dozen bottles of "old Madeira wine"; and two gallons of rum. These gifts "were very thankfully receiv'd," Franklin wrote, but he surely meant the memoir's earliest readers to view this profuse array of goods with some astonishment. Franklin and his son packed an imperial grocery list into each officer's parcel: tea from India or China, quite possibly imported on the same ships that Boston's mob would attack twenty years later at the outset of the Revolution; two varieties of sugar from the Caribbean; coffee and chocolate from Central America, Africa, or the East Indies; English cheese; rice from the Carolinas; butter from Pennsylvania or New Jersey; wine and rum in quantities calculated to warm the heart of Governor Clinton or William Denny. This is what the cultivators of the earth can produce for its merchants to transport around the globe, the memoir seems to suggest, when they are not engaged in annihilating one another. In place of George Washington on his cavalry mount, displaying America's martial prowess in the midst of a wilderness catastrophe, the memoir depicts a train of pack animals laden with the mix of luxuries and necessities that were the mark of a prosperous trading people.[12]

The carnage of Edward Braddock's defeat was all too real. Franklin tabulates the cost in the memoir's pages: 63 of 86 officers killed or wounded, 714 of 1,100 soldiers dead, "picked Men, from the whole Army," pushing ahead on the first leg of an ambitious campaign to capture all of western Canada, only to be cut off in ambush when they had scarcely begun (A, 225). As Franklin surely knew, any captives the Indians took during the chaotic retreat would have been tortured before being killed. The expedition that Governor Morris asked him to lead a few months later to reinter the victims of an Indian massacre at the Moravian settlement of Gnadenhütten and build a series of frontier forts gave him a firsthand look at the brutality of wilderness warfare. What is man at present, Benjamin Vaughan had asked in urging Franklin to finish his book: a reasonable and amendable creature or a vicious animal? The answer, he believed, would offer hope for the future.

The answer implied by Braddock's example is that we are both: reasonable and vicious, stubborn and amendable, the eater and the eaten, as Franklin had recognized in the memoir's first pages when he invoked an old truism to justify a sharp appetite for fresh cod. Like the young Franklin on his first ocean voyage, Braddock too enjoyed the convenience of reason as a reservoir of explanations and excuses. His overweening confidence in what Franklin oddly terms "the Validity of Regular Troops," coupled with his contempt for American militia and its Indian allies, combined to destroy him. The Indians in particular, Franklin notes, "might have been of great Use to his Army as Guides, Scouts, &c. if he had treated them kindly; but he slighted and neglected them, and they gradually left him" (A, 223). Franklin himself had considerable experience with the slights and neglect that English officials often inflicted on Americans, instead of the kindness that would have proved a far more useful means of securing their mutual interests. A gradual process of alienation begins with these events, one that works both ways (as so much of this portion of the memoir does) to depict an inward change that Franklin shares with the Indian scouts.[13]

Braddock originally envisioned dislodging the French from three of their wilderness strongholds before winter brought a halt to his operations, but Franklin "had conceiv'd some Doubts and some Fears for the Event of the Campaign," based in part on the knowledge of wilderness travel that he had acquired on excursions like the one to Carlisle, as well as on his reading, and on his respect for Indian tactics. But when he expresses these worries, Braddock's dismissive response puts an end to the discussion, a perfect illustration of the price that a dogmatist pays for his air of positive assertion: "He smil'd at my Ignorance," Franklin recalled, "and reply'd, 'These Savages may indeed be a formidable Enemy to your raw American Militia; but upon the King's regular and disciplin'd Troops, Sir, it is impossible they should make any Impression.' I was conscious of an Impropriety in my Disputing with a military Man in Matters of his Profession, and said no more" (A, 224). Modest, sensible men who do not love disputes leave opinionated people in possession of their errors. Braddock's realization that he was in the wrong comes too late to save the lives of his men, but the memoir includes an account of his death that portrays the process by which new "impressions" make their way past old prejudices:

> Capt. Orme, who was one of the General's Aid de Camps, and being grievously wounded was brought off with him, and continu'd with him to his Death, which happen'd in a few Days, told me, that he was totally silent, all the first Day, and at Night only said, *Who'd have thought it?* that he was silent again the following Days, only saying at last, *We shall better know how to deal with them another time*; and dy'd a few Minutes after. (A, 226)

Franklin makes no pretense of knowing what the dying man's long periods of silence might mean, or what changes he might have been experiencing, but his last words are almost completely free of the vanity that had kept him from attending to Franklin's worries or recognizing the value of Indian guides in this unfamiliar world.[14]

The memoir portrays Franklin's brief militia experience as a precise contrast to Braddock's fate. Unlike the professionally schooled military man, Franklin is an officer who scarcely ever issues an order, preferring to send various detachments of men to parts of the undefended frontier "with Instructions" to build forts for the security of the settlers. The men under his direct authority

Some Uses of Cunning 179

appear to need no instruction whatever, having long ago mastered the use of axes, shovels, and wagon axles as tools for cutting, moving, and planting heavy logs into a palisade adequate to deter Indians "who have no Cannon" (A, 224). Franklin's delight in observing this work echoes the pleasure that he took, as a boy, rolling construction stones into a fishing wharf:

> The next Morning our Fort was plann'd and mark'd out, the Circumference measuring 455 feet, which would require as many Palisades to be made of Trees one with another of a Foot Diameter each. Our Axes, of which we had 70 were immediately set to work, to cut down Trees; and our Men being dextrous in the Use of them, great Dispatch was made. Seeing the Trees fall so fast, I had the Curiosity to look at my Watch when two Men began to cut at a Pine. In 6 Minutes they had it upon the Ground; and I found it of 14 inches Diameter. Each Pine made three Palisades of 18 Feet long, pointed at one End. While these were preparing, our other Men, dug a Trench all round of three feet deep in which the Palisades were to be planted, and our Waggons, the Body being taken off, and the fore and hind Wheels separated by taking out the Pin which united the two Parts of the Perch, we had 10 Carriages with two Horses each, to bring the Palisades from the Woods to the Spot. When they were set up, our Carpenters built a Stage of Boards all round within, about 6 Feet high, for the Men to stand on when to fire thro' the Loopholes. We had one swivel Gun which we mounted on one of the Angles; and fired it as soon as fix'd to let the Indians know, if any were within hearing, that we had such Pieces; and thus our Fort, (if such a magnificent Name may be given to so miserable a Stockade) was finished in a Week, tho' it rain'd so hard every other Day that the Men could not work. (A, 233–4)

This passage deftly mirrors the separation of parts that Franklin recommends to the backcountry farmers when he is trying to arrange for Braddock's transportation needs, a segmented serpent that celebrates the handiwork of Franklin's men rather than his own leadership. Mr. Beatty's willingness to serve as steward of the rum is a further departure from the kind of traditional military practice that had given Braddock such confidence in the spurious validity of his Regulars.

The Moravian population that Franklin's men had come to protect discovered, during the early stages of the Seven Years' War, the fragility of some of its own assumptions. The massacre at Gnadenhütten had prompted the Moravians to make preparations to defend their primary settlement at Bethlehem even before the militia had arrived. They built a stockade, purchased weapons from New York, prepared piles of paving stones for their women to hurl on attackers from the windows "of their high Stone Houses," and organized their men into a garrison to stand watch. "I had suppos'd they were conscienciously scrupulous of bearing Arms," Franklin observed in the memoir, "But Common Sense aided by present Danger, will sometimes be too strong for whimsicall Opinions" (A, 232). August Spangenberg, the Moravian leader, told Franklin that his people were similarly surprised that their pacifism had collapsed so quickly in the face of threats. Braddock's poignant bewilderment—"Who'd have thought it?"—recurs among the settlers at Bethlehem, as they discover their own violent propensities, though a degree of cunning may have been involved in this misjudgment: "It seems they were either deceiv'd in themselves, or deceiv'd the Parliament," Franklin wrote, referring to the sect's exemption from military service.

During the visit that Franklin pays to Bethlehem on his way home from completing the fort at Gnadenhütten, his own whimsical opinions about the importance of a romantic bond in forming a happy marriage are tested by Moravian practices. When a young Moravian man feels inclined to get married, Franklin learns, he first approaches "the Elders of his Class," who then consult the "Elder Ladies" to establish the best fit between "the Tempers and Dispositions of their respective Pupils." Sometimes lots come into play in matching couples when several young women seem equally well suited for a given partner. Franklin is not satisfied with this approach to matrimonial treaties. Surely the "mutual Choice of the Parties" should decide the issue, he objects, otherwise some of these arranged marriages "may chance to be very unhappy." The reply of his Moravian host surprises and silences him: "And so they may, answer'd my Informer, if you let the Parties chuse for themselves.—Which indeed I could not deny" (A, 237).

This exchange, like Franklin's brief conversation with Braddock over military tactics, is a simple instance of choosing goodwill over victory. The wagon advertisement adopts the same approach to easing the potential antagonism between Pennsylvania's cautious farmers and their militant British visitors. For Franklin, the Seven Years' War offers opportunities for avoiding violence rather than deploying it, as he does when he convinces Mr. Beatty to combine his chaplain's duties with the liquor ration to sidestep a disciplinary issue, or when he and his men fire their small artillery swivel as soon as it is mounted on the palisade at Gnadenhütten to advertise their cannon's presence rather than to use it. The Indians were indeed within hearing when Franklin's men made this demonstration "to let the Indians know . . . that we had such Pieces" (A, 234). In patrolling the nearby countryside after the fort was finished, they found the signs that their audience had left behind:

> We met with no Indians, but we found the Places on the neighbouring Hills where they had lain to watch our Proceedings. There was an Art in their Contrivance of these Places that seems worth mention. It being Winter, a Fire was necessary for them. But a common Fire on the Surface of the Ground would by its Light have discover'd their Position at a Distance. They had therefore dug Holes in the Ground about three feet Diameter, and some what deeper. We saw where they had with their Hatchets cut off the Charcoal from the Sides of burnt Logs lying in the Woods. With these Coals they had made small Fires in the Bottom of the Holes, and we observ'd among the Weeds and Grass the Prints of their Bodies made by their laying all round with the Legs hanging down in the Holes to keep their Feet warm which with them is an essential Point. This kind of Fire, so manag'd, could not discover them either by its Light, Flame, Sparks or even Smoke. It appear'd that their Number was not great, and it seems they saw we were too many to be attack'd by them with Prospect of Advantage. (A, 234–5)

The memoir quietly stresses the extent to which the "proceedings" of the English and those of their observant enemies mimic one another, much as Franklin had mimicked the words of the Indian counselor at Carlisle. Each party practices a defensive "art" linked to the necessities of a hard life; each is skilled in the use of the ax or the hatchet to meet its needs; each manages fire with uncommon care in order to enhance its safety rather than its power of doing harm. Both the stockade and the fire pits awaken Franklin's love of measurement, his admiration for the little machines with which ingenuity and cunning address the threats to happiness or the incitements to curiosity that fill human experience.

CONCLUSION

Segmented Serpent

The pace of Franklin's narrative slows dramatically as he pieces together his account of the busy years between 1751, when he and Thomas Bond collaborate on building a hospital, and 1757, when he sails to England as the Pennsylvania Assembly's agent in its case at court against Thomas Penn. The bulk of the 1788 fragment of the memoir focuses on events that fall between the Carlisle treaty meeting in the autumn of 1753 and the immediate aftermath of the Braddock disaster a little over two years later. Franklin does not keep careful track of this month-by-month progression of incidents, and at several points in the story he appears to jumble names and meetings into confusion. The chronology is tightly coiled together, difficult to unravel, and even so it remains incomplete. In the course of discussing the Albany meeting and his plan of colonial union, Franklin never mentions the segmented serpent emblem and its provocative motto, "Join, or Die."[1]

The imperfect command of dates and details that this portion of his story displays is almost certainly a result of age and poor health, as well as a by-product of the extraordinary experiences that had filled the intervening decades. Franklin had a great deal to remember and to reflect upon in the clos-

Conclusion: Segmented Serpent 183

"Join, or Die," cartoon, *The Pennsylvania Gazette*, May 9, 1754.

ing months of his life. The opening stages of the Seven Years' War were more than thirty years in the past when Franklin began to reconstruct them. Nearly sixteen years of lobbying on behalf of the colonies in England, followed by nearly a decade of intense diplomatic activity in France, six ocean voyages, key roles in two continental conventions, and the associated personal and political stresses of a great revolution had all intervened to entangle the process of recollection. Even so the serpent emblem makes its presence felt in a variety of subtle ways during the closing pages of Franklin's book, not as a static political exhortation or an instrument of policy but as a figurative model for the devious paths of history. In sharing his apprehensions with General Braddock, as the expedition's baggage train was slowly taking shape, Franklin pictured the movement of the English army through the Pennsylvania woods as a variation on the serpent's image.[2]

After listening carefully to the general's ambitious plans for driving the French from the Ohio Valley in a four-month campaign, Franklin voiced his concerns:

> To be sure, Sir, if you arrive well before Duquesne, with these fine Troops so well provided with Artillery, that Place, not yet compleatly fortified, and as we hear with no very strong Garrison, can probably make but a short Resistance. The

only Danger I apprehend of Obstruction to your March, is from Ambuscades of Indians, who by constant Practice are dextrous in laying and executing them. And the slender Line near four Miles long, which your Army must make, may expose it to be attack'd by Surprize in its Flanks, and to be cut like a Thread into several Pieces, which from their Distance cannot come up in time to support each other. (A, 224)

An ambush is a tactical device, a tool that the Indians are "dextrous" in using, like the techniques they employ for keeping their gunlocks dry during weather that drenches Franklin's small militia detachment as it marches toward the massacre site at Gnadenhütten, or the charcoal pits that they dig for security and warmth as they watch Franklin's men build a frontier stockade. Many years earlier, Josiah Franklin had taught his restless son to admire and, eventually, to adapt just such skills to the construction of his own little machines. Constant practice and growing dexterity are equally applicable to the hypothetical problem of dismantling an army trying to wend its way through the wilderness, a challenge that Franklin cannot resist addressing, on the Indians' behalf, in this exchange with General Braddock.

The attack ultimately takes a different form from what Franklin had envisioned: not the surgical cutting of a slender thread, but the slaughter of soldiers "crowded together in a Huddle" and helpless without the guidance of their mounted officers, who had been "pick'd out as Marks" very early in the battle "and fell very fast" (A, 225). Remove the serpent's head, these Indian marksmen might have observed, and chaos results. But that ruthless lesson is not the implication of Franklin's emblem. Each segment of the serpent in his 1754 drawing is also an independent whole and in some instances more than a whole. From New England at one end to South Carolina at the other, the image is a map, a list, and a subtle form of prophecy, depicting the positions of separate communities, for the most part with separate governments, stretching from north to south along the North American seaboard.

In Franklin's day, this distance leaves the colonies too divided to support one another very readily in a common catastrophe, but the image suggests that each has a measure of self-sufficiency that equips it to survive on its own, and all are sufficiently attentive to their immediate neighbors to maintain a degree of sympathetic cohesion as a single political creature. The serpent's tail is a blank, not a menacing rattle, inviting the viewer to pencil in a new name, Georgia, which had just shed its status as a trustee province in 1752 to become a royal colony within a year or two of Franklin's drawing. Other blanks might succeed this one, with other names sketched in as the continental organism grew.

Franklin had visited most of these linked communities as deputy postmaster general—a title he had just assumed in 1753, the year before devising his emblem—and over his lifetime had played various roles in their affairs. He had financed the establishment of the first printer in South Carolina, prepared paper money for New Jersey, contributed to building an orphanage in Georgia, negotiated for cannon with New York, and been born and bred in Massachusetts, the chief member of a northeastern coalition that had considerable experience acting in concert to accomplish common goals. This northerly portion of the segmented serpent, at least, has already "joined" itself into the collective entity "New England," a dimension to Franklin's drawing that probably reflects his awareness of the experiments in confederation that the New England colonies had implemented, on various occasions, in the late seventeenth and early eighteenth centuries.[3] An attentive reader of Franklin's provocative cartoon, however, would not need to be well versed in history to note that his serpent is already changing: fusing together at one end and growing at the other, even in the absence of effective continental institutions to guide the design. It depicts a variety of social and temporal movements, as well as a geographic and political predicament.

This appreciation for the mixed significance of his emblem—its simultaneous embrace of several ongoing stories at once—lies behind the dismay that Franklin experiences when he encounters the dogmatic inflexibility of the English authorities whom he meets in the opening months of his long residence abroad. The final section of the memoir offers a brief glimpse of this experience. After a frustratingly slow departure for England as Pennsylvania's new colonial agent, followed by a harrowing adventure at sea, Franklin had barely settled into his London lodgings in 1757 when Lord Granville, the president of the Privy Council, arranged to see him so that Granville could deliver a lecture on the doctrines of imperial government, as he and his ministerial colleagues understood them. Acting as his own secretary, Franklin preserves Granville's words, as he does the speech of many other individuals, both prominent and obscure, in the course of telling his story:

> "You Americans have wrong Ideas of the Nature of your Constitution; you contend that the King's Instructions to his Governors are not Laws, and think yourselves at Liberty to regard or disregard them at your own Discretion. But

those Instructions are not like the Pocket Instructions given to a Minister going abroad, for regulating his Conduct in some trifling Point of Ceremony. They are first drawn up by Judges learned in the Laws; they are then considered, debated and perhaps amended in Council, after which they are signed by the King. They are then so far as relates to you, the *Law of the Land*; for THE KING IS THE LEGISLATOR OF THE COLONIES." (A, 261)

As far as the Americans are concerned, Granville argues, the body politic is a startling creature indeed: all royal head with very little need to consult other influential members of the Atlantic community, once England's learned judges, its counselors, and its king have had their say. "This was new Doctrine to me," Franklin noted in the memoir's closing pages, "I wrote it down as soon as I return'd to my Lodgings," anticipating the many written hints and records that would prove useful in the devious negotiations of the 1775 voyage letter.

But Granville's dismissive attitude is not so new to Franklin's reader. Edward Braddock had spoken in very similar terms of the unchallenged excellence of the king's regular troops, in contrast to the unprofessional colonial militia, and had displayed much the same indifference as Granville did to the importance of American advice. Four decades earlier, Josiah Franklin had thought it necessary to engage his twelve-year-old son's private inclinations in the momentous apprenticeship decision that he proposed for the boy. By contrast, as Granville portrays the imperial organism, the king and his Privy Council operate entirely without parliamentary involvement in governing the colonies and recognize no role for American inclinations at all. These circumstances seem suggestively similar to the near-fatal blindness that almost ends Franklin's diplomatic career before it had begun. A bow watchman on the packet ship carrying him to England was apparently so sleepy that despite many warnings to "*Look well out before, there*," he had failed to see a lighthouse signal marking the treacherous rocks off the Scilly Isles (A, 258). The packet captain was sound asleep, and only the quick action of another sea captain who was a passenger on the vessel prevented a wreck. "This Deliverance impress'd me strongly with the Utility of Lighthouses," Franklin drily remarks, but even a warning light "as big as a Cart Wheel" (the memoir implies) is useless if the watchman is asleep. This incident, like many in Franklin's book, quickly becomes a prophetic emblem for his diplomatic experience.

In the memoir's account, Franklin's first exchanges with Thomas and Richard Penn are every bit as unpromising as his encounter with Lord Granville. John

Fothergill plays the role of intermediary in arranging this meeting too, with no more success than he will have eighteen years later, as he and David Barclay convey Franklin's conciliatory "hints" to members of Parliament who hope to prevent civil war. In 1757, Franklin discovers, the Penns are not in a conciliatory mood. "The Conversation at first consisted of mutual Declarations of Disposition to reasonable Accommodation," he notes in his book, "but I suppose each Party had its own Ideas of what should be meant by *reasonable*" (A, 262). The wording echoes Franklin's account of the conveniences of being a reasonable creature when the savory odor of fried cod first begins to erode the principles of a young runaway apprentice. At this initial meeting with the Penns, a clash between reasonable creatures quickly ensues, with the proprietors refusing to respond at all to "the Heads of our Complaints in Writing" that Franklin had prepared, and Franklin in turn refusing to discuss the complaints with legal agents but only with the Penns themselves. The parties reach an impasse over the proprietors' insistence that Franklin had shown an offensive "want of Formality" in his dealings with them, though they eventually consent to a single taxation act by the Pennsylvania Assembly when Lord Mansfield, the king's chief justice, unexpectedly mediates a compromise.

This development proves to be a perfect application of Franklin's long-standing conviction "that *Truth, Sincerity and Integrity* in Dealings between Man and Man, were of the utmost Importance to the Felicity of Life," the lesson he had learned from the collapse of his early infatuation with Deism (A, 114). While lawyers for the Assembly and the Penns were arguing their positions before the Privy Council, Mansfield beckoned Franklin into a nearby clerk's chamber "and ask'd me if I was really of Opinion that no Injury would be done the Proprietary Estate in the Execution of the Act. I said, Certainly. Then says he, you can have little Objection to enter into an Engagement to assure that Point. I answer'd None at all" (A, 266). In the informal confines of the clerk's chamber, a simple "certainly," not a deferential "certainly, my lord," will do. Franklin's personal assurance proves good enough for Mansfield, much as a similar engagement on Franklin's part did for the Pennsylvania farmers who supplied wagons to Braddock's army a few years earlier. A written agreement is quickly drafted, and the Penns are forced for the time being to stifle their resentments.

These events bring Franklin's manuscript to a close. Had he lived to carry the narrative forward, through the genealogical trip that he and William took in 1758, the honorary degree from St. Andrews, his brief return to America in 1762, followed by a second mission to England and ending with the 1774 Privy Council experience, a far more complex sequence of disappointments and triumphs would have emerged, eventually arriving at Benjamin Vaughan's adulatory letter on the threshold of Franklin's departure from Paris at the end of the American Revolution. But the author of the memoir would have faced peculiar difficulties in writing about events involving many living witnesses to his conduct whose views of Franklin's performance would almost certainly have differed from his own. He would have confronted, as well, unusual temptations to make "Reprisals on my Adversaries," as the memoir admitted he was once tempted to do. And a discussion of his diplomatic career in England or his reception later by the French would have provided opportunities to gratify his vanity that few writers would have had the strength to resist.

Instead, Franklin compresses the full trajectory of his life story—from obscurity to fame, ridicule to praise—into the handful of pages that the memoir devotes to describing the circuitous growth of his scientific reputation. Manuscript evidence suggests that along with the memoir's account of the Pennsylvania hospital bill, and its treatment of the "trifling Matters" of paving and street cleaning, these are among the last passages of the book that Franklin wrote, probably sometime in the early months of 1789, before illness forced him to put the memoir aside.[4] Early in 1790, Franklin would add six paragraphs to the book, describing his negotiations with Lord Mansfield and the Penns, but the belated description of his interest in electricity, immediately following the Braddock episodes, has a scope and completeness that few other portions of the story can match. The account Franklin offers of "the Rise and Progress of my Philosophical Reputation" echoes the wording of his opening sentences so closely as to suggest that he intends this segment of the narrative serpent to echo the whole.

The story begins, as the memoir does, with the feelings of surprise and pleasure that Franklin experiences not in discovering little anecdotes of his Ecton ancestors but in first witnessing Archibald Spencer's electrical demonstrations during a trip to Boston in 1743. Shortly thereafter, Peter Collinson sends to the Library Company a glass tube for collecting charges of static electricity, along with a description of how to use this piece of apparatus to conduct simple experiments. Franklin quickly puts the pieces together: Collinson's tube and the procedures he describes, Spencer's Boston exhibits that Franklin learns to repeat, and a few new electrical demonstrations of Franklin's own devising—

all of which he practices performing at his home for delighted audiences "who came to see these new Wonders" (A, 241):

> To divide a little this Incumbrance among my Friends, I caused a Number of similar Tubes to be blown at our Glass-House, with which they furnish'd themselves, so that we had at length several Performers. Among these the principal was Mr. Kinnersley, an ingenious Neighbour, who being out of Business, I encouraged to undertake showing the Experiments for Money, and drew up for him two Lectures, in which the Experiments were rang'd in such Order and accompanied with Explanations in such Method, as that the foregoing should assist in Comprehending the following. He procur'd an elegant Apparatus for the purpose, in which all the little Machines that I had roughly made for myself, were nicely form'd by Instrument-makers. His Lectures were well attended and gave great Satisfaction; and after some time he went thro' the Colonies exhibiting them in every capital Town, and pick'd up some Money. (A, 241–42)

This account too is a narrative adaptation, in several phases, of the segmented serpent: Franklin first divides the experimental burden by duplicating Collinson's original tube several times over and distributing the copies among Philadelphia's electrical "Performers"; the lectures that he prepares for Kinnersley's use are ranged in a supportive sequence that ties the little machines together, like the portions of his 1754 cartoon; Kinnersley in turn becomes an itinerant lecturer, diffusing satisfaction through "every capital Town" of the colonies that the serpent emblem depicts, a common currency of interest that mimics the movement of the electric "fluid" that had originally captured Franklin's attention.

While Kinnersley goes on the road, his mentor goes to his desk and writes several letters to Collinson that describe "our Success" at using the glass tube that Collinson had sent, but these reports (unlike the original gift) meet with a mixed reception in England. When Collinson reads them to the Royal Society, the members dismiss Franklin's results as unworthy of appearing in the society's transactions. One of the members later writes him that his speculation "on the Sameness of Lightning with Electricity . . . was laught at by the Connoisseurs" (A, 242). This initial response repeats Braddock's patronizing amusement at Franklin's military advice and anticipates the scorn that the Penns express for his provincial rudeness, but Collinson and Fothergill arrange for Franklin's letters to appear as a published pamphlet that grows "by the Additions that arriv'd afterwards" to "a Quarto Volume, which has had five Editions" (A, 243). Segment by segment, letter by letter, the treatise that establishes Franklin's international reputation acquires scope and consequence, becoming both a scientific triumph and yet another similitude for the communities depicted in the serpent emblem, whose curiosity, ingenuity, and energy Franklin's letters embody.

An initial ambivalence similar to the ridicule of the Royal Society greets Franklin's work in France, charged with a degree of national as well as metropolitan resentment. The memoir charts this process as well, with particular care to note the vindication of modest diffidence that it provides. The Count de Buffon, a prominent admirer of Franklin's quarto volume, has the *Experiments and Observations on Electricity* translated into French, but the memoir records that the Abbé Nollet, "an able Experimenter, who had form'd and publish'd a Theory of Electricity which then had the general Vogue," resented this scientific competitor: "He could not at first believe that such a Work came from America," Franklin wrote, "and said it must have been fabricated by his Enemies at Paris, to decry his System" (A, 243). Once Nollet is convinced of his rival's existence, he tries to ignite a published dispute between them that Franklin declines to join, "believing it was better to spend what time I could spare from public Business in making new Experiments, than in Disputing about those already made" (A, 244). The outcome, Franklin reports, "gave me no Cause to repent my Silence." Other experimenters defend Franklin's book and oversee its translation into Italian, German, and Latin, until its "Doctrine" is "universally adopted by the Philosophers of Europe," while Nollet "liv'd to see himself the last of his Sect" (A, 244).

These incidents too give Franklin a chance to revisit many of the critical lessons of his story: his appreciation for the social value of silence and for the pervasive presence of vanity in human affairs, his wary view of sectarian blindness and the futility of disputes, his faith in the impact of associations as agents of change. The clash with Nollet echoes and recasts General Braddock's curious faith in the unshakable "validity" of English troops and anticipates Franklin's dismay at Lord Granville's stifling legal theory that the king was the Legislator of the Colonies. In time, the so-called *Philadelphia Experiments* would subdue all opposition; other investigators repeated Franklin's success at "procuring Lightning from the Clouds." The Royal Society named him a member, waived his dues, and awarded him "the Gold Medal of Sir Godfrey Copley for the year 1753," a turning point in imperial history as well as in Franklin's personal life, less than a year before the rejection of the Albany Plan of Union and the arrival of Edward Braddock's troops would set in motion the events that ultimately led to revolution.

Franklin scrupulously records the complete formal name of the Copley prize in his memoir, relishes the society's decision to waive his twenty-five-guinea membership fee, and takes note of the "very handsome Speech of the President Lord Macclesfield," in conferring the medal, "wherein I was highly honoured" (A, 246). The feeling of vindication must have been particularly gratifying in light of the thirty-five eventful years that had passed since Lord Macclesfield spoke. This scientific triumph forms a perfect counterweight to Franklin's public humiliation before the Privy Council in 1774, to the attacks leveled at his character from the floor of the House of Lords a year later, or to Richard Howe's bald attempts at bribery as Franklin is preparing to leave England in the spring of 1775—a final instance of the figurative scales that the memoir imposes on so much of Franklin's experience. In 1771 as he began to write his book, he had candidly admitted that in doing so he could at least indulge the natural "Inclination" of an old man to reflect upon his past. Eighteen years later, as Franklin looks back on his scientific legacy and adds a few more sentences to a manuscript that he will never live to finish, he takes comfort from this final interplay between the trifling satisfactions and great accomplishments of his life.

Notes

The references cited below offer a selective account of the most important commentary on Franklin's book, particularly work written on the memoir since the simultaneous appearance of the 1964 Yale edition and of Robert Sayre's pioneering study of American autobiography, *The Examined Self*. I have emphasized the sources that were most helpful to me, and I have tried to clarify the many instances in which this study differs from well-established lines of interpretation. Franklin's critics have not always shared his interest in curtailing verbal disputes, but it was my intent to keep to Franklin's standards of modest diffidence in the disagreements that I document here. Although each note number links to a specific place in the text, I have tried to replicate the experience of a bibliographic essay in the notes as a whole, so that readers who are inclined to do so may postpone consulting any annotation until they have finished the entire book.

INTRODUCTION: Accident and Design

1. Most modern paperback editions of Franklin's memoir give a brief description of its unfinished nature, but the introduction to the 1964 Yale edition, edited by Leonard Labaree and many colleagues, offers the most detailed, widely available account of this engrossing textual history. See *The Autobiography of Benjamin Franklin* (New Haven: Yale UP, 1964), pp. 25–36. I have assumed that Franklin intended the textual history of his manuscript to engage the reader's reconstructive energies precisely as it has engaged the attention of its editors for more than two hundred years. Two recent discussions of the erratic journey of Franklin's book into print are important supplements to the Yale introduction: James N. Green and Peter Stallybrass, *Benjamin Franklin: Writer and Printer* (New Castle, DE: Oak Knoll Press, Library Company of Philadelphia, and the British Library, 2006), pp. 145–71; and Christopher Hunter, "From Print to Print: The First Complete Edition of Benjamin Franklin's Autobiography," *Papers of the Bibliographic Society of America* 101 (December 2007): 481–505. See also Max Farrand's introduction to *Benjamin Franklin's Memoirs: Parallel Text Edition* (Berkeley: U of California P, 1949) and Steven Carl Arch, "Benjamin Franklin's Autobiography Then and Now," in *The Cambridge Companion to Benjamin Franklin*, ed. Carla Mulford (New York: Cambridge UP, 2008), pp. 159–64.

2. For a discussion of the James and Vaughan letters, as well as Franklin's "Notes of my Life," see J. A. Leo Lemay and P. M. Zall, eds., *The Autobiography of Benjamin Franklin: A Genetic Text* (Knoxville: U of Tennessee P, 1981), pp. 182–90 and 196–202. Neither of the original letters survives, and the "Notes" are a composite of corrections and additions that Franklin added to the copy that Abel James sent him in 1782. Lemay

and Zall insist that Franklin did not intend to print the "Notes," but nothing in the memoir itself or in the few letters where Franklin mentioned the memoir near the end of his life suggests any change in the structural intentions that he expressed in his manuscript. See the excerpts from the correspondence that Lemay and Zall collect in *Benjamin Franklin's Autobiography* (New York: W. W. Norton, 1986), pp. 205–7.

3. The "Notes," in other words, recast the figure of the segmented serpent in textual form. Franklin's failure to mention the emblem in the memoir itself has discouraged most readers from pursuing the comparison, though Karen S. Cook suggests some of the adaptive possibilities of the image in "Benjamin Franklin and the Snake That Would Not Die," *British Library Journal* 22 (1996): 88–111. Lester Olson's book, *Benjamin Franklin's Vision of American Community: A Study in Rhetorical Iconology* (Columbia: U of South Carolina P, 2004), explores Franklin's lifelong interest in emblems of social wholeness and fragmentation, including the segmented serpent (27–76). Timothy Shannon treats the image in the immediate context of the Albany Congress, along with the many variants that Franklin's cartoon inspired in other colonial newspapers. See *Indians and Colonists at the Crossroads of Empire: The Albany Congress of 1754* (Ithaca: Cornell UP, 2000), pp. 83–113.

4. Modern editors have cleared up the Riddlesden-Cornwallis confusion, but none have touched on the odd fact that Franklin used the alias in his "Notes" and "Riddlesden" in his text, when he was writing both documents during the same visit to the Shipley estate in 1771. Though he went over the "Notes" carefully after Abel James had supplied him with a copy, he never corrected this slip himself. A brief account of William Riddlesden's career appears in the appendices to the Yale edition (A, 296), with more detail provided by Lemay and Zall in their notes to the Norton edition of *Benjamin Franklin's Autobiography* (196).

5. The memoir has often struck readers as emotionally impoverished, particularly when Franklin touches on his children or his marriage. See, for instance, Eric Wertheimer's observation, in *Underwriting: The Poetics of Insurance in America, 1722–1872* (Stanford, CA: Stanford UP, 2006), that Franklin was unable "to account for sentiment" in his book or to confront the consequences of traumatic loss, a conclusion that neglects the complex effects of reticence that the narrative repeatedly exploits. Claude-Anne Lopez takes a far more subtle approach to Franklin's affective life, both in his correspondence and in his memoir, though she too struggles to capture its essence: "Neither demigod nor unfeeling egoist, this is the Franklin I have been groping to understand." See her "Subjective Preface" to Claude-Anne Lopez and Eugenia Herbert, *The Private Franklin: The Man and His Family* (New York: W. W. Norton, 1975). On the death of Francis Folger Franklin, see J. A. Leo Lemay, *The Life of Benjamin Franklin*, vol. 2: *Printer and Publisher, 1730–1747* (Philadelphia: U of Pennsylvania P, 2006), pp. 23–24.

6. See the text of Jefferson's autobiography in *Thomas Jefferson: Writings* (New York: Literary Classics of the United States, 1984), pp. 99–100.

7. Jefferson was particularly troubled by the dismissive attitude that William Temple Franklin displayed when Jefferson returned the manuscript: "As he put it into his pocket," Jefferson recalled, "he said carelessly he had either the original, or another copy of it, I do not recollect which. This last expression struck my attention forcibly, and for the first time suggested to me the thought that Dr. Franklin had meant it as a confidential deposit in my hands, and that I had done wrong in parting from it" (ibid.,

100). See Jennifer Kennedy's account of the episode in "Parricide of Memory: Thomas Jefferson's Memoir and the French Revolution," *American Literature* 72 (September 2000): 553–73. The editors of the Yale *Papers* call Franklin's 1775 narrative "one of the most vivid that he ever wrote" and conclude that Franklin intended it to be part of his autobiography. See P, 21.541.

8. For Tocqueville's comments on the "mother science" of association, see volume 2, part 2, chapter 5, in Alexis de Tocqueville, *Democracy in America* (1945; rpt., New York: Knopf, 1994), pp. 106–10. Eduardo Nolla's critical edition of Tocqueville's book includes Tocqueville's references to Franklin's work and to the anecdote in the memoir describing James Franklin's ruse for printing the *New England Courant* under Benjamin's name. See *Democracy in America*, ed. Eduardo Nolla, trans. James T. Schleifer (Indianapolis: Liberty Fund, 2010), 2. 674, 684.

CHAPTER 1: Great Works and Little Anecdotes

1. For the detailed and affectionate letter of September 6, 1758, that Franklin wrote to Deborah ("My Dear Child") describing this genealogical trip, see P, 8.133–46.

2. Modern readers often overlook the mix of public and private tension that lies behind the first part of the memoir. For a sense of the context in which Franklin wrote, see Claude-Anne Lopez and Eugenia Herbert, *The Private Franklin: The Man and His Family* (New York: W. W. Norton, 1975), pp. 188–96; Willard Sterne Randall, *A Little Revenge: Benjamin Franklin and His Son* (Boston: Little Brown, 1984), pp. 229–44; and Ormond Seavey, *Becoming Benjamin Franklin: The Autobiography and the Life* (University Park: Pennsylvania State UP, 1988), pp. 14–15. William Shurr suggests that Franklin took advantage of the memoir's first part in particular to attack William's character and mock him for his illegitimate birth, an instance of the strained antagonism that critics often bring to the reading of Franklin's book. See "'Now, Gods, Stand Up for Bastards': Reinterpreting Benjamin Franklin's *Autobiography*," *American Literature* 64 (September 1992): 435–51. Eric Wertheimer turns to Benjamin Vaughan's letter for evidence of the anxiety that Wertheimer believes Franklin strives to conceal in his narrative, but anxiety is implicit in nearly every feature of Franklin's opening sentences. See *Underwriting: The Poetics of Insurance in America, 1722–1872* (Stanford, CA: Stanford UP, 2006), p. 35.

3. The Interpreter's House is Christian's first stop after Good Will admits him through the Wicket-gate and his journey begins. After lighting a candle that signals his role as a source of illumination, the Interpreter schools Christian on how to read the similitudes on which Bunyan bases his narrative. Sixty years ago Charles Sanford called Franklin's memoir a secularized version of *The Pilgrim's Progress*, but he made very little effort to explore this broad, thematic judgment. See *American Quarterly* 6 (Winter 1954): 297–310. More recently William Spengeman treats the memoir as an allegorical successor to Bunyan, with "the rule of human Reason" as its object. See *The Forms of Autobiography: Episodes in the History of a Literary Genre* (New Haven: Yale UP, 1980), pp. 53–60. Myra Jehlen, in *Readings at the Edge of Literature* (Chicago: U of Chicago P, 2002), suggests that the memoir strives to tie Bunyan's trope of the *Pilgrim's Progress* to Poor Richard's "Way to Wealth," making "the world safe for a fertile selfishness and duplicity," as Jehlen puts it (31). None of these approaches seems to me to account for the obvious pleasure Franklin took in Bunyan's work—a riddle that the

balance of this chapter hopes to address. R. Jackson Wilson is more perceptive concerning Franklin's invocation of literary models, including Bunyan, though he focuses most closely on the intriguing links between Franklin's moral principles and Paul's letter to the Philippians, which Franklin cites in the 1784 fragment of the memoir. See *Figures of Speech: American Writers and the Literary Marketplace from Benjamin Franklin to Emily Dickinson* (Baltimore: Johns Hopkins UP, 1989), pp. 33–40.

4. See Leo Lemay's account of Browne's career in *The Life of Benjamin Franklin, Journalist*, vol. 1: *1706–1730* (Philadelphia: U of Pennsylvania P, 2006), pp. 222–23.

5. Edwin Wolfe expressed doubts about the attribution of the pamphlet collection to Franklin's uncle, based on his comparison of marginalia from a few of the recovered pamphlet volumes to some commonplace books "known to have been kept by Uncle Benjamin." But Franklin was convinced, by "the handwriting and various other circumstances" connected with the collection, that the volumes were assembled by his uncle (P, 18.176). I am inclined to accept Franklin's opinion, but see Wolfe's comment in "The Reconstruction of Benjamin Franklin's Library: An Unorthodox Jigsaw Puzzle," *Papers of the Bibliographical Society of America* 56 (1962): 1–26.

6. Robert Middlekauf sketches out this lifelong pattern of deep intellectual friendships at the beginning of *Benjamin Franklin and His Enemies* (Berkeley: U of California P, 1996), linking it to the unusual range and warmth of Franklin's bonds with men and women, children and adults, thinkers, tradesmen, artists, and politicians alike (1–21). By contrast, many literary and cultural critics insist on seeing Franklin as almost exclusively calculating in his personal life. See, for instance, Grantland Rice, *The Transformation of Authorship in America* (Chicago: U of Chicago P, 1997), pp. 45–69, or Michael Warner, *The Letters of the Republic* (Cambridge, MA: Harvard UP, 1990), who views Franklin's pleasure in the *Spectator* essays, for instance, as a cool manipulation of "printed artifacts" for instrumental purposes (78–79).

7. Stanley Fish stresses the intimate links between "reading and wayfaring" in Bunyan's book but neglects to point out that the frontispiece to *The Pilgrim's Progress* is itself a visual statement of this relationship, extending it to authors as well. Franklin invites us to consider the implications of this image when he recalls with such fondness the book's famous "cuts." See *Self-Consuming Artifacts: The Experience of Seventeenth-Century Literature* (Berkeley: U of California P, 1972), pp. 224–64. Fish, along with Wolfgang Iser in *The Implied Reader* (Baltimore: Johns Hopkins UP, 1974), is among the most useful students of Bunyan's figurative methods. Together Fish and Iser suggest models for understanding Franklin's adaptation of similitudes and parallels to his own story.

8. The memoir keeps "accounts" in several senses of the term, but beginning with Joseph Dennie's fierce attack, in an 1802 edition of his *Portfolio* magazine, on the "pitiful system of [spiritual] economics" that he believed Franklin represented, many critics have insisted on applying the ancient bookkeeping trope literally in treating the memoir. D. H. Lawrence is only the most famous of these hostile readers. For a recent instance, see Rekha Rosha, "Accounting Capital, Race, and Benjamin Franklin's 'Pecuniary Habits' of Mind in the *Autobiography*," in *Culture, Capital, and Representation*, ed. Robert J. Balfour (New York: Palgrave Macmillan, 2010), pp. 35–48. Grantland Rice quotes Joseph Dennie's attack in *The Transformation of Authorship in America*, p. 67.

9. Both of these public examinations continue to be popular dramatic vignettes with biographers, but the 1766 interview before Parliament was also famous in Frank-

lin's lifetime and helped restore his American reputation at the end of the Stamp Act Crisis. H. W. Brands opens his book with a re-creation of the 1774 Privy Council hearing. See *The First American: The Life and Times of Benjamin Franklin* (New York: Anchor, 2000), pp. 1–8. For biographical accounts of the role of Franklin's 1766 testimony in the repeal of the Stamp Act and the securing of Franklin's radical credentials, see Esmond Wright, *Franklin of Philadelphia* (Cambridge, MA: Belknap, 1986), pp. 194–97; Gordon Wood, *The Americanization of Benjamin Franklin* (New York: Penguin, 2004), pp. 118–20; Edmund S. Morgan, *Benjamin Franklin* (New Haven: Yale UP, 2002), pp. 156–59.

10. The Yale editors document Franklin's misattribution without comment, but this extended performance of the modest reader as reluctant editor is surely presented as a subtle piece of theater. Franklin appears to have confused the Earl of Roscommon's *Essay on Translated Verse* (1684) with the work of Pope, but within a few lines of the passage that Franklin transcribes, Roscommon offers a couplet on human self-entrapment that sheds an interesting light on Franklin's purposes: "But what a thoughtless Animal is Man, / How very Active in his own Trepan!"

11. This scene of reading has attracted the attention of Franklin's critics, many of whom see it as an example of the furtive influence of print in Franklin's narrative or of the paternalistic power of "text" in his story. See, for instance, Jennifer Kennedy's comments on the joint stool—Bible combination as a "machine . . . for deception" in "Death Effects: Revisiting the Conceit of Franklin's Memoir," *Early American Literature* 36 (2001): 211–12. Read as an emblem, however, the scene is a much more intriguing mental drama.

12. For an account of the history of the Breughel engraving and the proverb it illustrates, see Wolfgang Mieder, *Proverbs: A Handbook* (Westport, CT: Greenwood, 2004), pp. 34–43. Breughel's image is part of the family of emblems depicting the integration of parts into wholes to which the segmented serpent also belongs. The frontispiece to Hobbes's *Leviathan* is perhaps the most famous of these: an image of the king as a crowned head set on a torso composed of the aggregate heads of his subjects. The Library Company of Philadelphia owned Hobbes's book, probably the same "very scarce" edition that Franklin had advertised for sale from his printshop ten years before using the segmented serpent to dramatize the need for union at the Albany Conference. See *A Catalogue of Choice and Valuable Books* (Philadelphia: B. Franklin, 1744).

13. Franklin's "Notes of my Life" records his "return to eating Flesh" in its proper chronological place during his 1723 voyage from Boston to New York (A, 268). His decision to move the story keeps the fragmented nature of the narrative in the forefront of the reader's mind, as well as extending the implications of the Breughel emblem to portions of his life in Philadelphia. R. Jackson Wilson stresses this connection too, calling the episode a "parable" of eighteenth-century hierarchical social relations that signals Franklin's interest in becoming one of the "terminal predators" in the eating chain. See *Figures of Speech*, p. 48. John Lynen's metaphor of the "snapshot" scene strikes me as more applicable to this instance of Franklin's emblematic imagination. See *The Design of the Present: Essays on Time and Form in American Literature* (New Haven: Yale UP, 1969), p. 146. This particular snapshot is aimed less at social relations than at the psychological imbalance between principle and inclination that Franklin places on a figurative scale as he retells this story.

14. The curious absence of Deborah Read's father from this portion of Franklin's

book leads Leo LeMay to speculate that Franklin must have proposed marriage to Deborah at some point after John Read's death on September 2, 1724. But Franklin's decision not to mention this fact, at any point in the memoir, confers an unusual measure of authority on Deborah's mother, making her one of a series of influential women who help shape the first part of his story. See *The Life of Benjamin Franklin*, vol. 1: *Journalist, 1706–1730*, p. 257.

15. Franklin takes some pains, in these portions of his book, to establish a sense of dependency that many readers confuse with religious indifference. Revelation "as such" exerts no claim on his convictions, but revelation as a storehouse of psychological and moral truth does. The second part of the memoir makes clear that in Franklin's view this storehouse is not entirely the product of human accumulation. Many readers, though, see Franklin's religious life in sharply different terms. "The piety and the contrition of the early pages of the *Autobiography* are a rhetorical ruse," Mitchell Breitwieser bluntly declares in *Cotton Mather and Benjamin Franklin: The Price of Representative Personality* (New York: Cambridge UP, 1984), p. 239; Myra Jehlen largely agrees in *Readings at the Edge of Literature* (29). Nancy Glazener recently concluded that religious feeling was no more than a shadowy residue in Franklin's mind, replaced by a focus on the socially useful effects of mutual self-interest. See "Benjamin Franklin and the Limits of Secular Civil Society," *American Literature* 80 (June 2008): 223–25.

16. As the paragraphs that follow try to make clear, the memoir's vivid portrait of Josiah Franklin is one of the finest features of the 1771 fragment, concise and yet sufficiently rich in suggestive detail to convey the complexity and depth of this influential relationship. Jennifer Kennedy, however, is representative of many readers who detect a latent hostility in these episodes: "Franklin's sketch of Josiah Franklin does not bring him back to life, as his own autobiography does, but rather seals his grave." See "Death Effects: Revisiting the Conceit of Franklin's Memoir," *Early American Literature* 36 (2001): 218–19. One could just as easily argue that Franklin's narrative exposes the emotional texture of the epitaph that he wrote for his parents, filling in the intimate particulars that lie behind its conventional lessons and bringing the epitaph itself to life. That may be why Franklin breaks into the narrative immediately after transcribing the epitaph: to dramatize the power of memory over the impersonal claims of method. For a more favorable response to the portrait of Josiah, see Herbert Leibowitz, *Fabricating Lives: Explorations in American Autobiography* (New York: Alfred Knopf, 1989), pp. 37–38.

CHAPTER 2: Imposing Forms

1. The March 22, 1775, letter has remained in the Franklin papers, rather than joining the other parts of the memoir, despite the clear intentions expressed in "Notes of my Life" and in the deathbed exchanges with Thomas Jefferson that strongly suggest Franklin meant to include some form of the letter in his narrative. Its absence has led Christopher Looby, for instance, to conclude that Franklin sought to avoid writing about the Revolution altogether in the memoir. See *Voicing America: Language, Literary Form and the Origins of the United States* (Chicago: U of Chicago P, 1996), pp. 99–144. David Waldstreicher presents Franklin's 1775 departure from England as the culminating escape of a crafty "runaway," but even a cursory look at the story the March 1775 letter tells would have led him to dramatically alter that characterization.

See *Runaway America: Benjamin Franklin, Slavery, and the American Revolution* (New York: Hill and Wang, 2004), p. 208.

2. Jonathan Shipley's aphorism on admirable works and wretched tools suggests a model of the mixed nature of writing as well as a model of character. By contrast with the finished product that Benjamin Vaughan or Abel James had hoped to see, Franklin's surviving memoir-in-manuscript is a wretched compromise—as any book inevitably is—but, as such, the narrative blends principle with contingency, in its mixed form, very much as Franklin does in the ethical systems that he devises for himself. In this sense the memoir is more carefully shaped than it has seemed to be to many readers, though not in the "bifocal" fashion that R. Jackson Wilson suggests in *Figures of Speech: American Writers and the Literary Marketplace from Benjamin Franklin to Emily Dickinson* (Baltimore: Johns Hopkins UP, 1989), where he divides the book into halves that describe a trajectory from "being good" to "doing good," from "private" to "public" stories. Divisions are never that pure in Franklin's mind.

3. For the Collins dunking interpolation, see J. A. Leo Lemay and P. M. Zall, eds., *The Autobiography of Benjamin Franklin: A Genetic Text*, (Knoxville: U of Tennessee P, 1981), p. 33.

4. Characterizing Franklin's marriage as a love story is not a popular way of seeing the relationship. See, for instance, Ruth Bloch's assessment in "Women, Love, and Virtue in the Thought of Edwards and Franklin," in *Benjamin Franklin, Jonathan Edwards, and the Representation of American Culture*, ed. Barbara B. Oberg and Harry S. Stout (New York: Oxford UP, 1993), pp. 142–46. For a much fuller and more sensitive discussion of the marriage, see Claude-Anne Lopez and Eugenia Herbert, *The Private Franklin: The Man and His Family* (New York: W. W. Norton, 1975), pp. 16–41.

5. As the codfish-eating episode among others indicates, Franklin is interested in states of balance, and in the constant adjustments that a restless equilibrium requires, not in the notion of static cancellation—of "books" that are "closed"—that many readers adapt from a reductive model of the ledger and apply to Franklin's ethical system.

6. For an account of Bunyan's career and its literary range, as the Franklins of Ecton might have noted it, see Christopher Hill, *A Tinker and a Poor Man: John Bunyan and His Church, 1628–1688* (New York: Alfred Knopf, 1989), pp. 41–153. See too N. H. Keeble, "John Bunyan's Literary Life," in *The Cambridge Companion to John Bunyan*, ed. Anne Dunan-Page (New York: Cambridge UP, 2010), pp. 13–25.

7. See the note to this passage in A, 82.

8. Stanley Fish's observations in *Self-Consuming Artifacts: The Experience of Seventeenth-Century Literature* (Berkeley: U of California P, 1972), pp. 238–50, on the significance of what Christian clearly sees and what he only "thinks" he sees, as he begins his pilgrimage, suggest that Franklin may have derived this sly stress on what one "thinks" one likes or believes from *The Pilgrim's Progress*. The speckled ax story is frequently slighted by inattentive readers who take it to be a comparatively grim exhortation to grind relentlessly away at ineradicable faults. See, for instance, Wilson, *Figures of Speech*, p. 40, or Gordon Wood, *The Americanization of Benjamin Franklin* (New York: Penguin, 2004), p. 206.

9. For the most complete and perceptive account of Franklin's interest in an extended parallel between his memoir and the Letter to the Philippians, see Wilson, *Figures of Speech*, pp. 37–40.

10. The motto for Sincerity is an especially vivid instance of the manner in which Franklin's explanatory precepts repeatedly dramatize the constant and bewildering interchange between any given virtue and its opposite, not the silencing of economically disadvantageous traits that Mitchell Breitwieser detects in his admittedly "quick survey" of these complicated ethical statements. See *Cotton Mather and Benjamin Franklin: The Price of Representative Personality* (New York: Cambridge UP, 1984), pp. 282–85.

11. This motto contains the seeds of Robert Middlekauf's theme in *Benjamin Franklin and His Enemies* (Berkeley: U of California P, 1996).

12. Franklin thought highly enough of this prayer to include it in his daily regimen, yet even readers who do attend to it frequently slight its language. Nancy Glazener, for instance, finds in it only "the leftovers of religious feeling," the outcome of what she sees as "the deforming effects of interest-thinking" on Franklin's consciousness. See "Benjamin Franklin and the Limits of Secular Civil Society," *American Literature* 80 (June 2008): 225.

13. See Alexis de Tocqueville, *Democracy in America*, vol. 2, part 2, chap. 8 (1945; rpt., New York: Knopf, 1994), pp. 121–24.

14. Some readers see the precepts for Chastity and Humility, in particular, as representative of Franklin's pervasive insincerity. "Franklin's humility has no more to do with Christian humility than his purity has to do with Christian purity," Mitchell Breitwieser declares in *Cotton Mather and Benjamin Franklin: The Price of Representative Personality*, p. 284. Myra Jehlen is much less strident but no less dismissive when she suggests that Franklin meant "Imitate Jesus and Socrates" as a joke. See *Readings at the Edge of Literature* (Chicago: U of Chicago P, 2002), p. 8.

CHAPTER 3: The Scramble of Life

1. The degree to which the memoir is a unified or a disjointed performance divides its readers almost as sharply as the writing of the manuscript itself is divided and distributed across the last two decades of Franklin's life. Robert Sayre contends that the memoir displays only "a sense of order, no sense of form," presenting "three forms and identities" rather than a single authorial voice. See *The Examined Self: Benjamin Franklin, Henry Adams, Henry James* (Princeton: Princeton UP, 1964), pp. 15–16. Christopher Looby concurs in this "formal incoherence," attributing it to Franklin's inability or unwillingness to assimilate the story of the Revolution into his book. See *Voicing America: Language, Literary Form and the Origins of the United States* (Chicago: U of Chicago P, 1996), pp. 127–28. Edward White suggests that the book is both coherent and incoherent, reflecting as it does the shift in Franklin's ideological stance from the revolutionary "left" to the Federalist "right" in the memoir's long third section. See "Urbane Bifocals: The Federalist Sociology of Benjamin Franklin's *Autobiography*," *ALH* 11 (Spring 1999): 1–33. By contrast, in *The Design of the Present: Essays on Time and Form in American Literature* (New Haven: Yale UP, 1969), pp. 145–49, John Lynen finds a "firm pattern of causation" throughout the narrative, pointed toward describing the emergence of the revolutionary autobiographer who writes most of the book, and Ormond Seavey finds a single, consistent "consciousness" controlling the pages. See *Becoming Benjamin Franklin: The Autobiography and The Life* (University Park: Pennsylvania State UP, 1988), pp. 1–96. Few readers, however, pay much

attention to Franklin's own interest in the figures of unity and disunity, of joining and breaking apart, that pervade the memoir. These in turn suggest his determination to sustain the debate itself rather than settle its outcome. The Junto is not the first of these emblematic details, but it is among the most significant. In the final chapter of *The Implied Reader* (Baltimore: Johns Hopkins UP, 1974), Wolfgang Iser stresses "the building and the breaking of illusions" that mark the reader's "recreative" progress through any extensive narrative. Interruptions and discontinuity, Iser suggests, lend dynamism to the page. Franklin clearly exploits this dynamism wherever he can in the course of the memoir.

2. David Waldstreicher sees this incident as spurious, suggesting that Franklin carried with him his brother's discharge when he left Boston, but with or without such a document as a form of insurance, Franklin is still implicated in a pattern of broken "engagements" throughout this portion of his story. See *Runaway America: Benjamin Franklin, Slavery, and the American Revolution* (New York: Hill and Wang, 2004), p. 57.

3. At such moments, John Lynen suggests, Franklin is inviting the reader to appreciate the "beautifully managed gradations" by which the geopolitical crisis of the 1770s emerges from the narrative. See *The Design of the Present*, p. 146.

4. The anxieties that Vaughan and James express emerge from, rather than disclose, the pattern of shattered obligations that the first part of the memoir has systematically introduced, drastically expanding the scale of failure in preparation for the 1731 library memorandum that Franklin introduces into the book at the beginning of the 1788 section of his story. Vaughan, in other words, does not "give Franklin away," as Eric Wertheimer suggests; Franklin fits Vaughan carefully into his segmented vision. See *Underwriting: The Poetics of Insurance in America: 1722-1872* (Stanford, CA: Stanford UP, 2006), p. 35.

5. See the biographical note on Vaughan in the Norton edition of *Benjamin Franklin's Autobiography* (New York: W. W. Norton, 1986), p. 199.

6. The term *considerable* and Vaughan's emphasis on happiness, virtue, and greatness as the ideal outcomes a diligent reader might hope to attain by emulating Franklin are all pointedly different from mere "prosperity" or material comfort. Abel James does indeed stress the comparatively narrow goals of frugality and industry that he associates with Franklin's example. Vaughan's letter dramatically expands the scope of Franklin's didactic goals in a fashion that Franklin clearly intends to endorse by inserting the letter at this juncture of the narrative.

7. Christopher Looby's determination, in *Voicing America*, to present Franklin as being anxious to exclude the Revolution from his book requires Looby to conclude that the memo inserting the Vaughan and James letters into the memoir, along with "Notes of my Life," was never meant to be printed (127). Franklin's language and the shape of the manuscript, however, make clear that he wants to underscore this momentous interruption in every way possible, not paper it over. See J. A. Leo Lemay and P. M. Zall, eds., *The Autobiography of Benjamin Franklin: A Genetic Text* (Knoxville: U of Tennessee P, 1981), pp. 72-73, which confirms that Franklin entered the memo in the right-hand column of his draft and revised its wording, in a clear anticipation of its appearance in print with the rest of the book.

8. The Junto too is another instance of the scales that Franklin repeatedly invites his reader to envision as a model of the equilibria that mark ethical and social experi-

ence. Its meetings were designed to serve as instructive performances in themselves, as well as preliminary stages of social engineering or networking.

9. Michael Zuckerman emphatically makes the case that benevolence in the largest sense, not utility or "interest," characterizes Franklin's ethical performance. See "Doing Good While Doing Well: Benevolence and Self-Interest in Franklin's *Autobiography*," in *Reappraising Benjamin Franklin: A Bicentennial Perspective*, ed. J. A. Leo Lemay (Newark: U of Delaware P, 1993), pp. 441–44.

10. These scattered pieces of paper join the scattered "pie" of Franklin's Quaker history, the "scattered counsels" of Poor Richard that form "The Way to Wealth," or the scattered membership of the "united Party for Virtue," a "regular Body" dispersed over all nations, as a few of the memoir's many variations on the join-or-die motif.

11. "The Way to Wealth" is actually a collaboration between two avid collectors of scattered counsels, not one. Poor Richard concludes his account of Father Abraham's failure by explaining that "not a tenth Part of the Wisdom" that the old man had uttered was his own, "but rather the *Gleanings* I had made of the Sense of all Ages and Nations." See the preface to *Poor Richard Improved, 1758*, in *Benjamin Franklin: Writings* (New York: Literary Classics of the United States, 1987), p. 1302.

12. This phrase from the 1731 library memorandum reverberates through the third section of the memoir as a means of emphasizing Franklin's commitment not to "interest-thinking" (as Nancy Glazener terms it) but to anti-interest or "true interest" thinking, the phrase that Franklin's daily prayer to Powerful Goodness employs. The "one great error in communication" that the memoir commits, David Levin observed almost fifty years ago, is Franklin's failure to anticipate how easily readers might misunderstand his distinction between mere self-interest and the immaterial rewards of virtue that he associated with happiness. See "*The Autobiography of Benjamin Franklin*: The Puritan Experimenter in Life and Art," *Yale Review* 53 (1964): 258–75.

13. Alan Houston offers the most detailed and illuminating account of the relationship between *Plain Truth* and the circumstances that the pamphlet both addressed and shaped. See *Benjamin Franklin and the Politics of Improvement* (New Haven: Yale UP, 2008), pp. 60–105.

14. See Leo Lemay's report of the 1736 Philadelphia smallpox outbreak and the notice Franklin wrote for the December 30 issue of the *Pennsylvania Gazette* declaring the cause of his son's death in *The Life of Benjamin Franklin*, vol. 2: *Printer and Publisher, 1730–1747* (Philadelphia: U of Pennsylvania P, 2006), p. 456.

15. Readers who take the trouble to reconstruct the entire March 22, 1775, letter as Franklin intended it to be read by placing the inserts where he indicated they should go will find the analogy to the segmented serpent design almost unavoidable. The text and its pieces are all contained in volume 21 of the Yale *Papers*, with the body of the letter itself on pp. 540–99, and its inserts scattered throughout the preceding pages. The Library of Congress microfilm of the bound manuscript letter, in its collection of Franklin's papers, includes all the fragments in their places.

CHAPTER 4: *Litera Scripta Manet*

1. See the detailed timeline of publications and events in the "Chronology" of *Benjamin Franklin: Writings* (New York: Literary Classics of the United States, 1987), pp. 1486–87.

2. The Yale editors print the draft of annotations that Franklin prepared for Pitt's act. See P, 21.459–62. The wording of the annotations suggests that Franklin may have intended to call Pitt's attention to the 1754 Albany Plan of Union or at least take a copy of the plan itself to the meeting in which Pitt had intended to ask for Franklin's comments.

3. My comments throughout this chapter on Franklin's complex verbal world draw repeatedly but indirectly on Walter Ong's study, *The Presence of the Word: Some Prolegomena for Cultural and Religious History* (1967; rpt., Minneapolis: U of Minnesota P, 1981). In particular, Ong's chapter on "The Word and the Quest for Peace" (192–286) describes the gradual displacement of Late Latin oral polemic by the far less confrontational print culture of modernity—a transition that Franklin's memoir depicts in some detail, from his subordination of Latin to the study of modern foreign languages through his own lifelong struggle to control his combative oral gifts. The mix of written and spoken media, in Franklin's story, is almost as central to his self-portrait in the memoir as the more familiar prominence of print alone, beginning with his boyhood conflicts with John Collins through his astute observations on the verbal and written performances of George Whitefield.

4. By transcribing his parent's epitaph in the manuscript's opening pages and concluding with a brief Clerk's Chamber conversation in London, Franklin invites the reader to trace the progress of the memoir across the complete spectrum of fixed and ephemeral forms that words are capable of taking.

5. This genealogical oddity is the starting point for R. Jackson Wilson's account of what he sees as Franklin's systematic attack on the "entrenched and ominous system of social predation" in the memoir. See *Figures of Speech: American Writers and the Literary Marketplace from Benjamin Franklin to Emily Dickinson* (Baltimore: Johns Hopkins UP, 1989), pp. 43–44. But this form of "fixity" too is deceiving, as Franklin presents it. The privileged status of the eldest child is a ludicrously ineffective restraint on the migratory nature of individual gifts and individual character.

6. Franklin's famous account of this self-tutorial in how to write strikes many readers as an additional instance of his manipulative nature, of a desire (as Christopher Looby puts it) to become "an instrument of a language system" rather than a distinct voice in his own right. See *Voicing America: Language, Literary Form and the Origins of the United States* (Chicago: U of Chicago P, 1996), p. 117. The memoir, though, clearly stresses Franklin's ingenious efforts to teach himself how to play the "instrument" as well or better than Addison does, not how to become one.

7. Franklin invariably describes print as if it were continuous with, not distinct from, the social intimacy of speech. His interest in writing the Dogood letters springs from a desire to be part of his brother's convivial circle of printing house wits—an oral, not a textual, community. The letters themselves give "rubs" to James's critics in the Massachusetts Assembly, much as if Franklin relished the idea of manhandling them. In his London pamphlet he makes "Remarks" on Wollaston's book—a work of theology that he goes "into" very much as he does Thomas Tryon's printed account of vegetarianism or Cocker's arithmetic. Reading and writing are kinetic, physical activities as Franklin presents them in the memoir, a posture quite different from the sharp division between private writing and public print that Larzer Ziff presents in *Writing in the New Nation: Prose, Print, and Politics in the Early United States* (New Haven: Yale UP, 1991), pp. 83–106. By contrast, Michael Warner recognizes this tactile

relation to language in Franklin but sees it as a strictly utilitarian instinct: "[Franklin] does not just confront or see the texts; he handles them. And he handles them not for pleasure or for violence but in a strictly instrumental way" (79). The first part of this observation makes perfect sense; the second is to my mind inconsistent with the passion Franklin clearly brings to his reading and writing. See *The Letters of the Republic: Publication and the Public Sphere in Eighteenth-Century America* (Cambridge, MA: Harvard UP, 1990).

8. This reaction to the London pamphlet is especially illuminating, since it captures Franklin's recognition that print is not entirely subject to any measure of authorial control. In many ways, it is as laden with unpredictable potential as speech.

9. The figurative uses to which Franklin puts paper currency, in these passages, are far more varied and more playful than the grim account that Mitchell Breitwieser offers of what he calls the "spark and the dollar," electricity and money, in the memoir: "the Franklinian self," Breitwieser writes, "like the electrician and the economist, views the things and persons of its world as abstract quanta, as vessels that contain or lack amounts of the substance that the self epitomizes perfectly." See *Cotton Mather and Benjamin Franklin: The Price of Representative Personality* (New York: Cambridge UP, 1984), pp. 215–26.

10. The extraordinary lengths to which Franklin goes, in the memoir, to depict the verbal nexus of which print is only one part make a disproportionate stress on print alone seem especially inattentive to the book's performance. See, for instance, Michael Warner's conclusion that Franklin sought, throughout his career, to submerge his own voice in the "fictive speaking voice" of the "pseudonymous text" (*Letters of the Republic*, p. 96).

11. This interdependence of speech and print, as the memoir depicts it, is a far more volatile equilibrium than Larzer Ziff suggests, when he contends that Franklin divided the two expressive media into sharply divided spheres: speech for private relations and print for public business. See *Writing in the New Nation*, pp. 101–2.

12. "When will it suit you to have another interview," Whitefield wrote Franklin on January 21, 1768, while the two of them were pursuing their very different paths in England: "The College affair lies dormant." He went on to congratulate Franklin on the recent marriage of his daughter and to tease him with the expectation that, at their age, they could expect to "goe out" of the world at any moment and meet again at the apocalypse "to attend on the funeral of Time" together (P, 15.28–29). Religious differences do not seem to have affected the durability and the warmth of their friendship.

13. See J. A. Leo Lemay and P. M. Zall, eds., *The Autobiography of Benjamin Franklin: A Genetic Text* (Knoxville: U of Tennessee P, 1981), pp. 104 and 118, with the accompanying textual note, on Franklin's decision to move this detail to a later part of the memoir.

14. This famous scene in Franklin's book is a good example of the subtle roles that he allows money to play as an emblem of fine distinctions in character.

15. Grantland Rice touches on this passage concerning Whitefield's written and oral legacies as an indication of how the "objectification of the self in writing" could threaten individual autonomy. See *The Transformation of Authorship in America* (Chicago: U of Chicago P, 1997), pp. 66–67. But the memoir's discussion of Whitefield's example makes plain that neither speech nor print is entirely "objectified" or entirely autonomous; in different ways, each medium is carefully calibrated to the needs of the

speaker as well the audience, while each remains vulnerable to that audience's own carefully (or impulsively) calibrated responses.

CHAPTER 5: Some Uses of Cunning

1. In disclosing Franklin's own "cunning" this passage works both ways at least twice over by enticing the memoir's unwary reader to underestimate the productive interplay between generosity and self-interest that Franklin explores throughout this portion of his book. Cynthia Jordan, for instance, finds only verbal artifice and political expediency in the anecdotes Franklin includes in the 1788 fragment of the memoir—a stark conclusion that neglects the dramatic richness of these political vignettes. See *Second Stories: The Politics of Language, Form, and Gender in Early American Fictions* (Chapel Hill: U of North Carolina P, 1989), pp. 56–57. Edward White is clearly thinking of the hospital bill episode when he remarks on Franklin's "cunning antipathy to agrarian democracy" in the memoir's third part, but I find no indications of antipathy in this or any other anecdote that Franklin includes in this section of the book. See "Urbane Bifocals: The Federalist Sociology of Benjamin Franklin's Autobiography," *ALH* 11 (Spring 1999): 23. For an account of the hospital bill episode that stresses its relation to Franklin's personal candor rather than his "cunning," see Jennifer J. Baker, *Securing the Commonwealth: Debt, Speculation, and Writing in the Making of Early America* (Baltimore: Johns Hopkins UP, 2005), pp. 90–91.

2. David Levin's brief remarks on the Godfrey courtship are still the most sensitive reading of this skillfully crafted passage. See "*The Autobiography of Benjamin Franklin*: The Puritan Experimenter in Life and Art," *Yale Review* 53 (December 1963): 264.

3. Franklin's description of this incident is another interesting application of the idea of working both ways: with Governor Thomas's help, he is assisting in the creation of useful excuses.

4. The episodes in the memoir that toy with the emblematic or figurative uses of "fire" suggest Franklin's interest in extending the struggle to govern his private passions and appetites to the government of public "bodies." See Betsy Erkkila's account of the underlying continuity between the second and third parts of the memoir in "Franklin and the Revolutionary Body," *ELH* 67 (Fall 2000): 730–41.

5. *The Records of the Federal Convention of 1787*, vol. 2, ed. Max Farrand (New Haven: Yale UP, 1966), p. 222.

6. In *The Design of the Present: Essays on Time and Form in American Literature* (New Haven: Yale UP, 1969), John Lynen suggests that Franklin binds the memoir together in a common "atmosphere of relevance" that points toward Franklin's own emergence as a revolutionary leader. That goal may be part of the book's aim, but the Robert Hunter Morris episodes in particular suggest that Franklin is directing his words at the evolving consciousness of his contemporaries, not at his own ideological evolution.

7. See chapter 2 for a gloss on this analogy between the dusty room that cannot be cleaned and the heart's intractable nature (PP, 30). In recasting the emblematic scene, Franklin has added dramatic scope to its elements by preserving the street sweeper's speech, conferring on her a savvy intelligence that hints at the sense of latent force lying behind her performance, waiting to be tapped.

8. A willingness to acknowledge, and even to embrace, the hazardous implications

of radical democratic reform marked Franklin as a uniquely dangerous figure with his more conservative contemporaries. See Betsy Erkkila's stress on this aspect of his eighteenth-century reputation in "Franklin and the Revolutionary Body," p. 736.

9. Myra Jehlen is representative of many readers who see the precept for Humility as Machiavellian: a pragmatic fusion of humility and vanity, with economic ends in mind. But since martyrdom rather than profit or comfort is among the features shared by Jesus and Socrates, Franklin's motives in invoking their joint example seem much less worldly. See *Readings at the Edge of Literature* (Chicago: U of Chicago P, 2002), pp. 24–31.

10. See J. A. Leo Lemay and P. M. Zall, eds., *The Autobiography of Benjamin Franklin: A Genetic Text* (Knoxville: U of Tennessee P, 1981), p. 121, for Franklin's editorial polishing of the Old Counselor's speech at Carlisle. Betsy Erkkila sees this passage, too, as another signal on Franklin's part of his alertness to Benjamin Vaughan's post-Revolutionary anxieties, but the cultural narrative that the episode brings into play is much richer than these ideological uses require.

11. Jennifer Baker points to the Braddock wagon advertisement as another instance of the personal basis of credit that Franklin depicts in the third part of the memoir (*Securing the Commonwealth*, p. 92). See A, 228, for an account of Shirley's intervention in Franklin's financial plight.

12. This list was sufficiently important, in Franklin's eyes, that he transcribed it directly and without correction into the memoir. By contrast, early editors had to track down the broadside text of the wagon advertisement that Franklin prepared, since the "Quire Book of Letters," in which, he said, it could be found, had seemingly been lost. An anonymous British pamphlet published in 1755, purportedly reprinting letters from one of Braddock's officers, complained bitterly and at great length about the food the army encountered in America. The Pennsylvania delegation that arrived at the army's camp—"pure plump men, on brave fat horses"—were (this author claimed) "the first plump creatures I had seen in this country." It is possible that Franklin remembered this caustic account of colonial life when he itemized the luxurious contents of the junior officers' parcels. See *The Expedition of Major General Braddock to Virginia; with The Two Regiments of Hacket and Dunbar* (London: H. Carpenter, 1755).

13. This subtle identification with the Indian point of view begins with Franklin's account of the Carlisle treaty, where the Old Counselors illustrate the same principle that lies behind Franklin's boyhood experience with eating cod: how convenient a thing it is to be a reasonable creature whenever we are in search of excuses. The identification extends through the building of the fort at Gnadenhütten, when the memoir tacitly links the ingenuity of the Indian scouts with the independent skill and efficiency of Franklin's militia.

14. The report of Braddock's death has very little to do with the large political framework that shapes much of Franklin's account of the Duquesne expedition. It does, however, closely mimic the intimate experience of the eighteenth psalm writing contest in the memoir's 1771 fragment, where Franklin's friend Osborne anticipates Braddock's dying words: "But who would have imagin'd, says he, that Franklin had been capable of such a Performance" (A, 91). In attending so carefully to Braddock's reticence and to his bewilderment, Franklin confers an emotional complexity on this moment characteristic of many of his narrative's subtle dramatic scenes.

CONCLUSION: Segmented Serpent

1. The Yale editors note various places in the 1788 fragment where Franklin's memory seems to have failed him in reconstructing an accurate sequence of events (A, 193, 209, 250), but at least some of these lapses are surely intentional. The 1753 Carlisle treaty episode, for instance, is undated in the memoir, where Franklin includes it just before discussing the 1751 hospital bill instead of in the months immediately preceding the 1754 Albany Congress, where it properly belongs. This displacement allows the memoir to present Franklin's brief stint as a justice of the peace, the Carlisle negotiation, and the founding of a hospital as tightly linked experiences in addressing pathologies of the physical and communal "body."

2. Karen Cook first observed this similarity in "Benjamin Franklin and the Snake That Would Not Die," *British Library Journal* 22 (1996): 88–111.

3. The most ambitious of these federal experiments, the 1643 Articles of Confederation that formed the United Colonies of New England, lasted until 1690. Franklin could easily have learned its history from his father or from Cotton Mather's *Magnalia Christi Americana*.

4. For the dating and the compositional sequence of these last passages that Franklin wrote, see the introduction to *The Autobiography of Benjamin Franklin: A Genetic Text* (Knoxville: U of Tennessee P, 1981), p. xxiii, where Lemay and Zall place Franklin's writing about his scientific career between December 1788 and May 1789. After May 1789 he stopped adding to the manuscript and drafted only the few paragraphs of the final fragment in the last five months of his life.

Index

Adams, Matthew, 124, 127
Addison, Joseph: *Cato*, 66; *Spectator* essays, 5–6, 18, 89, 123–124, 140
"Advertisement" (BF's 1755 appeal for wagons), 119–120, 174–176, 206n.12
Albany Plan of Union (1754 colonial conference), 6, 157, 169, 182, 191
Allen, William, 103
American Philosophical Society, 101
American Revolution, 3, 9, 164, 166, 168, 176, 188; memoir's allusions to, 6, 105, 108, 151
"Articles of Belief and Acts of Religion" (BF's personal liturgy), 61, 138–139
Articles of Confederation, 105
"Art of Virtue" (BF's unfinished ethics handbook), 7, 22, 87, 97
association: memoir's treatment of, 10, 47, 85, 87, 99, 190; Tocqueville's emphasis on, 10, 195n.8

Baird, Patrick, 95
Banbury, Oxfordshire, Josiah Franklin's ties to, 53, 121
Barclay, David, 108–111, 113, 115, 117, 120
Beatty, Charles (BF's militia chaplain), 164–165, 179
Bethlehem (Moravian settlement), 179
Bigelow, John (1868 editor of BF's memoir), 1–2
Bond, Thomas, 151–152, 154, 182. *See also* Pennsylvania hospital project
Boston Grammar School, 41, 45
Boston Massacre, 25
Boston Tea Party (1773), 106, 119, 176
Braddock, Edward, 1755 expedition of, 164, 167–168, 172–180, 182, 186–187; BF's advice rejected by, 183–184, 189–190
Bradford, Andrew (Philadelphia printer), 33, 88, 154
Bradford, William (New York printer), 33, 138
Breintnall, Joseph, 84, 94
Breughel, Pieter, the Elder, "Big Fish Eat Little Fish" drawing, 30–32, 197n.12
Brockden, Charles, 76, 93–94, 98
Browne, John (innkeeper), 15–18, 40
Brownell, George, 41
Buffon, George-Louis Leclerc, Comte de, 190
Bunyan, John, 15, 28, 62, 90, 125, 167; portrait etching of, 20–21; preaching career of, 53–55. *See also Pilgrim's Progress*
Burnet, William (colonial governor of New York), 18
"Busy-Body" letters, 88

Camden, Charles Pratt, First Earl of, 112
Carlisle Treaty meeting (1753), 6, 169–172, 178, 181–182
Clinton, George (colonial governor of New York), 103, 170, 177
Cocker, Edward ("Book of Arithmetic"), 125
Coercive Acts (1774), 109, 119
Coleman, William, 84–85, 95–96
Collins, John (BF's childhood friend), 5, 35, 45, 82–83, 124; and BF in Philadelphia, 17, 150–151; BF's quarrels with, 32–33, 47–49, 51, 127, 169; BF's written debates with, 27, 124, 155
Collinson, Peter, 188–189
Constitutional Convention (1787), 7, 105, 159–160, 173
Copley Medal (1753), 190–191
counterpoise and counterweight: narrative tactic of, 34, 52, 85, 94–95; principle and inclination as instances of, 35–36, 40, 51, 83; scales as a figure of, 40, 52–53, 55, 58, 70–71, 99, 201n.8. *See also* equilibrium
currency, BF's printing of, 130–135

Index

Dartmouth, William Legge, Second Earl of, 114, 117–118
Decow, Isaac, 133
Defoe, Daniel, 17, 19
Deism, BF's interest in, 39, 187
Denham, Thomas, 75, 86–87, 117
Denny, William (provincial governor of Pennsylvania), 170, 177
Dissertation on Liberty and Necessity, Pleasure and Pain (BF's 1725 pamphlet), 17, 39, 127, 137
Dogood letters, 4–5, 203n.7
Don Quixote, 158
Dryden, John, 40
Dunkers (Pietist sect), 102–103

Ecton, Northamptonshire, BF's 1758 journey to, 13, 53, 121–122
"Edict by the King of Prussia" (1773), 119
eighteenth psalm, 78–80, 89
emblems: BF's employment of, 14, 24, 28–29, 50, 162; counterpoise as instance of, 52; in *Pilgrim's Progress*, 56–57, 60, 65, 68, 163; segmented serpent as instance of, 11, 85, 87, 104, 179, 190; speckled ax anecdote as instance of, 57. *See also* similitude
English Revolution, 16
equilibrium, BF's figurative use of, 96, 99, 104, 199n.5, 204n.11. *See also* counterpoise and counterweight
errata, BF's tabulating of. *See* excuses
Essay on Criticism. See Pope, Alexander
excuses, BF's narrative employment of, 150–153, 161, 170–171
exempla in *Pilgrim's Progress*, 56
Experiments and Observations on Electricity, 189–190

Farrand, Max (*Benjamin Franklin's Memoirs: Parallel Text Edition*), 6
Father Abraham ("The Way to Wealth"), 100, 104, 173, 195n.3
Federal Convention. *See* Constitutional Convention
First Continental Congress, 106
Folger, Peter (BF's grandfather), 17, 51
Fort Duquesne (1755 campaign), 164, 172, 183–184. *See also* Braddock, Edward

Fothergill, John, 162–163, 186–187, 189; BF's 1774–75 meetings with, 108–111, 113, 115, 117, 120
Franklin, Abiah Folger (BF's mother), 44–46, 52
Franklin, Benjamin (BF's uncle), 16–17, 29–30, 44, 74, 121; birthday poems by, 26–27, 39, 119; sermon and pamphlet collections of, 54, 196n.5
Franklin, Deborah Read (BF's wife), 16, 42, 86, 105–106; BF's courtship of, 36–38, 52, 76, 199n.4
Franklin, Francis Folger (BF's son), 5, 51, 104–105
Franklin, James (BF's brother), 45–47, 55, 86, 124, 132, 150
Franklin, John (BF's uncle), 53
Franklin, Josiah (BF's father), 40–46, 52, 55, 122–125, 151, 184; advice of, to BF on writing, 77, 127, 136; BF's apprenticeship arranged by, 45–46, 153–154, 186; BF's epitaph for, 44; dinner table practice of, 40, 43; religious nonconformity of, 29, 53
Franklin, Samuel (BF's cousin), 44
Franklin, Sarah (BF's daughter), 5
Franklin, Thomas (BF's uncle), 121
Franklin, William (BF's son), 5, 9, 29, 35, 108, 138, 176; BF's ideological differences with, 25, 106, 122; BF's 1758 journey with, 13–14, 41–42; illegitimacy of, 38, 52; memoir addressed to, 2–3, 15–16, 121, 129
Franklin, William Temple (BF's grandson), 8, 10, 194n.7

Gage, General Thomas, 111
Georgia, orphanage proposal for, 145–146; snake cartoon as accommodation for, 184–185
Gnadenhütten (Moravian settlement), 177, 179–180, 184
Godfrey, Mrs. Thomas, 154–155, 168
Godfrey, Thomas, 63, 84, 168
Grace, Robert, 84, 95–96
Granville, John Carteret, First Earl of, 185–186, 190
Great Awakening, 60

Hamilton, James (provincial governor of Pennsylvania), 157–159
Hemphill, Samuel, 104, 139–143, 148
Hesiod, 30

"Hints for *Conversation*" (BF's 1774 negotiation memorandum), 109–111, 113, 120
Hopkinson, Thomas, 145–146
House of Commons: BF's 1766 appearance before, 25, 196n.9; BF's critique of, 113, 115. *See also* Parliament
House of Lords, 108, 112–115, 191. *See also* Parliament
Howe, Caroline, 108–109, 113, 117
Howe, Richard, 108–109, 113, 117, 120, 191
Hutchinson, Thomas, 24, 106
Hyde, Thomas Villiers, Baron, 117, 120

Iroquois, 1754 Albany Conference with, 157

James, Abel, 6–8, 10, 23, 101–102; 1782 letter of, 2–4, 7, 87–91, 193n.2
Jefferson, Thomas, 8–9
"Join, or Die." *See* snake cartoon
"Journal of a Voyage" (1726), 129
Junto (BF's self-improvement association), 63, 94–97, 101, 109, 113, 167; currency discussions in, 134–135, 137; informal library of, 92–94; original members of, 82–85

Keimer, Samuel, 33, 36, 82, 138, 155; BF's quarrels with, 87, 130–133; character attributes of, 40, 52, 76; *Pennsylvania Gazette* established by, 84, 88; religious principles of, 34–35, 99
Keith, William (provincial governor of Pennsylvania), 5, 21–22, 35–37, 76, 86–87; financial promises of, 32–33, 46, 55
Kinnersley, Ebenezer, 189

Lady's Magazine, or Entertaining Companion of the Fair Sex (1793), 1
Lawrence, Thomas, 103
Lexington and Concord, battles of (1775), 106
Library Company of Philadelphia, 48, 92–94, 96–99, 104, 137, 188
Locke, John, BF's reading of, 125
Logic, or The Art of Thinking (translation of *Logique, ou L'art de Penser*, Antoine Arnauld and Pierre Nicole), 125
Lydgate, John, 30
Lyons, William (London surgeon and author), 127–128

Macclesfield, George Parker, Second Earl of, 191
Madison, James, 159–160
Mansfield, William Murray, Baron, 187–188
Massachusetts Assembly, 103; James Franklin's clashes with, 126, 150
Mather, Cotton (*Essays to Do Good*), 123
Maugridge, William, 84
memoir (BF's narrative): compositional history of, 2–6, 13–15, 71–72, 85, 105, 207n.4; critique of reason in, 30–37, 187; depictions of reading in, 15–18, 24, 27–30, 196n.7, 197n.11; disruption and fragmentation as elements of, 4–6, 14, 85, 97–100, 194n.7, 200n.1; editorial divisions of, 9–11; ethical self-discipline in, 55–71; historical context of Passy fragment (1784), 2–3, 88–90, 105; historical context of Philadelphia fragment (1788–1790), 6–9, 105, 157, 159–161, 164, 171; historical context of Twyford fragment (1771), 2, 13–14, 25, 27, 79–80, 135; historical context of voyage letter fragment (1775), 9, 48–51, 106, 119; manuscript appearance of, 32, 51–52; "Notes of my Life" (BF's "Outline") as part of, 3–6, 9, 91, 105, 193n.2, 197n.13; *Pilgrim's Progress* as influence on, 18–26, 30, 54–57, 59–60, 71, 74, 195n.3, 206n.14; publication history of, 1–4, 193n.1; religious elements in, 37–40, 43–44, 66–67, 198n.15, 200n.12; restraints on speech in, 165–167; role of feeling in, 43, 46, 81, 104–105, 114–117, 194n.5, 195n.6, 206n.14; voyage letter (BF to William Franklin, March 22, 1775) as part of, 8–9, 48–51, 105–120, 198n.1; Vaughan letter's formative role in, 88–92
Meredith, Hugh, 82–83, 94–96, 169
Mickle, Samuel, 60, 134
militia association of Pennsylvania, BF's founding of, 101–103, 156
Moll Flanders, BF's interest in, 17
Moravians, BF's 1755 contacts with, 179–180
Morris, Gouverneur, 157, 159–160
Morris, Robert Hunter (provincial governor of Pennsylvania), 157–161, 164, 169

Nature and Necessity of a Paper Currency (BF's 1728 pamphlet), 133–134, 173. *See also* currency
Navigation Acts (1774), 109, 119
New England Courant (James Franklin's Boston paper), 5, 86, 132, 135

Newton, Isaac, 86
Nollet, Jean-Antoine, 190
Norris, Isaac, 169
North, Frederick Lord (Second Earl of Guilford), 117, 120
"Notes of my Life" (BF's "Outline"), 3–6, 9, 85, 91, 105, 193n.2, 197n.13. *See also* memoir

"Observations on my Reading History in Library" (BF's 1731 memorandum), 102, 104–105, 109, 119, 137, 160, 176; BF's narrative uses of, 85, 97–100, 151
orality and oral performance, BF's interest in, 80, 138, 203n.3
Osborne, Charles, 76–82, 84, 86, 138

Palmer, Samuel (London printer), 126–127, 129
Pamela (Richardson), 17
parables. *See* emblems
Parliament, 93, 106, 109, 117–118, 120. *See also* House of Commons; House of Lords
Parsons, William, 84
Peace of Paris (1783), 89–90, 105
Penn, Richard, 186
Penn, Thomas, 9, 182, 186
Penn family (Pennsylvania proprietaries), 22, 158–159, 188
Pennsylvania Assembly, 22, 135, 169, 172, 176, 187; BF as London agent of, 182; BF as spokesman for, 157–160; hospital bill of 1751 in, 152–153
Pennsylvania fireplace, 100; BF's pamphlet on, 156–157
Pennsylvania Gazette, 84, 100–101, 104–105, 135–137, 140
Pennsylvania hospital project, 151–152, 154, 173, 188
Pennsylvania Society for Promoting the Abolition of Slavery, 159
Peters, Richard, 101, 169
Philadelphia, University of, 100, 101, 169
Philadelphia Academy. *See* Philadelphia, University of
Philadelphia city watch, BF's reform of, 100–101
Philadelphia Convention. *See* Constitutional Convention
Philippians 4:8, BF's interest in, 61, 66, 138–139

Pilgrim's Progress, 24–26, 53–57, 68, 71, 77, 98; Bunyan's verse "Apology" for, 22–23, 30; critique of legality in, 59–60, 63; House Beautiful in, 62, 65; Interpreter's House in, 15, 74, 163, 195n.3; similitudes in, 18–21, 24, 50–51, 61. *See also* Bunyan, John
Pitt, William (Lord Chatham), 108, 111–112, 114–115, 120
Plain Truth (BF's 1744 pamphlet), 102
Poor Richard's Almanac, 30, 100, 104, 140
Pope, Alexander: *Essay on Criticism*, 30, 165–166; *Dunciad*, 81
Potts, Stephen, 82–83
Presbyterian Synod of Philadelphia, 139–140, 142. *See also* Hemphill, Samuel
print, durability and ephemerality of, 121, 123, 129, 136–138, 147–148, 203n.7
Privy Council, 185–187; BF's 1774 examination by, 9, 24, 64, 106, 119, 188, 191; voyage letter's allusions to, 50, 108, 113–114
Public Advertiser, 119

Ralph, James, 21, 76–82, 84, 86, 129; eighteenth psalm version by, 80, 89, 138, 153
Read, John (Deborah Franklin's father), 36, 38
Read, Sarah White (BF's mother-in-law), 36–38, 40, 52
Reeve, Henry (Tocqueville's translator), 67
Restoration (1660), 53, 73
Richardson, Samuel, 17, 19
Riddlesden, William, 5
Robinson Crusoe, BF's interest in, 17
Royal Society of London, 189–190
"Rules by Which a Great Empire May be Reduced to a Small One," 119

Sandwich, John Montagu, Fourth Earl of, 114
Scull, Nicholas, 84
Second Continental Congress, 9, 115
segmented serpent, conceptual figure of, 4, 10, 11, 179, 182–185, 189–190, 194n.3. *See also* emblems; snake cartoon
Seven Years War, 108–109, 134, 157, 179–180, 183
Shaftesbury, Anthony Ashley Cooper, Third Earl of, 125
Shakespeare, William, 30

Shipley, Jonathan (Bishop of St. Asaph), 50, 51
Shirley, William (colonial governor of Massachusetts), 176
similitude: BF's use of, 22, 24–26, 33, 40, 65; Bunyan's use of, 19, 23–24, 28, 50, 56, 195n.3; cod-eating episode as instance of, 30; joint stool anecdote as instance of, 28, 39, 43. *See also* emblems
slavery, memoir's allusions to, 158–161
snake cartoon (1754), 4, 11, 96, 153, 182–184, 189. *See also* segmented serpent
Society of the Free and Easy, BF's vision of, 99–100
Spangenberg, August (Moravian leader), 180
Spencer, Archibald, 188
Stamp Act, 24
St. Clair, Sir John, 176

Taylor, Abraham, 103
Thomas, George (provincial governor of Pennsylvania), 156–157, 165
Three-fifths Compromise, 159–160
Tocqueville, Alexis de (*Democracy in America*), 10, 66–67
Tryon, Thomas, 125
Turgot, Anne-Robert-Jacques, 157

Union Fire Company of Philadelphia, 100, 153, 157
United Party for Virtue, BF's 1731 vision of, 99–100, 105, 151
United States Constitution, 105, 159–160, 174

Vaughan, Benjamin, 2–3, 6–8, 10–11, 23, 101–102; 1783 letter of, 87–92, 105, 113, 143, 177, 188, 193n.2
voyage letter (BF to William Franklin, March 22, 1775), 8–9, 10, 50–51, 97, 106–121, 130, 173

Walpole, Thomas, 118
Washington, George, 8, 173–174, 177
Watson, Joseph, 76–82
Watts, John (BF's London employer), 72–73, 75
"Way to Wealth." *See* Father Abraham
Webb, George, 82–84
Wedderburn, Alexander, 24
Welfare, Michael (Michael Wohlfart), 102–103, 138
Whitefield, George, 143–149, 153, 167–168, 171
Willcox, John (London bookseller), 128
Williams, Roger (*The Bloudy Tenant of Persecution*), 30
Wollaston, William, 126–127
writing, durability of. *See* print
Wycliffe, John, 30
Wygate, John (BF's London friend), 75–76

Xenophon, 125

Young, Edward (*Satires on Fame*), 129